WOMANPOWER

NATIONAL MANPOWER COUNCIL

WOMANPOWER

A STATEMENT BY THE

NATIONAL MANPOWER COUNCIL

WITH

CHAPTERS BY THE COUNCIL STAFF

NEW YORK 1957

COLUMBIA UNIVERSITY PRESS

COPYRIGHT © 1957 COLUMBIA UNIVERSITY PRESS, NEW YORK

First printing March, 1957
Second printing April, 1957

PUBLISHED IN GREAT BRITAIN, CANADA, INDIA, AND PAKISTAN
BY THE OXFORD UNIVERSITY PRESS
LONDON, TORONTO, BOMBAY, AND KARACHI

LIBRARY OF CONGRESS CATALOG CARD NUMBER: 56-12740

MANUFACTURED IN THE UNITED STATES OF AMERICA

65

THE NATIONAL MANPOWER COUNCIL[a]

PREFACE

THE NATIONAL MANPOWER COUNCIL was established at Columbia University in the spring of 1951, under a grant from the Ford Foundation, to study significant manpower problems and to contribute to the improved development and utilization of the country's human resources. This volume, the Council's sixth publication, is designed to contribute to a fuller understanding of the nation's manpower resources by illuminating the present role of women in the working population.

The Council is fully aware that much additional research is required before a comprehensive grasp of the distinctive nature of the country's resources of womanpower can be assured. The Council recognizes, moreover, that the manpower considerations which defined the scope of this study also limited the attention which could be paid to many social aspects of women's employment outside the home. As in the case of its two preceding studies, *A Policy for Scientific and Professional Manpower* and *A Policy for Skilled Manpower*, the Council will hold a national conference, in the fall of 1957, in order to secure critical evaluations of the conclusions emerging from its womanpower study and to stimulate discussions of the issues with which it deals.

Without the generous assistance provided by many individuals and organizations, both private and governmental, the Council's task could not have been pressed to completion within a two-year period. It need hardly be added that those who assisted the

Council bear no responsibility for the points of view expressed and the findings presented in this volume.

Those individuals who participated in the sixteen conferences conducted by the Council, who replied to special questionnaires or requests for information, and who provided help in still other ways, are listed in the Acknowledgments, where the many organizations which assisted the Council are also noted.

Throughout the study, the Council and its staff profited from the knowledge and judgment of five consultants: Miss Margaret Hickey, editor of the Public Affairs Department of the *Ladies' Home Journal;* Professor Everett C. Hughes of the University of Chicago; Professor Richard A. Lester of Princeton University; Professor Douglas McGregor of the Massachusetts Institute of Technology; and Dr. Anne G. Pannell, President of Sweet Briar College.

Miss Hickey also provided assistance in connection with three Council conferences: the February, 1955 and the January, 1956 conferences in New York, and the May, 1955 conference in St. Louis. President Millicent C. McIntosh of Barnard College not only presided at the Columbia University conference on womanpower held in March, 1955, but also consulted with the staff during the early stages of the study. Mr. James S. Schoff presided at the New York conference in March, 1955, and Dr. Sol W. Ginsburg played a major part in making possible the Council's New York conference in June of that year. The conferences held the following month in Los Angeles and San Francisco depended heavily on the advice and assistance provided by Mr. Karl R. Kunze and Mr. Frank P. Foisie, respectively. Mr. Charles B. Wade, Jr., cooperated in calling the regional conference in Asheville, N. C., in July, 1955. The Council is grateful to Mr. Carter L. Burgess, then Assistant Secretary of Defense, and to Mr. Gus C. Lee, of the Office of Manpower Utilization of the Department of Defense, for arranging the April, 1955 conference in Washington.

Two government departments contributed materially to the womanpower study by making personnel available for work with the Council staff. The Council is indebted to the Hon. Hugh M. Milton, II, Assistant Secretary of the Army, and to Col. Irene O. Galloway, formerly Director of the Women's Army Corps, for their willingness to assign Lt. Col. Irene M. Sorrough for this purpose. The Council is also indebted to the Hon. James P. Mitchell, the Secretary of Labor, and to Mrs. Alice K. Leopold, Director of the Women's Bureau, for assigning Miss Jean S. Campbell to the Council staff. Mrs. Leopold, as well as other members of the Women's Bureau, have provided valuable assistance to the Council staff throughout the study. They also read and commented upon virtually all the chapters prepared by the Council staff, which constitute Part Two of this volume.

Among others who read various chapters in Part Two, provided helpful criticisms of them, and also contributed to the work of the staff in other ways are Dr. Gladys L. Palmer of the Wharton School of Finance and Commerce, University of Pennsylvania; Professor Esther Lloyd-Jones of Teachers College, Columbia University; Mr. David L. Kaplan and Miss Gertrude Bancroft, both of the Bureau of the Census, Department of Commerce; Mr. Seymour L. Wolfbein, Mr. Harold Goldstein, and Mr. Stuart Garfinkle, all of the Bureau of Labor Statistics, Department of Labor; and Mrs. Ethel L. Ginsburg of the Citizen's Committee on Children of New York City.

Professor Mirra Komarovsky of Barnard College conducted and analyzed intensive interviews with college women for the purpose of providing additional information on the interrelationships among early marriage, college study, and employment. Professor Philip M. Hauser of the University of Chicago prepared a special memorandum on the female labor force and urbanization. Mrs. Edith Lynton interviewed a selected group of college-educated married women, now in their middle years, on their current attitudes toward employment. Mr. Louis Levine,

Assistant Director of the Bureau of Employment Security, Department of Labor, assisted by making available valuable data.

Mr. James K. Anderson, of the Conservation of Human Resources Project of Columbia University, and Dr. Douglas W. Bray, then also associated with the Project, prepared an analysis of the results of a questionnaire initiated by the School of General Studies of Columbia University, which illuminated certain aspects of college attendance by older students. Mr. Anderson and Dr. Bray also assisted on other aspects of the study.

The Council gratefully acknowledges the contributions to *Womanpower* made by the secretarial staff, Miss Reva Feldman, Mrs. Edith B. Garshman, and Miss Gloria Tofano.

A brief word must be said about the Council itself. It was fortunate in counting among its members the late Mr. William H. Harrison and Dr. Charles S. Johnson. With their deaths in 1956, the nation lost two distinguished citizens, and the Council wise and devoted members. Their contributions to this study, as to the Council's previous work, were invaluable, and are reflected in the Council's Statement on *Womanpower*.

In November, 1956, the Council reluctantly accepted the resignation of Mr. Robert B. Anderson, occasioned by his appointment as a trustee of the Ford Foundation. In January, 1957, three new members were appointed to the Council: Miss Margaret Hickey, Dr. Alonzo G. Morón, and Mr. Robert W. Woodruff.

Finally, I must note my resignation as Chairman of the Council, necessitated by my appointment as United States Ambassador to Italy, and the election of Mr. Erwin D. Canham as its new Chairman. I had the privilege of serving as Chairman for five years, and I look forward with pleasure to staying on as a member of the Council under his chairmanship.

JAMES D. ZELLERBACH

Rome, Italy

ACKNOWLEDGMENTS

ORGANIZATIONS

American Association of Industrial Nurses, Inc.
American Association of University Women
American Federation of Labor
American Home Economics Association
American Nurses' Association, Inc.
American Occupational Therapy Association
American Society of Women Accountants
Congress of Industrial Organizations
Democratic National Committee, Office of Women's Activities
Department of Commerce, Bureau of the Census
Department of Defense
Department of Health, Education, and Welfare, Office of Education
Department of Labor, Bureau of Employment Security, Bureau of
    Labor Statistics, Women's Bureau
Department of Labour, Ottawa, Canada
Department of the Air Force
Department of the Army
Department of the Navy, including U.S. Marine Corps
Elmo Roper & Associates
General Federation of Women's Clubs
National Association of Colored Women's Clubs, Inc.
National Consumers League for Fair Labor Standards
National Council of Administrative Women in Education of the Na-
    tional Education Association
National Council of Catholic Women
National Council of Jewish Women
National Council of the Churches of Christ in the U. S. A.

National Education Association of the United States
National Federation of Business and Professional Women's Clubs, Inc.
National Opinion Research Center
Republican National Committee, Women's Division
Young Women's Christian Association of the United States of America

CONFERENCE PARTICIPANTS

FEBRUARY, 1955

New York, New York

Eleanor C. French, The New York *Times*, New York, N. Y.
Eleanor Guggenheimer, Child Welfare League of America, New York, N. Y.
Margaret Hickey, *Ladies' Home Journal*, Philadelphia, Pa.
Mildred McAfee Horton, New York, N. Y.
Mildred Adams Kenyon, New York, N. Y.
Genevieve Rogers Riley, National Federation of Business and Professional Women's Clubs, Inc., New York, N. Y.
Marion Sheahan, National League for Nursing Education, New York, N. Y.
Savilla Simons, Young Women's Christian Association of the United States of America, New York, N. Y.
Anna Lord Strauss, New York, N. Y.
Ruth Streeter, Morristown, N. J.
Margaret Twyman, Association of Junior Leagues of America, New York, N. Y.

MARCH, 1955

New York, New York

Conrad M. Arensberg, Columbia University, New York, N. Y.
Harold F. Clark, Teachers College, Columbia University, New York, N. Y.
Nathan E. Cohen, New York School of Social Work, Columbia University, New York, N. Y.
Helen R. Downes, Barnard College, Columbia University, New York, N. Y.
Dr. Sol W. Ginsburg, New York, N. Y.
Louis M. Hacker, School of General Studies, Columbia University, New York, N. Y.
Ruth Houghton, Barnard College, Columbia University, New York, N. Y.

Dr. Lawrence C. Kolb, College of Physicians and Surgeons, Columbia University, New York, N. Y.

Mirra Komarovsky, Barnard College, Columbia University, New York, N. Y.

Robert D. Leigh, School of Library Service, Columbia University, New York, N. Y.

Esther Lloyd-Jones, Teachers College, Columbia University, New York, N. Y.

Millicent C. McIntosh, Barnard College, Columbia University, New York, N. Y.

Robert M. MacIver, Columbia University, New York, N. Y.

Phoebe Morrison, Barnard College, Columbia University, New York, N. Y.

Dr. Howard C. Taylor, Jr., College of Physicians and Surgeons, Columbia University, New York, N. Y.

MARCH, 1955

New York, New York

Grace Bamonte, B. Altman and Company, New York, N. Y.

Blanche Bernstein, Welfare and Health Council of New York City, New York, N. Y,

Courtney C. Brown, Columbia University, New York, N. Y.

Emory A. Coughlin, Cluett, Peabody and Company, Inc., New York, N. Y.

W. E. Foltz, New York Telephone Company, New York, N. Y.

Jack Frost, Manufacturers Trust Company, New York, N. Y.

Reuben Holland, Office of the Impartial Chairman of the Dress Industry, New York, N .Y.

Roger Hull, The Mutual Life Insurance Company of New York, New York, N. Y.

Jean Kennedy, New York State Employment Service, New York, N. Y.

Morris Krugman, New York City Board of Education, Brooklyn, N. Y.

Harvey Machaver, Montefiore Hospital, Bronx, N. Y.

Gertrude G. Michelson, R. H. Macy & Co., Inc., New York, N. Y.

James T. O'Connell, Publix Shirt Corporation, New York, N. Y.

Matthew Radom, Standard Oil Company (N. J.), New York, N. Y.

Joseph Schechter, Municipal Civil Service Commission, New York, N. Y.

James S. Schoff, Bloomingdale Bros., New York, N. Y.

Martha Scudder, Bloomingdale Bros., New York, N. Y.

Arnold K. Weber, Radio Corporation of America, Camden, N. J.

APRIL, 1955
Chicago, Illinois

Floyd S. Bordsen, Sadler and Associates, Chicago, Ill.

Ray E. Brown, University Clinics, The University of Chicago, Chicago, Ill.

Jane Burdick, Marshall Field & Company, Chicago, Ill.

Ruth Crowley, Ruth Crowley Syndicate, Lake Forest, Ill.

Patricia Darley, Chicago *Sun-Times*, Chicago, Ill.

Ruth Dunbar, Chicago *Sun-Times*, Chicago, Ill.

Frank S. Endicott, Northwestern University, Evanston, Ill.

Evangeline H. Fahy, National Federation of Business and Professional Women's Clubs, Inc., Chicago, Ill.

Margaret Filson, University Clinics, The University of Chicago, Chicago, Ill.

Harold Goldstein, Bureau of Labor Statistics, Department of Labor, Washington, D. C.

Paul F. Gorby, Marshall Field & Company, Chicago, Ill.

Alice Harwood, Harris Trust and Savings Bank, Chicago, Ill.

Robert MacRae, Welfare Council of Metropolitan Chicago, Chicago, Ill.

Ruth Moore, Chicago *Sun-Times*, Chicago, Ill.

Frances A. Mullen, Chicago Public Schools, Chicago, Ill.

Wilbur C. Munnecke, Chicago *Sun-Times*, Chicago, Ill.

Athlene Rowe, Illinois Bell Telephone Company, Chicago, Ill.

Adrienne Stokes, Marshall Field & Company, Chicago, Ill.

Seymour L. Wolfbein, Bureau of Labor Statistics, Department of Labor, Washington, D.C.

J. W. Young, Sears, Roebuck and Co., Chicago, Ill.

APRIL, 1955
Boston, Massachusetts

Robert A. Burns, General Electric Company, West Lynn, Mass.

Erwin D. Canham, *The Christian Science Monitor*, Boston, Mass.

Dr. John Conlon, Boston City Hospital, Boston, Mass.

Milton O. Corey, John Hancock Mutual Life Insurance Company, Boston, Mass.

Wynton R. Dangelmayer, New England Telephone & Telegraph Company, Boston, Mass.

James T. Dennison, Dennison Manufacturing Company, Framingham, Mass.

Dr. Jack Ewalt, Department of Mental Health, The Commonwealth of Massachusetts, Boston, Mass.

Frances M. Fuller, Radcliffe College, Cambridge, Mass.

Arthur C. Gernes, Bureau of Employment Security, Department of Labor, Boston, Mass.

Gertrude M. Gill, The First National Bank of Boston, Boston, Mass.

Daniel Goggin, Boot and Shoe Workers' Union, Boston, Mass.

Francis A. McCarte, Esso Standard Oil Company, Boston, Mass.

Forrest H. McKinley, Statler Corporation, Boston, Mass.

Lydia Marvin, Filene's, Boston, Mass.

Helen Tafe O'Donnell, Massachusetts Federation of Labor, Boston, Mass.

Henry G. Pearson, Polaroid Corporation, Cambridge, Mass.

Al Percoco, Rubber Workers Union, Watertown, Mass.

Mary J. Rizzitano, Cambridge Thermionic Corporation, Cambridge, Mass.

Viola Saltmarsh, Tufts College, Medford, Mass.

Hattiemay Smith, Department of Labor and Industries, Boston, Mass.

Leslie E. Woods, Raytheon Manufacturing Company, Waltham, Mass.

APRIL, 1955

Washington, D.C.

B. B. Bray, Office of Manpower Utilization, Department of Defense, Washington, D.C.

Lt. Commander W. A. Breathwit, Bureau of Medicine & Surgery, Department of the Navy, Washington, D.C.

Major Rachel Brinton, Directorate of Military Personnel, Department of the Air Force, Washington, D.C.

Carter L. Burgess, Department of Defense, Washington, D.C.

Lt. Colonel Marie Clark, Office of Personnel Policy. Department of Defense, Washington, D.C.

Lt. Colonel Hope Clowers, Office of the Assistant Chief of Staff, G-1, Marine Corps, Washington, D.C.

Colonel William Corbett, Manpower Controls Division, Department of the Army, Washington, D.C.

Commander Kathryn Dougherty, Office of Manpower Utilization, Department of Defense, Washington, D.C.

D. B. Dubois, Directorate of Personnel Procurement and Training, Department of the Air Force, Washington, D.C.

Lt. Colonel H. H. Dunwoody, Office of the Assistant Secretary, Manpower and Reserve Forces, Department of the Army, Washington, D.C.

Colonel Irene O. Galloway, WAC, Department of the Army, Washington, D.C.

Colonel Julia Hamblet, Women Marines, Marine Corps, Washington,
D.C.

G. H. Hieronymus, Office of Civilian Personnel, Department of the
Army, Washington, D.C.

Major Jeanne Holm, Office of Director, WAF, Department of the Air
Force, Washington, D.C.

Commander L. L. Isert, Bureau of Medicine & Surgery, Department
of the Navy, Washington, D.C.

Captain Leona Jackson, Nurse Corps, Department of the Navy, Washington, D.C.

Lt. Colonel Margaret Kimpton, Office of Director, WAC, Department of the Army, Washington, D.C.

Gus C. Lee, Office of Manpower Utilization, Department of Defense,
Washington, D.C.

Margaret Moore, Office of Industrial Relations, Department of the
Navy, Washington, D.C.

Lt. Colonel Manley Morrison, Office of the Surgeon General, Department of the Army, Washington, D.C.

Colonel Miriam E. Perry, Women's Medical Specialist Corps, Office
of the Surgeon General, Department of the Air Force, Washington,
D.C.

Jack Pockrass, Directorate of Civilian Personnel, Department of the
Air Force, Washington, D.C.

Lt. Colonel J. A. Prall, Office of the Assistant Secretary, Manpower and
Reserve Forces, Department of the Army, Washington, D.C.

George Price, Bureau of Naval Personnel, Department of the Navy,
Washington, D.C.

Lt. Colonel Elizabeth Ray, Defense Advisory Committee on Women
in the Services, Department of Defense, Washington, D.C.

Squadron Officer Barbara Turier, Office of Director, WAF, Department of the Air Force, Washington, D.C.

Commander C. S. Walline, Bureau of Naval Personnel, Department of
the Navy, Washington, D.C.

Major Harriet Werley, Army Nurse Corps, Office of the Surgeon General, Department of the Army, Washington, D.C.

Major Beatrice Whitcomb, Women's Medical Specialist Corps, Office
of the Surgeon General, Department of the Army, Washington, D.C.

Capt. Louise Wilde, WAVES, Department of the Navy, Washington,
D.C.

Colonel Verena Zeller, Air Force Nurse Corps, Department of the Air
Force, Washington, D.C.

MAY, 1955

St. Louis, Missouri

C. B. Allen, Southwestern Bell Telephone Company, St. Louis, Mo.
Julia Alsberg, Vocational Counseling Service of Greater St. Louis,
St. Louis, Mo.
Fred Bastman, Famous-Barr Company, St. Louis, Mo.
Ramon Beuc, First National Bank in St. Louis, St. Louis, Mo.
Ralph K. Brown, Emerson Electric Company, St. Louis, Mo.
Ruth Condon, Universal Match Corporation, St. Louis, Mo.
L. H. Diekroeger, Board of Education of the City of St. Louis, St.
Louis, Mo.
A. W. Evans, General American Life Insurance Company, St. Louis,
Mo.
Robert Gunnison, Military Personnel Records Center, St. Louis, Mo.
Nelle G. Hoffman, Civil Service Commission of the City of St. Louis,
St. Louis, Mo.
Annabelle Lamburth, Wagner Electric Corporation, St. Louis, Mo.
Frances Lamm, Miss Hickey's School for Secretaries, St. Louis, Mo.
Imogene Laswell, The Jewish Hospital of St. Louis, St. Louis, Mo.
R. F. McCoole, Monsanto Chemical Company, St. Louis, Mo.
Gladys Meyer, White-Rodgers Electric Company, St. Louis, Mo.
Mary Ryder, St. Louis Women's Trade Union League, St. Louis, Mo.
Julia Shanahan, Bindery Women's Union, St. Louis, Mo.
Edith Smith, Missouri State Employment Service, St. Louis, Mo.
Irvin Sobel, Washington University, St. Louis, Mo.
Arnie Solem, Bureau of Employment Security, Department of Labor,
Kansas City, Mo.
C. L. Windsor, McDonnell Aircraft Corporation, St. Louis, Mo.

JUNE, 1955

New York, New York

Dr. Grace Abbate, Brooklyn, N. Y.
Dr. Viola Bernard, New York, N. Y.
Ewan Clague, Bureau of Labor Statistics, Department of Labor, Washington, D.C.
Dr. John M. Cotton, New York, N. Y.
Dr. Margaret Craighill, New Haven, Conn.
Ethel L. Ginsburg, Citizens' Committee on Children of New York
City, New York, N. Y.
Dr. Sol W. Ginsburg, New York, N. Y.
Margaret Hickey, *Ladies' Home Journal,* Philadelphia, Pa.
Dr. Lawrence Hinkle, New York Hospital, New York, N. Y.

Johanna Hopkins, New York City Board of Education, New York, N. Y.

Dr. Edward Hornick, New York, N. Y.

Marie Jahoda, New York University, New York, N. Y.

Mirra Komarovsky, Barnard College, Columbia University, New York, N. Y.

Trude Lash, Citizens' Committee on Children of New York City, New York, N. Y.

Dr. Lena Levine, New York, N. Y.

Pearl B. Max, Board of Higher Education, New York, N. Y.

Marjorie Pleshette, New York, N. Y.

James S. Schoff, Bloomingdale Bros., New York, N. Y.

Dr. S. Mouchly Small, E. J. Meyer Memorial Hospital, Buffalo, N. Y.

Dr. Benson Snyder, Wellesley College, Wellesley, Mass.

Frances M. Wilson, New York City Board of Education, Brooklyn, N. Y.

JULY, 1955

Los Angeles, California

Cecelia Carrigan, United Automobile Workers, Los Angeles, Calif.

Albert W. Charles, Jr., AiResearch Manufacturing Company, Los Angeles, Calif.

Samuel L. Fick, Bureau of Industrial Education, State Department of Education, Sacramento, Calif.

C. M. Fleener, Pacific Finance Loans, Los Angeles, Calif.

Gordon Gilbert, Huntington Memorial Hospital, Pasadena, Calif.

John N. Given, Los Angeles Junior College of Business, Los Angeles, Calif.

H. V. Harris, The Pacific Telephone and Telegraph Company, Los Angeles, Calif.

Phyllis Harrison, Kwikset Locks, Inc., Anaheim, Calif.

C. Mansel Keene, Twelfth United States Civil Service Region, United States Civil Service Commission, Los Angeles, Calif.

Karl R. Kunze, Lockheed Aircraft Corporation, Burbank, Calif.

A. C. McGraw, International Association of Machinists, Los Angeles, Calif.

John D. McLean, Citizens National Bank of Los Angeles, Los Angeles, Calif.

Edward S. Marples, Marples Gears, Pasadena, Calif.

Raymond B. Parkhurst, Hughes Aircraft Company, Culver City, Calif.

Raymond F. Prinz, The Prudential Insurance Company of America, Los Angeles, Calif.

John F. Rood, Department of Employment, State of California, Los Angeles, Calif.

Paul H. Schrade, United Automobile Workers, Los Angeles, Calif.

Berlene Thompson, Coulter's, Los Angeles, Calif.

James E. Watson, Hartwell Manufacturing Company, Los Angeles, Calif.

Florence B. Watt, University of Southern California, Los Angeles, Calif.

Juliann Werle, Hughes Aircraft Company, Culver City, Calif.

James White, Rose Marie Reid Company, Los Angeles, Calif.

JULY, 1955

San Francisco, California

Margaret Kay Anderson, California Department of Industrial Relations, San Francisco, Calif.

John W. Bristow, California Processors & Growers, Inc., Oakland, Calif.

Vincent H. Brown, San Francisco Retailers' Council, San Francisco, Calif.

William B. Cobaugh, Fireman's Fund Group, San Francisco, Calif.

William W. Davison, Standard Oil Company of California, San Francisco, Calif.

James Dillon, Columbia-Geneva Steel, San Francisco, Calif.

Julian M. Edwards, The Pacific Telephone and Telegraph Company, San Francisco, Calif.

Frank P. Foisie, Federated Employers of San Francisco, San Francisco, Calif.

Margaret S. Gordon, Institute of Industrial Relations, University of California, Berkeley, Calif.

Thomas W. Harrell, Graduate School of Business, Stanford University, Stanford, Calif.

Gerald C. Henry, California Packing Corporation, San Francisco, Calif.

Alexander R. Heron, Crown Zellerbach Corporation, San Francisco, Calif.

Eleanor C. Hewlett, Oakland Junior College, Oakland, Calif.

Sam Kagel, San Francisco, Calif.

Daniel E. Koshland, Levi Strauss and Co., San Francisco, Calif.

M. D. Kossoris, Bureau of Labor Statistics, Department of Labor, San Francisco, Calif.

Karl R. Kunze, Lockheed Aircraft Corporation, Burbank, Calif.

Thomas P. Langdon, Hahnemann Hospital, San Francisco, Calif.

A. J. Noia, Pacific Gas and Electric Company, San Francisco, Calif.

Vernon L. Pankey, Cannery Workers Union, Oakland, Calif.

John L. Roberts, San Francisco Public Schools, San Francisco, Calif.

Herbert J. Sandstrom, American Trust Company, San Francisco, Calif.

Wesley P. Smith, State Department of Education, Sacramento, Calif.

J. M. Trickett, Food Machinery and Chemical Corporation, San Jose, Calif.

James D. Zellerbach, Crown Zellerbach Corporation, San Francisco, Calif.

JULY, 1955

Asheville, North Carolina

Charles P. Anson, Alabama Polytechnic Institute, Auburn, Ala.

Guy B. Author, Guy B. Author Associates, Tocoa, Ga.

J. A. Barksdale, University of Tennessee, Knoxville, Tenn.

A. L. Bechtold, Lance, Inc., Charlotte, N. C.

Ruth Current, North Carolina State College, Raleigh, N. C.

Annette Duchein, Spartan Mills, Spartanburg, S. C.

E. J. Eberling, Vanderbilt University, Nashville, Tenn.

Dale H. Gramley, Salem Academy & College, Winston-Salem, N. C.

Jackie Greer, First National Bank, Houston, Texas

Ernestine G. Hadaway, Spartan Mills, Spartanburg, S. C.

Ruth Hays, Tennessee Eastman Company, Kingsport, Tenn.

George M. Ivey, J. P. Ivey & Company, Charlotte, N. C.

Frank M. Malone, Southern Bell Telephone and Telegraph Company, Atlanta, Ga.

Mary B. Merritt, University of Miami, Coral Gables, Fla.

Fannie Y. Mitchell, Duke University, Durham, N. C.

Benjamin U. Ratchford, Duke University, Durham, N. C.

Dr. Logan T. Robertson, Asheville, N. C.

Josephine Schaeffer, Woman's College, University of North Carolina, Greensboro, N. C.

Susie Sharp, Superior Court, Reidsville, N. C.

Hammond B. Smith, Fifth United States Civil Service Region, United States Civil Service Commission, Atlanta, Ga.

Katherine Taylor, Woman's College, University of North Carolina, Greensboro, N. C.

Ruth Vaughan, Southeastern Clothing Regional Board, Amalgamated Clothing Workers of America, Knoxville, Tenn.

Charles B. Wade, Jr., R. J. Reynolds Tobacco Company, Winston-Salem, N. C.

Arthur M. Whitehall, Jr., School of Business Administration, University of North Carolina, Chapel Hill, N. C.

Ellen Winston, The North Carolina State Board of Public Welfare, Raleigh, N. C.

OCTOBER, 1955

    Washington, D.C.

Harold D. Barclay, Hotel & Restaurant Employees and Bartenders International Union, Washington, D.C.

Helen Berthelot, Communications Workers of America, Washington, D.C.

Selma Borchardt, American Federation of Teachers, Washington, D.C.

Catherine Brosnan, United Packinghouse Workers of America, Chicago, Ill.

Caroline Davis, Women's Bureau, United Automobile, Aircraft & Agricultural Implement Workers of America, Detroit, Mich.

Katherine Pollak Ellickson, Congress of Industrial Organizations, Washington, D.C.

Paula Goldberg, United Hatters, Cap and Millinery Workers International Union, New York, N. Y.

Joseph C. Goodfellow, International Glove Workers Union of America, Marinette, Wis.

Loretta Gordon, Boot and Shoe Workers' Union, Boston, Mass.

Sylvia B. Gottlieb, Communications Workers of America, Washington, D.C.

Peter Henle, American Federation of Labor, Washington, D.C.

Victor Hood, The Journeymen Barbers, Hairdressers, Cosmetologists and Proprietors International Union of America, Hyatsville, Ind.

Carl Huhndorff, International Association of Machinists, Washington, D.C.

John J. McCoy, American Federation of Hosiery Workers, Philadelphia, Pa.

Andrew W. Myrup, Bakery & Confectionery Workers' International Union of America, Washington, D.C.

Henrietta E. Olding, American Federation of Government Employees, Washington, D.C.

Henry Paley, United Paperworkers of America, Washington, D.C.

Iris Peterson, Air Line Stewards and Stewardesses Association, International, Chicago, Ill.

John P. Philpott, Retail Clerks International Association, Washington, D.C.

Nancy Pratt, American Federation of Labor, Washington, D.C.

Rowland K. Quinn, Jr., Air Line Stewards and Stewardesses Association, International, Chicago, Ill.

Roland R. Renne, Montana State College, Bozeman, Mont.

Herbert S. Shockney, Laundry Workers' International Union, Indianapolis, Ind.

Elwood Taub, International Brotherhood of Pulp, Sulphite & Paper Mill Workers, Washington, D.C.

Ruth Vaughan, Southeastern Clothing Regional Board, Amalgamated Clothing Workers of America, Knoxville, Tenn.

J. Belton Warren, Glass Bottle Blowers' Association of the United States & Canada, Philadelphia, Pa.

Anthony G. Weinlein, Building Service Employee's International Union, Milwaukee, Wis.

Henry T. Wilson, American Federation of State, County and Municipal Employees, Madison, Wis.

OCTOBER, 1955

New York, New York

Margaret F. Ackroyd, Department of Labor, State of Rhode Island, Providence, R. I.

Elwood C. Allen, American Telephone & Telegraph Corp., New York, N. Y.

Dr. Leo Bartemeier, The Seton Psychiatric Institute, Baltimore, Md.

Maurice E. Berthiaume, Cluett, Peabody and Company, Inc., Troy, N. Y.

Edith N. Cook, Solicitor's Office, Department of Labor, Washington, D.C.

Esther Cole Franklin, Young Women's Christian Association of the United States of America, New York, N. Y.

Mabel Fisher Garrahan, Joint Board of Shirt, Leisurewear, Robe, Glove, and Rainwear Workers, New York, N. Y.

Margaret Hickey, *Ladies' Home Journal,* Philadelphia, Pa.

Herbert Hill, National Association for the Advancement of Colored People, New York, N. Y.

Lucy Somerville Howorth, James Somerville and Associates, Washington, D.C.

Harry W. Jones, School of Law, Columbia University, New York, N. Y.

Isabella J. Jones, National Federation of Business and Professional Women's Clubs, Inc., Pittsburgh, Pa.

Alice K. Leopold, Women's Bureau, Department of Labor, Washington, D.C.

Beatrice McConnell, Bureau of Labor Standards, Department of Labor, Washington, D.C.

Elizabeth S. Magee, National Consumers League for Fair Labor Standards, Cleveland, Ohio

Margaret A. Mahoney, Department of Industrial Relations, State of Ohio, Columbus, Ohio

Emily Sims Marconnier, Department of Labor, State of New York, New York, N. Y.

Marion E. Martin, Department of Labor and Industry, State of Maine, Augusta, Maine

Alice A. Morrison, Women's Bureau, Department of Labor, Washington, D.C.

Phoebe Morrison, Barnard College, Columbia University, New York, N. Y.

Edward A. Nyegaard, Department of Labor, State of New York, New York, N. Y.

Helen Tafe O'Donnell, Massachusetts Federation of Labor, Boston, Mass.

Helen F. Southard, Young Women's Christian Association of the United States of America, New York, N. Y.

Henry W. Steinhaus, The Equitable Life Assurance Society of the United States, New York, N. Y.

JANUARY, 1956

New York, New York

Dr. Leo Bartemeier, The Seton Psychiatric Institute, Baltimore, Md.

Bess Bloodworth, Newburyport, Mass.

Helen D. Bragdon, American Association of University Women, Washington, D.C.

Frances T. Cahn, National Council of Jewish Women, New York, N. Y.

Catherine B. Cleary, First Wisconsin Trust Company, Milwaukee, Wis.

Margaret Divver, John Hancock Mutual Life Insurance Company, Boston, Mass.

Margaret Hickey, *Ladies' Home Journal*, Philadelphia, Pa.

Althea K. Hottel, University of Pennsylvania, Philadelphia, Pa.

Katherine G. Howard, Federal Civil Defense Administration, Washington, D.C.

Hazel McCalley, Camp Fire Girls, Inc., New York, N. Y.

Margaret Mealey, National Council of Catholic Women, Washington, D.C.

Thelma Mills, The Young Women's Christian Association of the City of New York, New York, N. Y.

Anne G. Pannell, Sweet Briar College, Sweet Briar, Va.

Nancy Pratt, American Federation of Labor, Washington, D.C.

Marguerite Rawalt, National Federation of Business and Professional Women's Clubs, Inc., Washington, D.C.

Zelia P. Ruebhausen, League of Women Voters of the United States, New York, N. Y.

Sarah Ann Stauffer, Association of the Junior Leagues of America, Inc., Lancaster, Pa.

Dorothy C. Stratton, Girl Scouts of the United States of America, New York, N. Y.

Anna Lord Strauss, New York, N. Y.

Janet M. Wilson, The American National Red Cross, Washington, D.C.

MARCH, 1956

Washington, D.C.

Wayne G. Althaus, Office of Defense Mobilization, Executive Office of the President, Washington, D.C.

Robert L. Clark, Office of Defense Mobilization, Executive Office of the President, Washington, D.C.

Brig. Gen. Carlton S. Dargusch, Office of Defense Mobilization, Executive Office of the President, Washington, D.C.

Bowen Dees, National Science Foundation, Washington, D.C.

John F. Hilliard, Office of Defense Mobilization, Executive Office of the President, Washington, D.C.

James M. Mitchell, National Science Foundation, Washington, D.C.

MARCH, 1956

Washington, D.C.

Homer D. Babbidge, Office of Education, Department of Health, Education, and Welfare, Washington, D.C.

Clara M. Beyer, Bureau of Labor Standards, Department of Labor, Washington, D.C.

S. M. Brownell, Office of Education, Department of Health, Education, and Welfare, Washington, D.C.

Millard Cass, Department of Labor, Washington, D.C.

Margaret J. Hagood, Agricultural Economics Division, Agricultural Marketing Service, Department of Agriculture, Washington, D.C.

John L. Kilcullen, Department of Commerce, Washington, D.C.

Alice K. Leopold, Women's Bureau, Department of Labor, Washington, D.C.

Gladys Miller, Bureau of Employment Security, Department of Labor, Washington, D.C.

Ralph E. Spear, Federal Civil Defense Administration, Washington, D.C.

Aryness Joy Wickens, Office of the Assistant Secretary, Department of Labor, Washington, D.C.

Seymour L. Wolfbein, Bureau of Labor Statistics, Department of Labor, Washington, D.C.

INDIVIDUALS*

Carrie Glasser Abramovitz, Palo Alto, Calif.
Wendell C. Allen, Office of Superintendent of Public Instruction, Olympia, Wash.
Ruth C. Anderson, San Francisco Unified School District, San Francisco, Calif.
Jarvis Barnes, Board of Education of the City of Atlanta, Atlanta, Ga.
C. S. Blackburn, Board of Education, North Little Rock, Ark.
Jesse P. Bogue, American Association of Junior Colleges, Washington, D.C.
Patricia Bond, Harry E. Wood High School, Indianapolis, Ind.
Miriam L. Boyer, Allentown High School, Allentown, Pa.
Carol P. Brainerd, Wharton School of Finance and Commerce, University of Pennsylvania, Philadelphia, Pa.
George W. Brooks, International Brotherhood of Pulp, Sulphite and Paper Mill Workers, Washington, D.C.
Lowell A. Burkett, American Vocational Association, Inc., Washington, D.C.
Ethlyn Christensen, Young Women's Christian Association of the United States of America, New York, N. Y.
Edith M. Clark, Los Angeles City Board of Education, Los Angeles, Calif.
Joseph G. Cohen, Division of Teacher Education, The College of the City of New York, New York, N. Y.
Mary M. Condon, State Department of Public Instruction, Helena, Mont.
Herbert S. Conrad, Office of Education, Department of Health, Education, and Welfare, Washington, D.C.
Sophia Cooper, Bureau of Labor Statistics, Department of Labor, Washington, D.C.
Howard H. Cummings, Office of Education, Department of Health, Education, and Welfare, Washington, D.C.
Richard C. Date, San Francisco Unified School District, San Francisco, Calif.
John J. Desmond, Jr., State Department of Education, Boston, Mass.
Eleanor F. Dolan, American Association of University Women, Washington, D.C.
Galen N. Drewry, Chattanooga Public Schools, Chattanooga, Tenn.
Marguerite E. Dunn, New Orleans Public Schools, New Orleans, La.
William H. Dunstan, Schenectady Public Schools, Schenectady, N. Y.

*Not previously listed.

P. K. Whelpton, Scripps Foundation for Research in Population Problems, Miami University, Oxford, Ohio

John B. Whitelaw, Office of Education, Department of Health, Education, and Welfare, Washington, D.C.

Sam Wiggins, George Peabody College for Teachers, Nashville, Tenn.

Richard C. Wilcock, Institute of Labor and Industrial Relations, University of Illinois, Champaign, Ill.

W. S. Wilwerding, Art Instruction, Inc., Minneapolis, Minn.

Helen Womack, Bedford County Schools, Shelbyville, Tenn.

Harold Wool, Office of the Assistant Secretary of Defense, Department of Defense, Washington, D.C.

The figures in Part Two were prepared by Mr. Vincent Kotschar.

CONTENTS

Contents

TABLES

FIGURES

PART ONE

A STATEMENT BY THE
NATIONAL MANPOWER COUNCIL

SUMMARY OF RECOMMENDATIONS BY THE NATIONAL MANPOWER COUNCIL

Women constitute not only an essential but also a distinctive part of our manpower resources. They are essential because without their presence in the labor force we could neither produce and distribute the goods nor provide the educational, health, and other social services which characterize American society. They constitute a distinctive manpower resource because the structure and the substance of the lives of most women are fundamentally determined by their functions as wives, mothers, and homemakers.

A revolution in women's employment has occurred in the course of the present century. Today, one third of all the women in the United States, aged fourteen and over, are in the labor force in any given month, and well over two fifths—some 28 million—work in the course of a year. Three out of every ten married women are now working, and nearly two out of every five mothers whose children are of school age are in the labor force.

The skills and the capacities of our people depend on the opportunities for development available to each individual. The effective utilization of those skills and capacities is crucial to the strength of our manpower resources. Both more effective development and utilization rest upon increasing our knowledge about our manpower resources.

With respect to expanding the opportunities for the effective development of womanpower, the National Manpower Council recommends that:

1. School and college officials, boards of education, and Federal, state, and local governments expand and improve educational and vocational guidance in order to help young women make sound decisions with respect to their self-development, the growing and changing employment opportunities open to them, and the probability that paid employment will occupy a significant place in their adult lives

2. The Federal and state governments, employers, unions, and voluntary organizations cooperate to increase occupational guidance and placement services for mature women who want to work, in order to help them make sound decisions in the light of their individual interests, capacities, and employment opportunities

3. The Federal and state governments, employers, labor unions, voluntary groups, and individuals expand their support of scholarship and fellowship programs, in order to enable more young women of high ability to continue their formal education in college or in professional or graduate schools

4. State governments, in cooperation with local communities, educational institutions, employers, and labor unions, initiate surveys to determine whether existing training facilities are adequate to meet the needs of mature women who want to work, and in what ways mature women can be helped to meet the requirements for employment in professional or semiprofessional occupations where manpower shortages exist.

With respect to expanding the opportunities for the effective utilization of womanpower, the National Manpower Council recommends that:

1. Employers hire, assign, train, and promote all individuals regardless of sex on the basis of their personal qualifications; labor unions strive to implement for all individuals the principle of equality of opportunity in employment; and both employers and unions take additional steps to apply the principle of equal pay for equal work

2. Employers review their hiring, assignment, training, and promotion practices in light of the changes which have taken place in the education, skill, age composition, and work interests of women in the labor force, in order to insure that they make effective use of their women employees

3. Employers experiment further with part-time and flexible work arrangements, so that they can draw upon the potential supply of women who want to work, but are not available for regular, full-time employment

4. Management associations and personnel groups undertake studies for the purpose of appraising the experiences of business organizations which have developed new practices for utilizing their women workers more effectively and make their findings broadly available for use by employers

5. The Secretary of Defense direct the Secretaries of the Army, Navy, and Air Force to review jointly their experiences with the utilization of women in uniform and to make their significant findings available for use by employers.

With respect to increasing knowledge about the effective development and utilization of womanpower, the National Manpower Council recommends that:

1. Universities, foundations, and government encourage and support research dealing with the impact of the increased employment of women upon family life, the rearing of chil-

dren, and the self-development of women; upon the process of occupational choice among both younger and older women; upon the prosperity of the economy and living standards; and upon the availability of volunteer workers for community service functions

2. The Secretary of Labor initiate a comprehensive study of the maximum use which could be made of the actual and potential resources of womanpower in the event of a national emergency

3. The Secretary of Labor take the initiative in establishing a commission to review, in the light of recent changes in technology and the economy and in the composition of the female labor force, the consequences and adequacy of existing Federal and state laws which have a direct bearing on the employment of women.

A STATEMENT BY
THE NATIONAL MANPOWER COUNCIL

IN RECENT YEARS, Americans have developed a new understanding of the extent to which their nation's strength and security depend upon its manpower resources—that is, upon the skills, capacities, and creativeness of its people. The search for immediate solutions to pressing problems of manpower shortages has been accompanied by a growing awareness of the rich contribution which the more effective development and utilization of our manpower resources can make to the future progress of the nation and to the well-being of each individual.

Today, we are troubled by the waste of human abilities. We recognize the need to expand our resources of highly trained manpower. We seek ways of raising the skill level of the population as a whole. We find our national investment in education sorely inadequate for developing our potential manpower resources. We realize that we must expand the opportunities for education and training in the light of our manpower needs and make certain that all our people have equal access to them. We are dissatisfied with traditional ways of utilizing manpower which waste capacities and competence or do not contribute to the acquisition of new skills.

THE NEW CONCERN WITH MANPOWER

The emergence of a conscious and continuing concern with manpower development and utilization, and not merely with immediate problems of shortages of highly trained personnel, affirms a truth long taken for granted but also long ignored—that the nation's most precious resource is its people. Today, Americans are better armed than ever before with understanding and a sense of common purpose to respond to the challenge implicit in this truth. Man's capacity for development is still an open frontier which we have only begun to explore. That exploration, undertaken with the vigor and imagination it deserves, could initiate a new era in the nation's history.

During the past decade, current or anticipated shortages of highly trained personnel, especially in scientific and professional occupations, have prompted efforts to expand the supply of college-educated young men and women and to improve the quality of secondary education. At the same time, there has been a growing appreciation that the urgent manpower problems which have caught the nation's attention since World War II are interrelated, and, even more important, that they will not be solved by simple panaceas. Our manpower problems, it is now recognized, must be attacked upon many fronts at the same time and with as much regard for long-range consequences as for short-run gains. Energetic campaigns and special incentives to increase the supply entering an occupation may be successful, but they may also result in contracting the number of men and women preparing for employment in other fields.

These broad considerations have been stressed by the National Manpower Council in previous studies devoted to our resources of scientific, professional, and skilled manpower. In each of these segments of the nation's labor force, women are represented. In some occupations—in nursing, teaching, and secretarial work, for example—women constitute almost all or the major portion of the available manpower supply. In others—as in medicine, engineering, and most skilled trades—they comprise only a small part of the supply. The role which women now play in the nation's working population of 70 million merits separate study if we are to have an adequate understanding of our total manpower resources, not only as they now are but as they may be developed in the future.

Women constitute not only an essential, but also a distinctive part of our manpower resources. They are essential because without their presence in the labor force we could neither produce and distribute the goods nor provide the educational, health, and other social services which characterize American society. They constitute a distinctive manpower resource because the structure and the substance of the lives of most women are fundamentally determined by their functions as wives, mothers, and homemakers.

THE "REVOLUTION" IN WOMEN'S EMPLOYMENT

Work outside the home has been a salient aspect of a broad and continuing effort to secure for women greater equality and freedom in all spheres of life. The changes which have taken place in women's employment are an integral part of basic transformations in American life. To make clear the variety and the complexity of the factors which have affected the demand for and the supply of women workers during the present century would require retelling the history of the United States. Growth and change in the economy, advances in science and technology, an expanding urban population, developments in education, the role of government as an employer, the crisis situations of war and depression, social values and attitudes, patterns of marriage, childbearing, and life expectancy—all have contributed significantly to the revolution in women's employment.

In 1890, the 4 million women in paid employment accounted for about one sixth of the working population. In 1956, about 22 million working women were reported by the Census, and they comprised almost one third of the civilian labor force. In 1890, about one sixth of all women ten years old and above were working. Today, one third of all the women aged fourteen and over are in the labor force in any given month, and well over two fifths—some 28 million—work in the course of a year.

At the close of the last century, about half the adult women never entered paid employment. Now, at least nine out of every ten women are likely to work outside the home in the course of their lives. Women who reached adulthood around the turn of the century participated in paid employment, on the average, for 11 years in the course of their lives. Those who reached adulthood just before World War II are likely, on the average, to work over 20 years. Today's schoolgirls may spend 25 years or more in work outside the home.

In 1890, out of every ten women who did work, seven were single and five were under 25 years old. Today, only one fourth of the female labor force consists of single women. About six out of every ten women now working are married, and five out of ten are over 40 years of age. Three out of every ten married women are now working. Even more striking is the fact that nearly two out of every five mothers whose children are of school age are in the labor force.

These changes in the number of women workers and in their age and marital characteristics have been accompanied by alterations in the occupational and industrial structure of the female labor force. While the relative importance of unskilled and semi-skilled manual work for women has declined, that of white-collar employment has risen. More than one third of all women workers are today employed in secretarial, clerical, and sales occupations, compared to about one twentieth in 1890. In that year, one out of every five gainfully employed women was an agricultural worker, but now the ratio is one in twenty. Better than eight out of every ten employed women who did not work on farms in 1890 were found in domestic and personal service, teaching, and in the clothing and textile industries. These are still important fields of women's employment, but they now claim only one out of every three women workers. Domestic service, which claimed about half of all employed women in 1890, now accounts for less than one tenth.

Since the end of the last century, the proportion of proprietors, managers, and officials in the female labor force has increased threefold. In professional employment, the most prominent change has been the decline in the relative importance of teaching as an occupational field for women. Six or seven decades ago, four fifths of all women professional workers were teachers, compared to about two fifths today.

WOMEN'S EMPLOYMENT TODAY

Today, one fifth of the nation's income in the form of wages and salaries is earned by the women in the labor force, and they are responsible for more than one fourth of the total number of man hours worked in the course of a year. In 1955, for example, women received an estimated $42 billion in wages and salaries and worked an estimated 130 billion man hours.

Currently, women are found in virtually all occupations listed by the Bureau of the Census. They are represented in every professional field, and they hold top posts in management and government. They are regular members of the armed services. They handle baggage, work in railroad yards, and are teamsters. They are atomic physicists and engineers, bankers and real estate agents, clergymen and college presidents, artists and automobile mechanics. They run newspapers and hospitals. They work on assembly lines and farms and in offices, stores, and restaurants.

They are psychologists and mathematicians. They operate hydraulic presses and electronic computers. Hardly any significant area in the world of work still carries the tag "For Men Only."

Even more significant than the wide-ranging distribution of women workers among occupations and industries is the degree to which they are concentrated in a small number of employment fields. In 1950, two out of every five women in the labor force were found in five occupations, and better than seven out of ten were accounted for by twenty occupations. Clerical work now claims the largest share of all women workers, almost 29 percent. Another 17 percent are employed as semiskilled operatives, largely in manufacturing plants; 13 percent are employed in a variety of service occupations; almost 11 percent are professional and semiprofessional workers; and 8 percent are in sales. Two professional occupations alone—teaching and nursing—claim about 8 percent of all employed women, and about 5 percent hold managerial positions, are government officials, or are business proprietors.

Women constitute a majority in fifteen of the twenty occupations in which most employed women are found. In some of these occupations, women predominate so strongly that the men workers are numerically unimportant. Thus, women represent practically all the workers classified as professional nurses, telephone operators, private household workers, and stenographers, typists and secretaries. Women comprise better than four fifths of those working as waiters, cashiers, and operatives in the manufacture of apparel and other fabricated textile products. About three fourths of the teachers and bookkeepers are women, as are three fifths or more of the laundry and dry-cleaning operatives. Finally, women account for more than half of the factory operatives in several manufacturing fields and for a majority of all cooks. In two of the major occupational groupings of the labor force, women are poorly represented—farm owners and workers and managers, officials, and business proprietors. They are least well represented among both skilled craftsmen and foremen and among unskilled laborers.

FORCES OF CHANGE

An expanding and constantly changing economy and a growing national income have constituted the bases for a rising level of demand for women workers. Advances in science and technology have led to the appearance of new production processes, products, services, occupations, and skills, and have contributed to reducing the length of the working day and week and to improving the conditions of employment. These developments in turn have influenced the demand for women workers, the fields of their employment, and the kinds of work regarded as suitable for women. The replacement of muscle power by mechanical power has increased the number of jobs open to women, while the availability of women for work outside the home has encouraged technological innovations designed to eliminate physically demanding labor.

The demand for women office and clerical workers has been influenced by the increasing scale of industrial and commercial activity, by growth in the size and complexity of business enterprises, and by greater specialization in managerial functions. It has also been directly stimulated by innovations in systems of communications and record-keeping which have had far-reaching implications for the employment of women by government as well as private industry. Vastly expanded responsibilities and functions of government during the emergency years of depression, war, and cold war also enhanced the demand for women white-collar workers.

The number and variety of jobs held by women have grown because women have been employed in jobs once open only to men, because new industries, services, and occupations have ap-

peared, and because job opportunities have expanded in older
fields of work involving functions traditionally performed by
women. The education and training of children, the preparation of food, the making, repairing, and cleaning of clothing, the
care of the sick—these are still in major part the responsibilities
of women, whether they are fulfilled through paid employment
or within the home.

As the society became more urban and industrial—and less
rural and agricultural—large numbers of women were absorbed
in paid work associated with their traditional functions. While
the growth of urban centers creates new demands for women
workers, urban life also tends to make more women, particularly
more married women, available for paid employment by encouraging higher standards of living and by making housekeeping
easier and less time-consuming.

The spectacular growth of secondary and higher education in
the twentieth century has also brought about changes in women's
employment. For decades, girls have accounted for a majority of
our high school students and graduates. They have used their
school years to equip themselves for employment in a variety of
fields, as well as to prepare for their future responsibilities as
wives, mothers, and citizens. For decades, too, young women
have been so strongly represented among our college students
that in 1950 they accounted for more than two fifths of all college
graduates 25 years old or more. The predominance of women in
office, clerical, and other white-collar work has been made possible by the great number of girls graduating from high school.
The importance of women in the professions rests upon the large
proportion of young women among college graduates.

Social values and attitudes exert a pervasive influence upon
women's employment. They are reflected in changing conceptions
of when and under what circumstances it is appropriate for a
woman to work outside the home. They underlie judgments about

the kinds of jobs and the conditions of employment which are harmful to women and about the impact of their working upon their maternal functions. Such judgments are reflected in the adoption of laws specifically designed to protect women workers.

The entrance of women into fields of employment previously closed to them required, just as it mirrored, changes in conventional views about the types of work which are suitable for women and about the capacities of women for performing certain kinds of tasks. The undermining of the belief in the innate inferiority of the female sex, and continuing changes in popular ideas about the intellectual capacities and emotional traits of women, have been inextricably interwoven with the changing nature of women's employment. In sharp contrast to older conceptions, which had a restrictive effect upon employment opportunities, is the contemporary view that measurable variations between men and women with respect to intelligence, abilities, and aptitudes are probably not determined by sex, but are produced by differing interests, expectations, and cultural experiences.

The disposition of women to work outside the home is inevitably conditioned by widely shared values and attitudes. Americans view the man in the family as the primary breadwinner and, when jobs are scarce, are inclined to believe that women workers should not compete with men who have families to support. Americans also believe that mothers should personally care for their children during their early formative years. Consequently, even though there are today over 2.5 million mothers in the labor force whose children are under six, there is still little sympathy with the idea of mothers holding full-time jobs when their children are of preschool age, unless they are compelled to do so by economic necessity.

The attitudes of the society which affect the participation of women in paid employment are deeply rooted and resist change, but they are far from immutable. They have altered sufficiently to make it easier for married, as well as for single, women to work outside the home without feeling that they are violating social conventions. The idea that young women will work before they marry is now taken for granted. For them to continue to work after marriage until the birth of the first child is typical. The married women who takes a full-time job when her children have reached school age is rarely censured, even when her family could get along on her husband's earnings alone. The desire to achieve a richer life for the family, measured not only in physical goods and possessions but also in more education and better medical care, has such widespread approval that it provides a generally acceptable reason for married women, whose responsibilities at home do not absorb all their time and energy, to go to work.

Just as the depression years of the 1930's strengthened employment policies favoring the man with a family to support over the married woman worker, so manpower needs during World War I and, more particularly, World War II, made the recruitment of women workers necessary if the nation was to meet its war production goals. World War II not only saw an explosive and unprecedented expansion of the female labor force, but it also influenced the future character of women's employment. The female labor force increased from 14 million in 1940 to a peak of 20 million in 1945. World War II demonstrated the importance of wives and mothers as a manpower reserve. When the war began, less than one tenth of the mothers in the country were working. When it ended, one fifth of the mothers whose children were 18 or younger, and one eighth of the mothers whose children were under 6, were in the labor force.

World War II also witnessed the entrance of women into jobs formerly reserved for men; occupational shifts within the female labor force; the opening of special training programs to women; the establishment of publicly supported, as well as private, facilities to provide care for the children of working mothers; and the enlistment of some 350,000 women in the armed services of the United States. Wartime experiences challenged employers to examine their traditional ways of utilizing women workers. Preconceptions about what women could and could not do received little confirmation, and difficulties expected to arise with mixed work forces frequently did not eventuate. In labor unions, too, traditional fears were allayed as the influx of women workers did not result in endangering union wage rates and working conditions, and as hundreds of thousands of women became union members. The wartime experiences of women workers—especially of wives and mothers—encouraged more positive attitudes toward work outside the home, and many of them looked forward to remaining in the labor force after the war. The successful utilization of women in uniform laid the basis for integrating the women's services into the regular military establishment on a permanent basis in 1948.

THE RECENT GROWTH IN WOMEN'S EMPLOYMENT

Since 1947, a period marked by international tension and crisis and high levels of employment, women have accounted for most of the growth of the nation's working population. Between 1930 and 1940, the civilian labor force increased by 5.4 million persons, and men accounted for about 55 per cent of the net growth. But between 1940 and 1950, the labor force increased by 8.6 million, and women were responsible for 55 percent of the net growth. Even more arresting is the role played by women in the expansion of the civilian labor force between 1950 and 1956. During these years, the male labor force rose by more than 1.2 million, an increase of 3 percent, while the female labor force grew by about 3.1 million, an increase of 17 percent.

Since 1950, the largest single source of workers for expanding the labor force has been women in their middle and later years, whose homemaking responsibilities do not absorb so much of their time and energy as to prevent them from going to work, if they want to. In the past, if a woman worked at all, the chances were good that she did so when she was in her late teens and early twenties, and the likelihood of her being employed diminished as she grew older. As recently as 1940, the chance that a woman would be in the labor force was almost one out of two if she was in her early twenties, but less than one of out four if she was around 50.

Today, peak participation in paid employment occurs among young women of 18 and 19. Among those who are older, the proportion working declines, but only up to age 30. After that year, the percentage of women in the labor force rises for each successive age group through to the early fifties. Currently, the chances are about as good that a woman of 50 will be working as one of 20. In 1940, more than half of all employed women were under 25 and one fifth were over 45. Now, one fifth are under 25 and almost two fifths are over 45.

The importance of women in their thirties, forties, and fifties as a new source of workers, on the one hand, and the significance of paid employment in the lives of these women, on the other, are closely linked to the aging of our population and to changes in patterns of marriage and childbearing. The ratio of older to younger people has risen not only because we live longer than we used to and because birth rates declined between 1890 and the mid-1930's, but also because we have placed restrictions on immigration since the 1920's.

Ten years have been added to the average span of adult life since the close of the nineteenth century, and the great majority of women who are now 25 years old will witness the advent of the twenty-first century. At the same time, there has been a reduction not only in the size of the average family, but also in the number of years during which the lives of married women revolve around the bearing and rearing of children. The birth rate has risen and the age of marriage has fallen since 1940. The tendency for families to have all their children during the earlier years of marriage has been accentuated. Two long-run developments have been intensified: one is the decline in the number of years young women work full-time before marriage; the other is the rise in the number of years of employment among a growing proportion of wives and mothers.

The median age at which young women now leave school is 18, and that of marriage is just over 20. Current patterns of child-bearing mean that many women may be free enough from the pressure of work at home to take a job as early as ten to fifteen years after they marry, if not sooner. It is now common for women to be in their middle twenties when their families are completed, and to be in their early thirties when the youngest child enters school. At the turn of the century women who had several children were likely to be past 30 when their last child was born, almost 40 when that child entered school, and in their mid-fifties when the youngest child married.

WHO WORKS AND WHY

Age and marital status help determine whether or not a woman is likely to work outside the home and what kind of job she is likely to hold. So do the level of her education, her economic status, her race or ethnic origin, and her place of residence.

The fifteen-year-old girl who takes a part-time job while in high school in order to earn additional spending money; the twenty-year-old wife who is willing to help her husband complete college by holding a secretarial job, but who looks forward to being a full-time housewife and becoming a mother; the woman of forty-five who took a job in an airplane factory during the war, and has since remained in the labor force; the mother who returns to the teaching profession when her children are of school age; the grandmother in her late fifties who has been practicing medicine throughout her adult life; the sixty-year-old woman who, having just lost her husband, takes a job as a housekeeper; the wife who carries on her husband's real estate business when he is ill; the wife and mother who is a migratory farm worker; the middle-aged mother who works in a department store during the holiday season in order to provide additional family income; the woman who has been a machine operator in garment factories all her adult life; the hourly domestic worker—these only begin to suggest the diverse circumstances and motives which influence the participation of women in paid employment and the nature of their attachment to the labor force.

The proportion working among single women is almost as high as among single men. Older single women are likely to remain as firmly attached to the labor force as men, in the sense that they continue to work until they retire. In this group, substantial numbers are employed in professional or skilled occupations, conduct their own enterprises, or hold jobs as officials, managers, and supervisors. The vast majority of young, single workers are in clerical, sales, and service jobs, or work as operatives, and only one in ten of them is found in professional and semiprofessional employment. For most of them, work outside the home stops either temporarily or permanently with marriage or just before the birth of their first child.

And almost all of them do marry and marry young—half of them before they reach 21. Only 7 percent of all women never marry. Among young married women without children, about three fifths are working, but among young wives whose children are not yet of school age, only a small proportion is employed —about one eight. Because of their responsibilities at home, many of them hold part-time jobs or work part of the year, and are likely to leave and re-enter the labor force several times in a relatively short period. The likelihood that mothers will work outside the home increases sharply once their children reach school age. About one fifth of the female labor force now consists of women with children between the ages of 6 and 17. These wives and mothers, the majority of whom hold jobs for which little training is required, are relatively less well represented in professional occupations and clerical work than are single women.

Almost three fifths of the women under 65 who are widowed, divorced, or separated from their husbands are working. Among those who have children over 17, an even higher proportion is in the labor force. Among women separated from their husbands, two fifths of the mothers whose children are still below school age are working. Divorced women are likely to be found holding the same kinds of jobs as working wives and mothers. Widows and women separated from their husbands are usually found in unskilled and poor-paying jobs.

The influence exerted by formal education upon work outside the home is linked to that of marital status and age. Many young women have some experience with part-time work while they are still in school. The vast majority of them, however, seek full-time employment as soon as they leave school. Consequently, the lower the level of education, the earlier in their lives do young women enter the labor market. On the other hand, the more education adult women have had, the more likely they are to be working. In part, this tendency reflects differences in marriage and childbearing patterns. Women college graduates tend to marry later than less well-educated women, and to have fewer children. A relatively high proportion of women college graduates, moreover, remain single. College graduates are better represented than high school graduates in the adult female labor force, just as the proportion of high school graduates employed exceeds that of women who never went beyond elementary school. College graduates comprise the majority of women workers in professional and technicians' occupations. While high school graduates are characteristically engaged in clerical work, the majority of those with only elementary schooling hold jobs as operatives and service workers.

Economic circumstances is a major determinant of employment among women. Over half of those who work either support themselves or are primarily responsible for the support of their families. Most single women and those who are widowed, divorced, or separated from their husbands work out of necessity. Where the husband's income is very low, economic necessity is again the compelling reason why mothers, including those with children under school age, seek employment. As the husband's income rises, the mother with young children is less likely to be employed. Among women with children past school age, the proportion working falls when the husband's income goes above $5,000. When the husband's earnings amount to $10,000 a year or more, however, the percentage of working mothers rises.

Nearly half the women now working are married to men who are the chief breadwinners in their families. However, in many instances, it is the additional income provided by the wife which safeguards the family against hardship and deprivation. In others, where the family could live in modest comfort upon the husband's earnings, the wife's willingness to take a job, even when it imposes heavy demands upon her time and energy, is nourished by a desire to assure a better life for herself and for her family. This motive for working outside the home is a distinguishing feature of women's employment. Today, probably more than half of the families in which both husband and wife work have incomes of $5,000 or above, and in two out of every five families with incomes between $6,000 and $10,000, both husband and wife are employed.

When their responsibilities in the home no longer consume

most of their time and energy, and when employment opportunities exist, women may be prompted to seek employment for quite different reasons than the desire to achieve higher living standards. Some may believe that they can realize their potentialities only if they work outside the home in addition to fulfilling their functions as wives and mothers. Others may look to work as a means of satisfying a need for adult companionship or for personal independence. Some may find their homemaking tasks dull and unrewarding. Some may feel troubled that they are not making fruitful use of the free time at their disposal, even though they may be helping to provide valuable community service as volunteer workers. Others may have originally planned to resume the careers which they readily interrupted in order to marry and raise a family. Still others, as in the case of those trained to be teachers or nurses, may be impelled to return to work because the professional skills they possess are sorely needed by the community. Some may be apprehensive that their lives will be empty when their children are grown and no longer live at home, and they hope to insure against this possibility by finding a place for themselves in the world of work.

The reasons for working are many and diverse. In the absence of economic compulsions, probably most wives and mothers who enter or return to employment do so in response to a combination of motives. Their decision to work outside the home is an act of individual choice, for there are other meaningful activities in which they could and frequently do find satisfaction. It is, consequently, of major significance that more and more married women have been deciding to work outside the home as the opportunities for employment have expanded.

Variations within national patterns of employment indicate that where a woman lives and the racial or ethnic group to which she belongs affect both the range of job opportunities open to her and her participation in the labor force. Women in urban communities are much more likely to be in the labor force than those in agricultural and rural areas. The proportion of women working is smaller in cities dominated by heavy industries than where a diversified urban economy with light manufacturing industries and a variety of business enterprises presents many more job opportunities. Where women tend to marry young, as they do in Southern and Western cities, the proportion of married women in the labor force is slightly above the national average. How great a difference there may be in the ratio of single to married women workers from one city to another is illustrated by Boston, where less than half of the working women are married, and Los Angeles, where three fourths are married.

Women of native parentage are somewhat better represented in the female labor force than those of foreign origin, and a higher proportion of them are found in better paying and more skilled jobs. There are also discernible differences with respect to employment among groups of women of foreign origin or parentage. Thus, a higher proportion of women of Southern and Eastern European origin or parentage, than of Western and Northern, are in the labor force. Variations in labor-force participation among women in minority groups reflect differences in the kinds of job opportunities to which they have access, as well as the influence of such key factors as marital status, education, and economic circumstance. Thus, although employment opportunities have expanded in other fields, about two fifths of all Negro women workers are still found in domestic service, and Negro married women are heavily represented in the female labor force, in part because of the relatively lower earnings of Negro men. The jobs held by women in almost all minority groups tend to be concentrated on the lower rungs of the skill and pay ladder.

LOOKING AHEAD

If present patterns of marriage and childbearing persist, and if positive attitudes toward work outside the home by wives and mothers continue to grow in strength, employment among women in their middle and later years is likely to become even more common than it now is. Recent tendencies indicate that work at this stage of women's lives will be even more a matter of choice and less a product of necessity than in the past. In consequence of these developments, girls will take it increasingly for granted that they will be likely to work during two stages of their lives—immediately after they leave school and after their children are old enough to go to school.

The impact of automation upon future employment opportunities cannot be forecast with any certainty. The technological innovations now represented by that term are, however, expected to require the development of new skills, to reduce the need for semiskilled workers engaged in routine tasks, many of whom are women, and to result in the temporary displacement of some workers. Yet, a contraction in total employment opportunities is not expected to occur as long as the economy continues to grow, especially if further reductions in the length of the working day or week occur as a result of gains in productivity. Moreover, automation is not likely to have a drastic effect in the near future upon women's employment in service, sales, and secretarial jobs, or in such professional occupations as teaching and nursing.

With a social climate favorable to the employment of women, a continued expansion of the economy promises a further growth in the female labor force not only in absolute numbers, but also in relative size. And much of this growth would result from the higher proportion of women returning to or entering employment for the first time when they are past 30. Women over 45 are now working outside the home to an extent which was, only a few years ago, not expected to be achieved until almost 1970. This demonstrates how risky prediction is, but it also testifies to the power of those social and economic forces which have brought about rapid alterations in what had been fairly stable patterns of behavior.

If past developments provide a key to future trends, the continued growth of the female labor force seems assured. Present expectations are that there will be 10 million more persons in the labor force by 1965 than there were in 1955, and that women will account for at least half of the increase. Recent Census Bureau estimates indicate that if the rate at which women participate in paid employment continues to increase as rapidly as it did during the years 1950-55, the female labor force could total 33.6 million by 1975.

LABOR FORCE CHARACTERISTICS

The vast majority of women have some experience with paid employment in the course of their lives. Relatively few, however, spend all of their adult lives in work outside the home. Even today, less than half of the adult women in the nation participate in paid employment, however briefly, during the course of a year. Work outside the home is characteristic at certain stages of a woman's life, and not throughout her life, as it normally is with a man. Moreover, when she is a member of the labor force, she is far more likely than a man to work only part of the year, or to hold a part-time job. Of all employed women, a little more than one third hold full-time jobs—which means that they work 35 hours a week or more—and work throughout the year. About one third work full time, but for only part of the year. The others hold part-time jobs for varying periods during the year.

The labor force behavior of women is characterized by discontinuity in work and by part-time work. These are the direct results of the home and family responsibilities which women fulfill. These responsibilities influence the frequency with which women leave and re-enter the labor force within short periods of time as well as in the course of their lives. Marriage may bring a brief, if not a more lasting, break with paid employment. Pregnancy marks at the very least a suspension in work, and, more generally, means withdrawal from the labor force for a number of years or even permanently. The illness of a child or of a relative may also bring an interruption of work outside the home. The work which women do at home helps determine the extent to which they work part of the year or hold part-time jobs. To undertake full-time, regular employment in addition to running a household, particularly one in which there are young children, is frequently an intolerable burden for a woman to assume.

The extent to which women work part time helps to explain why their annual wage and salary earnings are, on the average, well below those of men. Another reason is their concentration in jobs at the lower end of the skill ladder, in factory, service, sales, and office work. When the earnings of full-time women workers are compared with those of men in the same or similar jobs, the differences in favor of the men are small. In recent decades, wage differentials in favor of men for the same kind of work have been significantly reduced in both private and public employment, and the principle of equal pay for equal work is winning increasing acceptance. Action by employers, unions, and government, as well as the educational efforts of many women's organizations, have all contributed to the greater realization of this principle.

When a man leaves a job, particularly if he is between 25 and 44 years old, the chances are overwhelming that he will remain a member of the labor force. When a woman leaves a job, she may also be withdrawing from the labor force. Consequently, total labor force turnover rates—which measure the extent to which workers enter and leave the labor force in a given period of time—run substantially higher for women than for men.

It is widely believed that women workers are also likely to leave their jobs more frequently than men. The view that most women workers are tenuously attached to their jobs is in large measure a carry-over from the past, when the female labor force was composed far more than today of young, single women. However, it is not supported by recent information, which shows no appreciable difference in the average quit rates for all employed men and women. In some fields of employment, women quit jobs at about the same rates as men; in others, women's quit rates are higher; and in still others, they are lower. In manufacturing generally, differences in quit rates—which at one time were substantial—have been growing much smaller. Among groups of women whose participation in paid employment is characterized by continuity, the tendency to quit a job is about as strong, or as weak, as among comparable groups of men workers.

As a general rule, absence from work is also far more common among women workers than men. The contrast in absenteeism rates between men and women appears to be due less to differences in the actual incidence of illness than was once thought to be the case. Moreover, not all women workers are equally likely to stay away from work because of illness, fatigue, or obligations at home.

Women hold high-level positions in many fields of employment. Nevertheless, they are poorly represented in most skilled trades and in supervisory and managerial jobs. This feature of women's employment is largely a product of discontinuity in work, part-time work, the prevailing beliefs of workers and employers, and the concentration of women in employment fields and jobs which offer limited opportunities for promotion. Training opportunities, work experience, and seniority, which are important in the acquisition of skill and in promotion to supervisory positions, are jeopardized by interruptions in employment. Systems of promotion are not part of the structure of part-time work, and opportunities for promotion are lacking in many semiskilled occupations in which women predominate, as in the case of routine factory, office, and service jobs.

Women who subordinate the claims of work outside the home to their obligations and functions in the home will not make the effort required to move up the ladder of skill and responsibility. Employers who are persuaded that their women workers are temporary members of the labor force are reluctant to make an investment in providing training opportunities for them. Consequently, even women who do remain strongly attached to the labor force are often deprived of this necessary means for promotion. If employers also believe, as many do, that women are not likely to have the qualities required to be competent supervisors, and that women and men alike prefer to be supervised by men, they will be unwilling to plan to promote their women employees to positions of greater responsibility and authority.

The return to work by women in their middle and later years has added a new dimension to the nation's total manpower resources. These women constitute a source of supply for new workers in a wide range of fields. They have been especially important in increasing the number of professional workers in at least two occupations marked by persistent shortages. In part, supply has lagged behind demand in teaching and nursing because many women leave these professions when they become wives and mothers. If the new supply for these and other professions, such as social work and library service, had been made up solely of young college and professional school graduates, the shortages would be even more acute. The availability of qualified older women for employment in teaching and nursing, and the establishment of special training programs in order to facilitate their return to these professions, have been important factors in expanding the supply.

MANPOWER POLICY OBJECTIVES

The size and occupational composition of the female labor force indicate how essential the functions which women perform as workers outside the home are to the life of the nation. The radical changes which have occurred in women's employment have altered the significance of women as an actual and potential manpower resource. These changes reflect the convergence of two developments: the need of the economy for more workers and the willingness of more women to enter paid employment.

The greater the needs of the society for manpower, the more willing we have been to abandon traditional ways of developing and utilizing our human resources. The more we come to understand how heavily the skills and the capacities of our people depend upon the opportunities for development available to each individual, the more willing we should be to enrich these opportunities and to establish greater equality of access to them. The more we realize how vital to the development of our manpower resources is each individual's freedom to choose his or her occupation and work, the more determined we should be to make that freedom effective.

These considerations apply to all our people without regard to race, religion, ethnic origin, or sex, and they establish the guideposts for manpower policies in a free society. Therefore, the National Manpower Council has set forth in its previous studies specific recommendations designed to achieve the following broad manpower objectives:

To provide more equal opportunities for all individuals to acquire skill

To strengthen the contributions made by secondary education to the acquisition of skill

To develop more effective programs for vocational guidance

To improve the facilities and methods used to train skilled and technical manpower

To strengthen the institutions through which scientific and professional manpower is educated and trained

To expand the opportunities for capable young men and women to secure a higher education.

OPPORTUNITIES FOR THE EFFECTIVE DEVELOPMENT
OF WOMANPOWER

In preparing young women not only for the obligation of citizenship and for a rich adult life, but also for work, our secondary schools play a critical part in manpower development. In 1956, girls accounted for just over half of almost 700,000 secondary school graduates, but for many decades they comprised an even larger proportion of the students completing high school. The high schools have long placed a strong emphasis upon vocational courses in which large numbers of girls have been enrolled. The secondary school experience of girls has in part been designed to prepare them not only for the functions of women in the home, but also for initial employment after they leave school.

The expectation that their lives as adults will be defined primarily by marriage and motherhood, and that their experience with paid employment will occur when they leave school and will be of short duration, leads many girls to pursue commercial and other vocational curricula. Existing patterns of employment strongly influence them to prepare for work chiefly in the small number of fields in which women are already heavily concentrated. Fewer girls than boys plan to go to college, and this is reflected in the fact that they are less well represented in high school curricula which prepare for college entrance. Because so many girls do not intend to go to college, and because there is a tradition that they have neither the interest in nor the aptitude for work in mathematics and the physical sciences, they are less well prepared than boys in these subjects.

The choices of high school girls with respect to curricula and subject matter seem frequently to be attuned more to older patterns of women's employment than to its present and emerging characteristics. It is uncertain how much awareness a high school girl can be helped to acquire of the new place which work occupies in the lives of women. It is difficult for an adolescent girl to make educational and vocational plans which take into account not only employment before or early in marriage, but also the probability that she will return to work when she is in her thirties or later. Nor is it an easy task for those who carry responsibility for vocational guidance and counseling to provide reliable information about future, as well as present, employment opportunities and skill requirements. Nevertheless, a greater awareness than now exists of the revolution in women's employment and of the place of work in women's lives is essential, if each high school girl is to have the opportunity to make sound decisions about her courses of study and about continuing her formal education.

If this awareness were present, some girls might decide to complete high school instead of dropping out earlier; others might plan to enroll in a junior or community college or set their sights on a college degree; some might think of preparing for work in fields which now attract few women. A greater knowledge of the future prospects, as well as of the current realities, of women's employment would in effect expand the opportunities open to young women for their self-development and for the acquisition of skills useful not only in paid work, but also in volunteer community service.

More effective guidance at the high school level could also contribute to reducing the waste of high ability among young women as among young men. Potential ability ignores sex lines, and the proportion of those capable of high accomplishment is no smaller among women than among men. Our society's needs for capable, highly trained persons are so great that we do ourselves a disservice by neglecting any reservoir of undeveloped talent and ability. The chief, but not the only, means by which potential ability is developed is through formal education. Consequently, it is significant that, of all the young women capable of doing college work, only about one fourth graduate from college, and only one woman out of every three hundred capable of earning a Ph.D. degree actually does so.

Yet, women have long taken advantage of the opportunities for higher education. They comprise over a third of the students enrolled in junior and community colleges. In the past few years, they have accounted for over one third of our college graduates, for about one third of the recipients of master's degrees, and for about one tenth of those who earn doctoral degrees. Women are found in virtually all fields of undergraduate and graduate study, but are heavily concentrated in a small number of them. Thus, about half of all the bachelor's and first professional degrees earned by women are in four fields of study—education, nursing, library science, and home economics. At the master's degree level, only five fields of study account for about four fifths of the degrees earned by women: education, English, home economics, nursing, and fine arts. A similar pattern of concentration is found among women who earn doctoral degrees, about 30 percent of which are in the field of education alone.

The concentration of women in a few fields of professional employment is sharply mirrored in the choices among fields of study made by women college and university students. But these choices are also profoundly influenced by the weight of tradition, and by the fact that many young women look upon a college education as preparation not for work primarily but for a meaningful adult life. Guidance at the college level which stresses the likelihood of employment at a later stage of a woman's life, and which calls attention to the emergence of employment opportunities for women in technological and scientific occupations, might lead more young women to consider specializing in less conventional fields, or to plan to continue with graduate study.

The return to work of wives and mothers has raised a series of new guidance and educational problems. Adults as well as young people require assistance in making wise educational and vocational decisions. The choice of an occupation or a field of work is the result of an extended and complex process, and not of a single act early in life. The choice of a satisfactory field of employment by a mature woman who has never worked or who has not held a job for fifteen years, and who seeks to relate her interests and skills to available job opportunities, may be very difficult. Existing facilities for guidance and counseling—whether provided by the schools, government, employers, or others—are largely designed to serve the needs of younger people. The degree to which adults, particularly mature women, also need the help such services can provide still remains to be fully recognized.

Our colleges now enroll thousands of students who are well past the age of the typical college graduate, as do other post high-school educational institutions. The growth of educational facilities geared to the needs of adults has contributed to the strength of our manpower resources. The return to work of mature women merely emphasizes the extent to which opportunities for education and training available to adults constitute a significant factor in manpower development.

These opportunities are numerous, but so little is known about them that a reliable judgment on their adequacy cannot be reached. Such efforts as have been made to provide special refresher courses and training programs for mature women who want to return to employment have paid worthwhile returns. How much more should be done to establish new training facilities which could contribute to the development of skills later in life warrants exploration.

With respect to expanding the opportunities for the effective development of womanpower, the National Manpower Council recommends that:

1. School and college officials, boards of education, and Federal, state, and local governments expand and improve educational and vocational guidance, in order to help young women make sound decisions with respect to their self-development, the growing and changing employment opportunities open to them, and the probability that paid employment will occupy a significant place in their adult lives

2. The Federal and state governments, employers, unions, and voluntary organizations cooperate to increase occupational guidance and placement services for mature women who want to work, in order to help them make sound decisions in the light of their individual interests, capacities, and employment opportunities

3. The Federal and state governments, employers, labor unions, voluntary groups, and individuals expand their support of scholarship and fellowship programs, in order to enable more young women of high ability to continue their formal education in college or in professional or graduate schools

4. State governments, in cooperation with local communities, educational institutions, employers, and labor unions, initiate surveys to determine whether existing training facilities are adequate to meet the needs of mature women who want to work, and in what ways mature women can be helped to meet the requirements for employment in professional or semiprofessional occupations where manpower shortages exist.

OPPORTUNITIES FOR THE EFFECTIVE UTILIZATION OF WOMANPOWER

History and habit, which determine practices governing the utilization of all workers, have left their mark in the distinctions made between "men's" and "women's" jobs. It is conventional to think of both men and women as being peculiarly suited or ill-suited for certain kinds of work. It is also conventional to think of particular jobs as demanding specific qualities characteristic of one sex or the other. Preconceptions about differences between men and women with respect to their aptitudes and capacities, as well as social attitudes toward the appropriateness of particular jobs for women, influence the hiring, assignment, training, and promotional practices of employers. These practices affect the manpower resources available to employers no less than they do the employment opportunities open to women.

Under pressure of the need for manpower and as a result of technological, attitudinal, and other changes, traditional conceptions of differences between "men's" and "women's" jobs have broken down, and new utilization practices have been introduced. World War II encouraged the abandonment of many conventional—and restrictive—employment practices. The armed services have experimented successfully with new practices in utilizing women in uniform by employing them in all but a few assignments, and by providing them with an exceptionally wide range of opportunities for training and promotion.

Many employers have learned that maternity-leave programs help them retain married women workers. Some have developed promotional systems which do not discriminate between men and women workers. Others have recognized that cherished views about women workers in general may make it impossible to utilize fully the skills and competences of the particular women in their employ. Many have introduced part-time work arrangements in order to hire women whose responsibilities at home prevent them from taking full-time jobs. Still others have discovered that they gained by establishing the same wage rates for men and women who do the same kind of work. Many of these developments have encouraged women workers to become more interested in their jobs and to make the effort to advance themselves. Much still remains to be learned, however, about other ways of achieving the more effective utilization of womanpower.

With respect to expanding the opportunities for the effective utilization of womanpower, the National Manpower Council recommends that:

1. Employers hire, assign, train, and promote all individuals regardless of sex on the basis of their personal qualifications; labor unions strive to implement for all individuals the principle of equality of opportunity in employment; and both employers and unions take additional steps to apply the principle of equal pay for equal work

2. Employers review their hiring, assignment, training, and promotion practices in light of the changes which have taken place in the education, skill, age composition, and work interests of women in the labor force, in order to insure that they make effective use of their women employees

3. Employers experiment further with part-time and flexible work arrangements, so that they can draw upon the potential supply of women who want to work, but are not available for regular, full-time employment

4. Management associations and personnel groups undertake studies for the purpose of appraising the experiences of business organizations which have developed new practices for utilizing their workers more effectively and make their findings broadly available for use by employers

5. The Secretary of Defense direct the Secretaries of the Army, Navy, and Air Force to review jointly their experiences with

the utilization of women in uniform and to make their significant findings available for use by employers.

INCREASING KNOWLEDGE ABOUT WOMANPOWER

If the outlines of the revolution in women's employment are already clearly visible, the full range of its implications for many aspects of American life still remain to be disclosed. It would be naïve to assume that the presence of so many wives and mothers in the labor force does not have consequences for patterns of family life, the development of children during their formative years, or the greater sharing of homemaking functions by husband and wife. Some concern has already been expressed that existing child care facilities, provided either by voluntary organizations or governmental agencies, might be inadequate in the light of the large number of working mothers. But whether there is in fact a genuine need for more facilities of this kind is not known.

Past conceptions of the reserve of womanpower which could be drawn upon in the event of a national emergency were based upon the assumption that many married women not in the labor force would be available for paid employment. The age, marital status, and family responsibilities of those women who are not in the labor force, however, may require significant revision of this view. Much of the legislation regulating the employment of women was enacted when the size and composition of the female labor force, as well as the economy and the technology, were very different from what they now are. It is not yet clear what bearing the growth of women's employment has upon the number of women available for volunteer work with organizations providing community services, or whether such services need to be expanded because so many wives and mothers work outside the home. Only with the clarification of these and still other issues will we grasp the full meaning of the revolution in women's work.

With respect to increasing knowledge about the effective development and utilization of womanpower, the National Manpower Council recommends that:

1. Universities, foundations, and government encourage and support research dealing with the impact of the increased employment of women upon family life, the rearing of children, and the self-development of women; upon the process of occupational choice among both younger and older women; upon the prosperity of the economy and living standards; and upon the availability of volunteer workers for community service functions

2. The Secretary of Labor initiate a comprehensive study of the maximum use which could be made of the actual and potential resources of womanpower in the event of a national emergency

3. The Secretary of Labor take the initiative in establishing a commission to review, in the light of recent changes in technology and the economy and in the composition of the female labor force, the consequences and adequacy of existing Federal and state laws which have a direct bearing on the employment of women.

PART TWO

CHAPTERS BY THE COUNCIL STAFF

HENRY DAVID, *Executive Director*

ELI GINZBERG, *Director of Staff Studies*

DALE L. HIESTAND

ROBERT W. SMUTS

BRYNA BALL	BERNARD ROSHCO
JEAN SCOTT CAMPBELL	IRENE M. SORROUGH
ANN CRICHTON	ALBERT R. VOGELER

1. THE NEW CONCERN WITH MANPOWER

FOR THE PAST DECADE and a half, public attention increasingly has been centered on various manpower issues—shortages of scientists and engineers, difficulties in staffing schools and hospitals, losses to the armed services of technically trained personnel who return to civilian life, to name a few. The growing awareness of the importance of manpower resources is exemplified by the fact that a section of the President's 1956 Budget Message, under the heading "Manpower," dealt with a series of proposals for strengthening the nation's human resources by improving the skills of the working population and by insuring an adequate supply of highly trained personnel.

Earlier in the nation's history, governmental policies affecting immigration and education were developed to achieve, among other objectives, a strengthening of the nation's manpower resources. During the nineteenth century, it was recognized that the expansion of the economy would be accelerated if additional labor could be secured from abroad. The emphasis placed on the development of a free public educational system reflected the belief that in a democracy all young men and women should be helped by the schools to prepare for their adult responsibilities as workers as well as citizens. The establishment of the land-grant colleges, and, much later on, of vocational education in the high

come many of its manpower shortages. With only a brief interruption at the war's end, the rapid increase in women's employment has continued ever since.

The extent to which the United States today depends on the
presence of more than 22 million women in the labor force is not
always appreciated. One way of illustrating the importance of the
part they play in the production of goods and services is to ask
what would happen to the operation of the nation's schools and
hospitals if there were no women workers; how many offices and
stores would be able to function without women secretaries and
salesgirls; and where the textile and clothing industries—to men-
tion only two—would find an adequate labor supply if they could
not hire women.

The significance of women for the economy is not limited to the
contribution they make as workers. Their substantial earnings
have made it possible for millions of families to buy homes, automobiles, and household appliances, and to achieve higher standards of educational and health services. This higher level of consumers' spending has helped to accelerate the expansion of the
economy, which in turn has made a larger number of jobs available to women.

WOMEN AS MEMBERS OF THE LABOR FORCE

Recognition of the important part which women play in the
economy of the nation should not obscure the fact that most
women continue to be primarily concerned with their functions
as wives and mothers. Today, as in the past, their activities in
the home, together with the contributions many make to essential
community services as volunteer workers, absorb a very large
part of the time and energy of the majority of American women.

"Work" is a word of many meanings. One meaning is any pur-
poseful expenditure of energy directed toward a socially useful
end. In this sense, it stands in sharp contrast to play or leisure.

But common usage has associated the term "work" with the earning of a livelihood, and it is frequently used as a synonym for a job. The woman who runs her home, however, evidences by the language she uses that she thinks of herself as one who works. A housewife remarks to her husband on his return home from work that she had "some job with the children today—they never gave me a moment's rest." Another says she is very tired because she "worked so hard straightening out the closets." A third comments that "I worked almost all day just mending clothes." Housewives have no doubt that they work, and many of them are quick to point out that they work much longer and harder than their husbands. Women who serve as volunteers helping to take care of the patients in Veterans Administration hospitals, or selling in a church bazaar the cakes they baked earlier, have no question that they are engaged in useful work.

There are very few adults who do not "work," in the sense of performing useful activities, but most women do not work for pay. The women who do work for pay earn more than $42 billion annually. A comprehensive measure of all the useful work which women perform would also have to include the value of the goods and services for which they are responsible both in the home and in connection with their volunteer work in the community. Some indication of the scale of such work is suggested by the simple fact that, at any time during the year, the number of women who are not employed is nearly twice as great as the number who are. During 1955, more than half of the 60 million women fourteen years of age and over in the nation had no contact whatever with employment, not even to the extent of holding a job for a few weeks in the summer months or before the Christmas holidays.

How much is accomplished by women volunteer workers is suggested by the fact that they comprise the vast majority of some 15 million persons engaged in the fund-raising campaigns of the Community Chest and similar joint appeals, as well as in the work of agencies supported by these efforts. The National Foundation for Infantile Paralysis and the American Red Cross also depend very much on women volunteers. Perhaps 10 million women are members of organized church groups. From the point of view of many women, volunteer work may sometimes serve as training for paid employment. Others engage in volunteer work only because it provides an opportunity for service, and are not interested in working for pay.

Although it would not be easy to estimate in dollar terms the value of the work which women perform at home or as volunteers, it is possible to appraise their contribution within the economy proper, that is, as members of the labor force. A person in the labor force, according to the definition of the Bureau of the Census, is one who worked, or sought work, for pay or profit during a given week. The high school girl who baby-sits Saturday nights is included, as is the young woman who has never held a job but is currently looking for one. So, too, is the woman who helps in the family-owned store and the woman who helps to run her family's farm, if she spends at least 15 hours during the week in these activities.

During the course of a year, some people enter and others leave the labor force. The total of all persons who worked at any time during a year is always larger than the total in the labor force in any one week. In 1955, a total of almost 28 million women were in the labor force at some time during the year. The peak figure for a single week during that year, however, was about 22 million.

A person who is unemployed and looking for a job, or who works only a few hours during the course of the week, is counted as a member of the labor force. Consequently, it is important to distinguish between labor-force participation and regular full-time employment. Only slightly more than a third of all women who work hold full-time jobs throughout the year. About a third hold full-time jobs, but do not work throughout the year; and slightly less than a third work during part or all of the year on a part-time basis, which is defined as less than 35 hours a week.

WOMEN AS A MANPOWER RESOURCE

Women constitute so significant a part of the working population that an understanding of their behavior in the labor force and of the factors which influence it is essential for an adequate appraisal of the country's total manpower resources. Some men in their active working years enter and leave the labor force from time to time, or work part time rather than full time. The vast majority of adult men, however, remain more or less steadily in the labor force until they retire. Moreover, a man is likely to be not only a member of the labor force, but actually holding a full-time job unless he is ill, is on vacation, out on strike, or has left or lost his job and not yet found another. Although a few women work steadily from the time they leave school until they retire, the pattern for most women is markedly different. The majority enter paid employment after they leave school, but stop working before their first child is born. Many return after longer or shorter intervals, and some of them leave and reenter employment several times in later years in response to the needs of their families, or for other reasons. The fact that most women are not the principal breadwinners of their families means that they are relatively free to choose between paid work, on the one hand, and volunteer work, work in the home, or leisure, on the other hand.

Prevailing conceptions about the proper role of women in society establish the boundaries within which decisions about work are made. There are many parallels between the ways in which men and women prepare for work. But there are also many differences, some of which have their origins in early child-

hood—in the games which children play and the ideas they begin
to form about their roles in adult life. The adolescent girl and
boy think differently about the place of work in their future lives.
This affects their attitudes toward school and the type of educational program they select. The fact that girls do not expect to
bear the main responsibility for supporting a family also influences
their decisions about preparing for work.

The job structure and the practices employers follow in hiring
and utilizing different groups of workers help to shape the plans
of young people who are currently preparing for work. Thus, the
prevailing distribution of jobs between the sexes is reflected in
the fact that most students enrolled in vocational courses in auto-
motive mechanics are boys, while the majority of those pursuing commercial studies are girls. Both the aspirations of young
people and their awareness of job requirements established by
employers enter into their decisions about the kind and amount
of education they will seek. If a young man who wants to gain
a foothold on the executive ladder learns that his chances are
very slim unless he possesses a college degree, he is likely to go
to college. If a young woman has a serious interest in nursing
administration and has been advised that jobs in the field are
filled by those with a bachelor's degree, she is likely to follow
the four-year college course rather than a three-year program
leading to a diploma. As the schools place more emphasis on
guidance and counseling, the information they make available
to young women about the range of available jobs is an increasingly important influence on their preparation for work.

Formal schooling provides the basic preparation for work, but
the specific skills of workers are acquired mainly on the job as
a result of experience and training. The opportunities of women
to acquire skill in this manner depend directly on the hiring,
training, and promotional policies of employers. The extent to
which an individual takes advantage of the opportunities which

are available, however, depends upon his own attitudes toward work, responsibility, and promotion.

The particular circumstances affecting the ways in which women prepare for work and respond to job opportunities have an important bearing on current manpower shortages. Knowing that science and engineering are "men's" professions, some young women with aptitude for these fields do not prepare for them. On the other hand, because they marry and have children, many women who have been trained for teaching or nursing never enter the profession, or delay entrance, or leave the field for longer or shorter periods.

Underlying many of the differences between the patterns of men's and women's work are the attitudes of the society toward the propriety of work for women, and prevailing beliefs about their fitness for particular kinds of work. During the last half century, changes in these attitudes and beliefs have contributed to steady modifications in the hiring, assignment, training, and promotion of women. These changes in the utilization of women workers have an immediate effect on women who are already at work, and slower, but equally important consequences for the ways in which girls and young women prepare for work. Two illustrations of the close connection between changes in prevailing attitudes about women and the effectiveness with which they are utilized can be found in the mobilization experience of World War II and in the more recent developments in the women's services of the armed forces. Under the pressure of events, conventional ideas were abandoned, with the result that many opportunities were opened to women in new types of work and at higher levels of responsibility.

INDIVIDUAL PROBLEMS AND SOCIAL ISSUES

To separate the problems involved in considering the paid employment of women from those associated with their functions as wives and mothers is impossible. Ever since women first began to enter factory employment with the advent of the Industrial Revolution, questions have been raised about the meaning of work to the individual woman and the impact of her working upon her family. Most contemporary studies of the problems of individual and social adjustment facing wives and mothers devote a good deal of attention to paid employment.

More than a century ago, the movement for equal legal, political, social, and economic rights for women gained momentum throughout most of the Western world. In the United States particularly, the advocates of equal rights placed great stress on broadening the work opportunities of women. The leaders of the movement to emancipate women saw a need to break down discrimination, particularly in the professions, for they believed that careers offered one of the best ways for securing freedom and equality. It is difficult for one living in the middle of the twentieth century to realize that not so long ago women were second-class citizens, unable to vote or hold office. Only a few vestiges remain of a former system of law which made married women and their property subject to the direct and almost unlimited control of their husbands.

The feminist leaders believed that a woman's inferior status was partly grounded in her economic dependence—initially on her father, later on her husband. They held that she could gain independence only if she prepared herself for and was permitted to enter all fields of paid employment on the same terms as men. It was not long, however, before others, though sympathetic with the aims of the feminists, questioned whether a career was a satisfactory alternative to marriage. This was the point made by Miss Ida M. Tarbell in *The Business of Being a Woman,* published in 1912. She maintained that women were convinced that their "destiny" was "to bear and to raise . . . to know that upon them depend the health, the character, the happiness, the future of certain human beings—to see themselves laying and preserving the foundations of so imposing a thing as the family." Describing militant feminism as a movement which urged women to devote themselves to careers and behave like men, she declared that "instead of increasing in favor [it] has declined. There is little likelihood now that any great number of women will ever regard it as a desirable working formula for more than a short period of their lives." Nevertheless, she added, the movement will remain influential "in a modified form. . . . For, while the Uneasy Woman has practically demonstrated that 'making a man of herself' does not solve the problem, she has by no means given up the notion that the Business of Being a Woman is narrowing and unsatisfying."

Decade by decade, outright discrimination against women in all phases of American life, including work, has diminished to a point where today most of the objectives of the early feminists have been secured. There are now few insuperable barriers facing a woman who is determined to pursue a career in almost any field of work. Nevertheless, as has been seen, many employers still apply different hiring, training, and promotion policies to women workers. A report by the Commission on the Education of Women, published in 1955, stressed this fact, and maintained that, even where there is no discrimination, the ways in which girls are brought up and educated, together with the continuing responsibilities of women in the home, make it difficult for women to achieve a high order of self-development and fulfillment in work. The report continues: "This poses a basic problem: How can current restrictive attitudes and concepts about women workers in general be so changed that women who wish careers will have unfettered opportunities to pursue them solely on the basis of their own abilities?" The Commission observes that almost all women are primarily concerned with marriage and homemaking, but it points out that "they are also motivated, as are men in our culture, to use all of their abilities and energies throughout their lives, and many have an incentive to achieve status and to amass financial resources as individuals in their own right." There is a strong line of continuity between the importance which the early feminists attached to women's working outside the home as a means of self-realization and the Commission's recognition that some women will be able to realize themselves only if, in addition to marriage, they are able to have a career.

Several students of contemporary society have speculated about how the employment of married women may affect the relations between husbands and wives. Although modern psychology, sociology, and anthropology have cast doubt on older assumptions about the range of differences between men and women, the experts still disagree over whether there are in fact basic differences in the needs, capacities, and interests of the sexes. Some authorities feel that it would contribute to the stability of marriage and the true satisfaction of husbands and wives if married women continued to concentrate on homemaking functions. There are many who believe that the employment of married women means that men, as a result of assuming more responsibilties around the home, tend to become more "feminine," and that women become more "masculine," as a result of working under the competitive pressures prevailing outside the home.

The impact of married women's working on the welfare of their children has probably received more widespread attention than any other issue growing out of the increasing employment of women. There is widespread agreement with the position taken in a recent publication of the World Health Organization that "the infant and young child should experience a warm, intimate, and continuous relationship with his mother (or permanent mother-substitute) in which both find satisfaction and enjoyment." Many observers have been quick to attribute the reported rise in juvenile delinquency to the absence of working mothers from the home. But others—who also stress the importance of the mother to the child's development—believe that several questions must be answered before a balanced judgment can be reached about the consequences of the employment of mothers for children. How old must a child be—two, six, eighteen —before the mother can safely leave the home for part or all of the day? Under what conditions can others be relied upon to share some of the mother's responsibility? Do working mothers also have the physical and emotional resources to provide the care and love their children need?

Most people readily grant that it is best for children to be nurtured by the love of both parents, but they know that this ideal is more easily stated than attained. They know, too, that it is not always clear what will be best for a child in a particular family situation. Certainly, the consequences for children of the employment of their mother will vary enormously with the circumstances of the family. In one case, the mother, deserted by her husband, may be forced to go out to work if her family is not to starve. She is grateful to her neighbor, who promises to keep an eye on her two young children when they return from school. In another, a happily married woman physician may return to work when her children are four and six, having first added to her household an excellent nursemaid.

The point has been made that the employment of mothers may profoundly affect the emotional well-being of future generations and alter values, attitudes, and behavior with respect to family life and the rearing of children. At some time in the future it may be possible to determine whether this view is well founded. At present, however, there is little reliable knowledge about how the participation of mothers in paid employment specifically affects the development of their children.

INDIVIDUAL CHOICE AND SOCIAL CHANGE

The remarkable increase in the employment of women has

come about because more and more women have made a personal decision to work. Before the turn of the century, women worked primarily before marriage. Older women worked only if they were forced to by adversity. Today, of course, some women work because they must support themselves and others, but ever larger numbers work because they choose to.

The changes which have occurred in the role of women in paid employment since the turn of the century can be explained only in terms of the many developments in American life which have provided women with vastly expanded opportunities to find their own place in the economy. In the future, as today, the personal decisions of individual women will determine how many will work, at what times in their lives they will work, how intensively they will work, and what goals they will seek to realize through work. Undoubtedly, the environment in which women will grow up and live—especially with regard to education, marriage, family structure, and employment opportunities and practices—will continue to change and to present them with new and varied choices concerning work.

The following chapters provide information about and analyses of the changes which have occurred and are now taking place in women's work and in the place it occupies in their lives. These changes were brought about by, and in turn contributed to, the major transformations which have taken place in the American economy and society during the first half of this century. A deeper understanding of the origins and consequences of these changes may help to indicate the character of major social and economic developments in the decades ahead.

ii. WOMEN IN THE LABOR FORCE TODAY

Although few exclusively male strongholds are left, the occupational structure is still divided into jobs that are primarily "men's" and others that are primarily "women's." In 1950, there were twenty occupations, each of which employed no less than 1 percent of the women in the labor force. These twenty occupations, as Table 1 shows, accounted for almost three fourths of all employed women. Over half of all women workers were in the eight leading occupations. Most women, moreover, were employed in occupations dominated by women. One quarter of all working women were in occupations in which at least 90 percent of the workers were women, and nearly half were in occupations in which at least three fourths were women.

The traditional functions of women—care of the sick, training of the young, making and caring for clothing, and preparing and serving food—are involved in many of the paid occupations which employ the largest numbers of women. As these functions were gradually removed from the home, they were still performed by women, although in new surroundings and, usually, in quite different ways. This generalization applies to professional work, where two thirds of the women were teachers or nurses in 1950; to manufacturing, where over half the women operatives were in the food, textile, and apparel industries; and, most obviously, to the service occupations. Nevertheless, there are millions of women working in jobs which have no relation to their traditional functions in the home. Over a third of all employed women are now in the secretarial, clerical, and sales occupations, which are

Table 1. Occupations Employing 1 Percent or More of All Employed Women, 1950

	Occupation	Thousands	Percent of All Employed Women	Percent of Total in Occupation
1	Stenographers, typists, and secretaries	1,501	9.5	94
2	Clerical and kindred workers, n.e.c.	1,440	9.2	49
3	Private household workers	1,334	8.5	95
4	Salesmen and sales clerks, n.e.c.	1,260	8.0	38
5	Teachers, n.e.c	835	5.3	75
6	Operatives, apparel and other fabricated textile products manufacturing	655	4.2	81
7	Bookkeepers	556	3.5	77
8	Waiters and waitresses	546	3.5	82
9	Nurses, professional	389	2.5	98
10	Operatives, textile mill products manufacturing	355	2.3	53
11	Telephone operators	342	2.2	53
12	Farm laborers, unpaid family workers	318	2.0	35
13	Service workers, except private household, n.e.c.	311	2.0	62
14	Laundry and dry-cleaning operatives	288	1.8	67
15	Cooks, except private household	242	1.5	56
16	Retail proprietors	242	1.5	17
17	Barbers, beauticians, and manicurists	190	1.2	50
18	Operatives, food and kindred products manufacturing	186	1.2	38
19	Cashiers	184	1.2	81
20	Operatives, electrical machinery, equipment and supplies manufacturing	180	1.1	54
	Total	11,354	72.2	

n.e.c.=not elsewhere classified
Source: U.S. Bureau of the Census

thought of as "women's" work, but which were once dominated by men.

Because the women in the labor force differ from each other in many important ways, because they are engaged in nearly every occupation, and because some work all their adult lives while others are employed briefly or intermittently, they can be described only by concentrating on a few aspects of their behavior in connection with paid employment. After considering the occupations in which women are employed, this chapter deals with the relationships between their employment and five other factors: their position within the family group, their financial circumstances, their education, their race or ethnic background, and their place of residence.

The relationships between these factors and the employment of women are far from simple. Thus, the state of the labor market for both men and women may affect the age at which they marry and have children, the finances of their families, the education received by their children, the opportunities of minority groups, and even the geographic distribution of the population. Each of these, in turn, helps to determine not only whether or not individual women work, but also what kinds of work they do. Because the American economy and society are always changing, the relationships between these factors and employment are also subject to constant change—usually slow, but sometimes, as in the last fifteen years, quite rapid. Here, however, the primary purpose is to examine various groups in the female labor force today, rather than to illuminate changes in the employment of women.

A word of caution is in order at this point. The Census data on women's employment show their employment in a single given week, but, as has been seen in Chapter I, women are constantly entering and leaving the labor force in large numbers. Consequently, the number of women who fall into any particular labor force category over the course of a year is considerably larger than the number reported, and the number who remain constantly in any one category for an extended period of time is considerably smaller.

THE OCCUPATIONS OF WOMEN WORKERS

The procedures used to gather and present data on employment make use of broad rather than narrow occupational categories wherever women workers predominate. This has the effect of exaggerating the extent to which women are concentrated in relatively few fields of employment. On the whole, women workers do not acquire the range of specialized skills that men do, but occupational distinctions often are not made which would reveal differences among women workers. The skills of a secretary and a typist, for instance, are far from identical, but these titles are used so loosely that they are grouped together by the Census. Nevertheless, under any reasonable system of classification, most women workers would be found in a narrower range of occupations than most men.

The extent to which working women are concentrated in occupations where women predominate is not exaggerated by the statistical procedures employed. In fact, the statistical aggregates help to conceal the extent to which jobs are differentiated according to the sex of the worker. Men comprised 25 percent of the 1.1 million teachers reported in the 1950 Census, but most men teach in high schools while most women teach in elementary schools. In high schools the physical sciences and some of the social sciences are usually taught by men, while languages and literature are usually taught by women. In vocational, commercial, and industrial arts classes and physical education, men generally instruct boys, while women teach girls.

Women are a majority in two of the major groups of occupations shown in Figure 1—clerical workers (including typists and secretaries) and domestic service workers. They are a substantial minority of the workers—from a third to a half—in four other

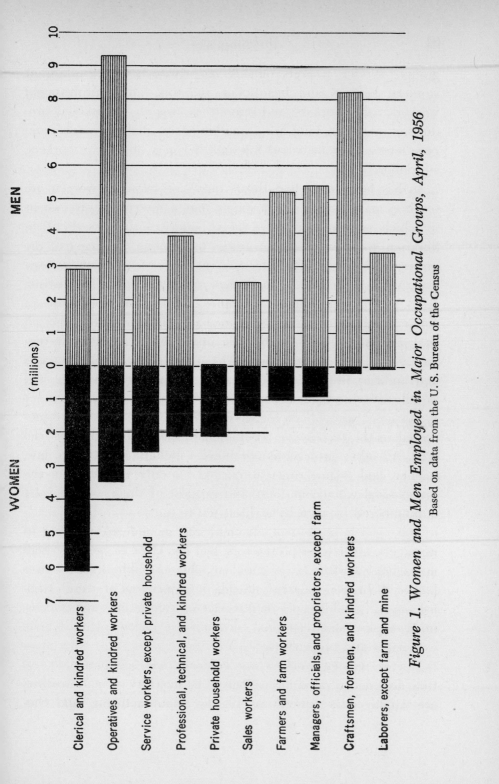

Figure 1. Women and Men Employed in Major Occupational Groups, April, 1956

Based on data from the U. S. Bureau of the Census

groups: service workers outside of private homes (restaurant workers, barbers and beauticians, janitors, etc.); professional workers; sales workers; and operatives (mainly semiskilled production workers). They are a small minority of the managers and proprietors, craftsmen and foremen, farmers and farm workers, and laborers.

As has been seen, two thirds of all professional women are teachers or nurses. Table 2 shows that a few other professions in which women were in a large majority—such as dietitian, librarian, social worker—accounted for another 9 percent of the professional women. One fourth of the professional women, however, work in fields in which they are a minority. The artistic fields and higher education employ substantial proportions of women, and women have also gained a foothold in certain specialized professional fields in the business world, particularly in personnel and labor relations work. The great majority of accountants and auditors are men, but because accounting is a large and rapidly growing field, it has become one of the more important professional occupations for women. Women are also well represented in the technician occupations, especially in the medical field. All other professions combined—including medicine, law, science, and engineering—accounted for only 7 percent of the professional women in 1950, and in most of them women were outnumbered by men by at least ten to one.

Less than 5 percent of all employed women are working as managers, officials, or proprietors, and less than 15 percent of all managerial workers are women. In 1950, as Table 3 shows, over half of them were salaried officials or proprietors of retail establishments. Retail and personal service establishments and government employment accounted for almost seven out of ten female executives and proprietors.

Just as women workers are concentrated occupationally, so they are concentrated industrially. The majority of male workers are employed in agriculture, mining, manufacturing, and construction—the industries which produce physical goods. Almost three fourths of all women workers, however, are employed in industries which distribute goods or provide services. Manufacturing, nevertheless, is the largest single employer of women workers. Women, moreover, constitute at least 10 percent of the total office and production labor force in all but two of the twenty

Table 2. Women Employed in Professional, Technical, and Kindred Occupations, 1950

Occupation	Thousands	Percent of All Workers in Occupation	Percent of All Women Professional Workers
Teachers, n.e.c.	835	75	43
Nurses and student nurses, professional	463	98	24
Dietitians and nutritionists	21	94	1
Librarians	49	89	3
Religious, social and welfare, and recreation and group workers	88	66	5
Dancers, actors and actresses, and entertainers	21	45	1
Artists, art teachers, designers	40	34	2
Musicians and music teachers	78	51	4
Authors, editors, reporters	35	35	2
College presidents and teachers	29	23	1
Personnel and labor relations workers	15	29	1
Accountants and auditors	56	15	3
Medical and dental technicians and therapists	55	55	3
Other technicians	21	21	1
Natural scientists	13	12	
Architects	1	4	
Dentists	2	3	
Draftsmen	8	7	3
Engineers	6	1	
Lawyers and judges	6	4	
Pharmacists	7	8	
Physicians and surgeons	12	6	
Other	78	13	3
Total	1,939	40	100

n.e.c.=not elsewhere classified
Source: U.S. Bureau of the Census

major manufacturing industries listed by the U.S. Bureau of Labor Statistics—lumber and primary metals. About one eighth of the workers in the transportation equipment (automobiles, aircraft, etc.) and nonelectrical machinery industries are women, but since these are the two largest manufacturing industries, they are among the leading employers of women. In most other branches of manufacturing, at least one worker out of five is female. In the leather, apparel, and tobacco industries, women are a majority of all workers.

Table 3. Women Employed as Managers, Officials, and Proprietors, 1950

	Thousands	Percent of All Workers in Occupation	Percent of All Women in Managerial Occupations
Proprietors of retail establishments	242	17	36
Buyers, department heads, and other salaried officials of retail establishments	120	18	18
Proprietors of personal service establishments	39	27	6
Government officials and administrators	26	17	4
Salaried managers and officials of manufacturing establishments	26	6	4
Building managers and superintendents	22	34	3
Salaried managers and officials of personal service establishments	22	33	3
Postmasters	17	43	2
Salaried managers and officials, banking and finance	12	10	2
Salaried managers and officials, insurance and real estate	12	17	2
Credit men	7	22	1
Proprietors of insurance and real estate businesses	6	13	1
Salaried managers and officials, business services	5	18	1
Proprietors, business services	5	14	1
Lodge, society, and union officials	3	11	--
All other managers, officials, and proprietors	113	6	16
Total	677	14	100

--=less than 0.5 percent
Source: U.S. Bureau of the Census

Although women workers are widely distributed throughout manufacturing, the great majority of them are concentrated in particular kinds of clerical or semiskilled production jobs. In 1950, women accounted for one fourth of all workers in manufacturing. But only 7 percent of the managers, officials, and proprietors, only 10 percent of the foremen, and less than 4 percent of the skilled workers were women. In the rapidly expanding electrical machinery and equipment industry, which is now the third largest manufacturing employer of women, operations involving the fabrication and assembly of small parts are performed almost exclusively by women. Other manufacturing industries in which such operations are the principal work of women employees include nonelectrical machinery, transportation equipment, instruments, ordnance products and accessories, and other fabricated metal products. Together, these industries account for about one third of all the women in manufacturing.

MARITAL CHARACTERISTICS AND WORK

For both men and women, the likelihood of being in the labor force is affected by the individual's familial status. Almost all married men who have not reached the age of retirement are in the labor force. Single men are somewhat less likely to be working. Single women are almost as likely to be in the labor force as single men. Women who have been married are considerably less likely to work than single women, even if they are widowed, divorced, or separated from their husbands. Least likely of all to be in the labor force are married women living with their husbands. Among women who have been or are married, those who have never had children are more likely to work than mothers, and mothers of older children are more frequently employed than mothers of young children.

If a woman is single and has finished school, or if she is no longer living with her husband and has no minor children, the chances are about four out of five that she is working, provided she is under 45. If she is the mother of children under 6 and is living with her husband, the chances are about the same that she is not working. But among all other groups of women, substantial proportions are found both within and outside of the labor force. Because the family circumstances of women are closely related to their age, the following pages frequently deal directly or implicitly with women of different ages. It is important to note that the data and the conclusions refer to women in different age groups at the present time, not to the work experience of the same women during different periods of their lives.

Today, the work experience of many girls begins while they are still in school. About one fifth of the girls and young women over 14 who were enrolled in school in the fall of 1955 were also in the labor force, but the great majority of them were part-time workers. During the summer months, the proportion employed is considerably higher, and more of those who are employed work full time. Nevertheless, paid employment is a secondary activity for most young women and young men while still in school.

When they leave school, the overwhelming majority of young women go to work, unless they are already married or plan to marry very shortly. As long as they remain single, most women are likely to stay at work. Between the ages of 20 and 65, the proportion of single women at work is not a great deal lower than the proportion of single men. In 1955, in the age group 35-44, 82 percent of the single men and 81 percent of the single women were in the labor force.

In the United States today very few women remain single long after they leave school. Women stay in school longer than they do in any other country, and there are few countries where women marry at a younger age or where more women eventually marry. Half of all women marry before they reach 21, and by the time they pass 35, all but 7 percent have been married. Those who are both out of school and unmarried constitute less than half of the total in every age group. On the average, the interval between school and marriage is only about two years. One third of the women who received bachelor's degrees in June, 1955, were married within six months thereafter.

The single women in the labor force, therefore, may be divided into two groups. The larger group is composed of young women under 30, the great majority of whom will marry within a short time. The smaller group, about 40 percent of the total, consists of unmarried women over 30, most of whom will remain single and at work until they reach retirement age. Together, these groups constitute only one fourth of all women in the labor force.

The younger and the older single women workers occupy quite different positions in the labor force. Of the single women workers under 25, half are in clerical or sales jobs and 35 percent are operatives or service workers. Only about 10 percent are in jobs that require considerable training and responsibility, and most of these are teachers or nurses. Among single women aged 45 to 54, on the other hand, about 36 percent are employed in the upper levels of the occupational structure—as professional workers, as managers, supervisors, or owners of businesses, or as foremen and skilled workers. Of the male workers in the same age group, about 45 percent are in these occupational categories. Only about one fourth of the men, but over one third of the women, are professional workers, managers, or owners of businesses.[1] The men in these occupational groups have higher-level, better-paying jobs than most of the women. Nevertheless, it is clear that the relatively few women who remain single and stay at work for many years often achieve substantial advancement.

Although some women stop working when they marry, it is the arrival of children, rather than marriage, which exercises the greatest influence on their participation in the labor force. Most

[1] These and other data indicating the major occupational groups of women by age and marital status are derived from unpublished tables especially prepared for the National Manpower Council by the U.S. Bureau of the Census and are for April, 1954.

young wives continue to work until shortly before their first child is born, but the great majority of mothers do not work while their children are young. Among women aged 20 to 24 in 1951, for instance, 76 percent of those who were single were in the labor force, compared to 60 percent of those who were married, living with their husbands, and childless. Of those in this age group who had children under 6, only 13 percent worked.

Most women have their first child soon after marriage. In 1950, about 40 percent of the women married for between one and two years had at least one child. Of those married between two and three years, about 60 percent had a child. Like the single women in the labor force, therefore, the childless married women may be divided into two quite dissimilar groups. One is a constantly changing group of women under 30, the great majority of whom will have a child in the near future and will then stop working for some time. They constitute well under 10 percent of the female labor force, and their occupational distribution resembles that of the young, single working women. About half of them are clerical or sales workers, and very few hold positions requiring extensive training or responsibility. The second group consists of childless wives over 30. Most of them will probably not have children and will remain in the labor force until they are ready to retire. Recent studies by P. K. Whelpton of the Scripps Foundation indicate that among married women born since World War I, no more than 10 percent will never have a child. Among older married women, the proportion who are childless is much higher—about 20 percent, for instance, for women now in their fifties. Childless wives, aged 30 or over, were about one eighth of the female labor force in 1950. Only a little over half of this group of working women, however, were still married to and living with their first husbands. The others were separated, divorced, widowed, or had remarried.

When their children are in school, a great many mothers enter or reenter the labor force. Of mothers living with their husbands and with children aged 6 to 17 (but not under 6), 35 percent were working in 1955. Since the majority of women marry before they are 21 and have their first child soon afterwards, a great many mothers no longer have children of preschool age by the time they reach 30. Today, it has been estimated, the average mother is only 32 when her last child reaches school age.

Probably about one fourth of all women workers are wives and mothers over 30 years old, whose children are all of school age or older. By comparison with single women of the same ages, these working mothers of older children are heavily concentrated in sales, nonhousehold service, and, especially, operative jobs. The proportions in professional and clerical work are only about half as great as they are among single women. In part, this difference can be traced to the fact that their employment was interrupted and that they cannot devote as much time or attention to work as single women. In part, it is probably due to the preference of mothers for jobs that they can hold part time or intermittently.

Mothers of children of school age or older are not the only mothers who work. Only 16 percent of the mothers living with husbands and with children under 6 are in the labor force, but there are so many women with young children that the number who work is significant. Almost 2.5 million women with children under 6 are in the labor force, and they constitute, therefore, about one eighth of all working women. Most of them, as will be seen later, are married to men whose earnings are low, and many are working because the family needs additional money. Almost one fifth of them are widowed, divorced, or separated from their husbands. Perhaps three fourths of them are under 35. Because they are young, because their time and interests are divided between children and work, and because most of them come from the lower socio-economic groups, they are concentrated in low-paying jobs. But there are a few whose careers are so important to them that they are unwilling to interrupt their work for more than the necessary minimum period to have a child.

When women are widowed, divorced, or separated from their husbands, the likelihood of their working is considerably increased. Of the total number of women who have ever been married, nearly one fourth are either no longer married or not living with their husbands. Among those who are between 20 and 65, nearly 60 percent work. Many of the younger ones do not work because they have small children to care for, and some of the older ones receive income from children or from pensions, or may be able to live on savings. Among those between 25 and 44 who do not have children under 18, about 80 percent are in the labor force. About 65 percent of the entire group—widowed, divorced, and separated—are widows, however, most of whom are over 65. Since few women work at this age, less than 40 percent of the whole group are in the labor force.

Largely because of economic necessity, mothers who are no longer married or who are not living with their husbands are much more likely to work than mothers whose husbands are present. In 1955, among mothers of school-age children, about 35 percent of those with husbands present worked, but of the others, over 60 percent worked. Even when their children were under school age, 40 percent of the mothers who were not living with husbands were at work.

Widows, divorcees, and women who are not living with their husbands constitute about 23 percent of all women in the labor force. The jobs held by divorced women resemble those of wives and mothers rather than of single career women. Widows and women who are separated from their husbands are more heavily concentrated in low-paying jobs than any other groups. About 60 percent are operatives, private household or other service workers, farm workers, or nonfarm laborers. The concentration of these women at the bottom of the occupational ladder reflects the fact that many of them suddenly found themselves, at a fairly advanced age, with no other means of support and with no particular skills.

FAMILY INCOME AND THE EMPLOYMENT OF WOMEN

Today, women who have little or no responsibility for the care of a home or family are generally expected to support themselves. This group includes widows, divorcees, and women separated from their husbands who are young enough to work and do not have small children, as well as unmarried women. Many other women work because they belong to families in which there is no man able to support the family. A 1946 study by the Census found that about one fifth of all women workers in nonfarm families were either the sole earners in their families or earned more than any other member. In about one family in eight, women received half or more of the total income. A few exceptional women in this group may have been earning more than their husbands, even though the latter's earnings were fairly high, but the great majority worked because their husbands' earnings were very low. Together, these groups of women—those who are expected to support themselves and those who provide the main support for a family—probably account for over half of the female labor force. Somewhat less than half of all working women, therefore, are married to men who are the main support of the family. Even in these families, of course, the man's earnings are sometimes so low that the wife is also compelled to take a job. It is impossible to draw a clear distinction between a woman who works because of economic necessity and one who works so that her family may enjoy a higher standard of living or for some other reason. Nevertheless, some estimate of the relative importance of these several factors can be gained by comparing the extent to which wives work and the incomes of their husbands.

In 1951 the Bureau of the Census collected data on the employment of wives aged 20 to 44 in relation to both husbands' income and the presence or absence of children of different ages. When there were small children in the family, the employment of the wife was inversely related to the earnings of the husband throughout the entire range of income. Among mothers of children under 6, employment fell steadily from about 25 percent when the husband earned between $1,000 and $1,500, to 7 percent at $5,000, and then to 5 percent when he earned over $7,000. This suggests that financial need is an important reason for the employment of mothers of small children. When there were no small children in the family, the husband's income had little effect on the probability of his wife's working, unless he made over $5,000. Up to this level, between 50 and 60 percent of the wives were in the labor force when there were no children under 18, and between 30 and 50 percent when there were children of school age. In the income range between $5,000 and $10,000, the proportion of wives at work fell sharply. In the $7,000 to $10,000 bracket, only 9 percent worked when there were no children under 18, and only 4 percent when there were school-age children. When the husband made over $10,000, however, the proportion of wives in the labor force was more than double the proportion when he was in the $7,000 to $10,000 income bracket.

These findings suggest that a great many older wives work in order to raise the standard of living of their families. Both husband and wife were in the labor force in 9.8 million families in 1955. These families amounted to three out of four of all families in which husband and wife were living together and in which at least one member of the family, in addition to the husband, was in the labor force. The effect of supplementary employment on family living standards is illustrated by a recent *Fortune* study which found that in 1953 about two fifths of the nonfarm families whose total income after taxes was between $4,000 and $7,500 would have had less than $4,000 except for the earnings of workers other than the head of the household. Of families with income over $7,500, over half would have been in a lower bracket without supplementary earnings. Census data indicate that, in families with total income before taxes ranging between $6,000 and $10,000 in 1954, nearly 40 percent of the wives were in the labor force. This is a substantially higher proportion than among families in both lower and higher income brackets. Most working wives are in families where the husband's earnings are neither very high nor very low, but where the addition of the wife's earnings enables the family to live in fairly comfortable circumstances. Of all families where the husband and wife were both working in 1954, about 55 percent had a combined income before taxes of at least $5,000, and more than one fourth had at least $7,000.

The relationship between the employment of women and family income is actually far more complex than these data suggest. The economic position of a family depends, of course, on expenditures as well as income, and both of these are interrelated with the employment of women in a number of direct and indirect ways. Husband and wife are most likely to be working at the same time at the beginning of marriage, before children are born. Neither are likely to be making very much, but expenses are also moderate. In most families, economic stringencies are most likely to occur during the decade or so after the first child is born. The husband's income is not yet likely to have reached its maximum, and the wife usually stops working just when expenditures are rising rapidly.

After the husband and wife reach their middle thirties, the situation is likely to be somewhat easier. The husband's earnings generally continue to increase, and frequently the wife returns to work. In many families, as the parents approach 50, college education for the children adds a major expense, with no increase in income likely unless the wife, if she has not been working, now enters the labor force. If the children do not go to college, however, husband, wife, and children may all be income earners for a short time. In most families, the last child has married and left home before the parents reach 50. At this point, however, the newly established families of the children are encountering financial problems and are frequently helped by the parents. When the parents are past 65, their earning power usually declines rapidly or disappears, and the mother is likely to be widowed. But at this time the children may begin to help their parents.

EDUCATION AND THE EMPLOYMENT OF WOMEN

Attendance at school keeps many young women out of the labor force, but once a girl completes school, the more education she has, the more likely she is to work. Among women aged 25 to 64 in 1952, less than 30 percent of those who had no more than elementary school, 37 percent of those who were high school graduates, and 47 percent of those who were college graduates were in the labor force.

There are several reasons why better-educated women are much more likely to work than other women. The more education a woman has, the longer she is likely to remain single, and the more likely she is never to marry. In 1950 almost one fifth of the women college graduates in their early thirties were single, compared to less than one tenth of those in the same age group who had no more than a high school education. An even higher proportion of older college women were unmarried. This does not mean, of course, that a well-educated woman is less likely to marry simply because she is well educated. As a result of their education, some women may develop such a strong interest in a career that they turn their backs on marriage and motherhood. But women who have strong career drives or who are not strongly motivated to marry and have children are also more likely to prolong their schooling.

Well-educated women are also more likely to postpone having children for several years after they marry. Among white women under 45 who had been married between two and three years in 1950, about one third of those with only an elementary school education, but over half of the college graduates had not yet had a child. In the recent past, a high proportion of married college women never became mothers. Today, however, they are only slightly more likely than other women not to have children by the time they reach their early thirties.

Whether the well-educated woman who marries and has children is more or less likely to be employed than the mother who has less education is not known. The better-educated woman is certainly more likely to have had some work experience, and she may seek opportunities to put her special training and skills to use by returning to work. Both men and women in the upper socio-economic groups seem more likely to approve of the employment of wives and mothers. Moreover, even though she begins her family at a later age, the college woman is likely to have fewer children and to have her last child at a younger age than other women. On the other hand, the college woman is less likely to seek employment because her family's financial needs are pressing. It may also be difficult for her to find a job commensurate with her education as she approaches 40 years of age.

Table 4 shows that college women are much more likely than women with little education to work at the beginning of marriage

Table 4. Percent of Married Women[a] in Labor Force, by Age and Years of School Completed, 1950

Age	Eighth Grade or Less	High School Graduates	College Graduates
22-24	18	29	50
25-29	19	23	31
30-34	22	21	27
35-44	25	27	34
45-54	20	26	37
55-64	12	15	26

[a] Husbands present
Source: U.S. Bureau of the Census

and when they are past 35. This characteristic may be explained largely in terms of different patterns with respect to marriage and fertility. Most of the younger college women have not yet had their first child. More of the older college women are childless, and those who have had children have had fewer. The proportion in the labor force is also significantly higher for college women, however, in the 30-34 year age group—even though the proportion childless and the average number of children are almost the same for high school graduates in this age group.

Women who work have more schooling on the average than those who do not work and, as Table 5 shows, considerably more than men. Nevertheless, one third of all women over 25 who were in the labor force in 1950 had not been to high school, and a majority of all working women were not high school graduates.

Table 5. Education of Persons Aged 25 and Over, by Labor Force Participation, 1950

	All Women	Women in Labor Force	Men in Labor Force
No more than elementary school	46%	37%	47%
High school, 1-3 years	18	18	18
High school, 4 years	23	26	20
College, 1-3 years	8	10	7
College, 4 years or more	5	9	8
	100%	100%	100%

Source: U.S. Bureau of the Census

The amount of education that a person has exercises a strong influence on the type of job he holds. Of the working women over 25 with no more than elementary schooling, nearly seven out of ten were employed as operatives or in service work in 1950. The more education a woman has, the less likely she is to be employed in such work. Clerical and sales work claimed a majority of the women who were high school graduates in 1950 and a large minority of those who had attended but did not graduate from high school or college. Of the college graduates, 70 percent were professional or technical workers, and most of the rest were clerical or sales workers. No matter how much or little education a woman has, she is not likely to be employed as a laborer, agricultural worker, skilled worker, or foreman. The relationship between education and occupation is less direct for men, who have much more opportunity to enter a wide variety of fields regardless of their educational handicaps.

RACIAL AND ETHNIC DIFFERENCES

Negro women are more likely to be in the labor force than white women. In 1950, 28 percent of all white women, but 37 percent of all nonwhite women were in the labor force. Among women who were or had been married, the difference was even greater—23 percent for white women and 37 percent for nonwhite women. Among single women, however, the opposite was true. Nearly half of all white single women worked, but among nonwhite single women, only 36 percent were in the labor force.[2]

There are a number of reasons why so many Negro women who have been married are in the labor force. In the first place, 36 percent of the nonwhite women who had ever been married were no longer married or no longer living with their husbands in 1950. This was true of only 21 percent of the white women. Moreover, among women living with their husbands, a substantially higher proportion of Negro than white wives were childless. Even among Negro mothers living with their husbands, however, the proportion in the labor force is much higher than for white mothers. This is true even though Negro mothers have more children than white mothers. The high labor-force participation of Negro mothers, even when living with their husbands, reflects the lower incomes of Negro men, the long tradition of employment for married Negro women, and the strong demand for women willing to work as domestic servants. There is no reliable information to explain the relatively low proportion of single Negro women reported in the labor force. It is likely that misreporting of both

[2] Some Census data are available for all nonwhites together, but not separately for Negroes. Since Negroes constitute 95 percent of the nonwhite population, data for nonwhites represent a close approximation of data for Negroes alone. The Census Bureau believes that there was a substantial undercount in 1950 of the number of Negro women of all ages in the labor force.

marital status and labor-force status is responsible for at least part of the difference.

Table 6. *Selected Characteristics of White Women and Women in Minority Groups, 1950*

	White	Negro	Indian	Chinese	Japanese	Puerto Rican [a]	Mexican [b]
Total aged 14 and over (thousands)	51,404	5,499	100	28	49	113	700
Percent in urban residence	68	68	17	93	74	86	70
Percent of urban women in labor force	32	43	28	31	48	40	25
Occupational Distribution of Employed Urban Women (percent)							
Professional, managerial, supervisory, and skilled workers	20	7	13	20	14	5	10
Clerical and sales workers	44	7	17	40	31	9	26
Operatives, service workers, farm workers, and laborers	36	86	70	40	55	86	64

[a] Urban data are for New York City only.
[b] White persons with Spanish surnames in Arizona, California, Colorado, New Mexico, and Texas.
Source: U.S. Bureau of the Census

In addition to the 5.5 million Negro women in the nation in 1950, there were about one million women in the five other minority groups shown in Table 6. The percentage living in urban areas—where employment opportunities for women are greatest—is much higher for some of these groups than for others. The table, therefore, shows employment data for urban women only. The proportion in the labor force was highest among Japanese-American women—nearly half. Negro women were second, closely followed by Puerto Rican women in New York City. Indian women and women of Mexican background, however, were less frequently found in paid employment than white women.

Of all these groups, the Chinese-American women appear to resemble most closely the white majority, both in terms of the proportion working and their occupations. With this exception, the women members of minority groups are heavily concentrated in undesirable jobs. Negroes and Puerto Ricans clearly have the poorest job opportunities. Almost nine out of every ten were operatives, service workers, or laborers in 1950. The jobs held by women in these two groups, however, were quite different. Over three fourths of the women from Puerto Rico were operatives, mainly in factories, but two thirds of the Negro women were service workers. Only about 17 percent of the Negroes were employed as operatives, and over 40 percent worked as servants in private households.

Although immigration from Europe fell off sharply after World War I, women of foreign birth or parentage still constitute one third of the urban female population. On the whole, they are slightly less likely to be in the labor force than women of native parentage. Differences among women of foreign background with respect to employment, however, are quite marked. Among urban women who came, or whose parents came, from each of the ten countries which contributed the largest number of immigrants, the proportions in the labor force in 1950 ranged from 26 to 36 percent. In general, women with Southern and Eastern European backgrounds were more likely to be working, while those from Britain, Scandinavia, and Germany were less likely. The highest proportion in the labor force, however, was among French Canadians in the United States, and the lowest was among those of Russian origin.

There are significant differences between women of native and of foreign parentage with respect to the place of work in their lives. Women of foreign parentage marry, on the average, several years later than women of native parentage. Consequently, more of them are single, and more of the single women among them are no longer in school. It is not surprising, therefore, that the proportion in the labor force among young women is considerably higher for women of foreign than of native background. Among urban white women under 25, 46 percent of those of foreign parentage, compared to 37 percent of those of native parentage, were in the labor force in 1950. On the other hand, among older women of recent immigrant origin, relatively fewer are in the labor force.

As Table 7 shows, the proportion employed in professional work is lower among women of foreign parentage than it is among those of native parentage. Although more of the women of foreign

Table 7. Occupational Distribution of Employed Urban White Women, by Parentage, 1950

Occupational Group	Native Birth and Parentage	Foreign Birth or Parentage
Professional, technical, and kindred workers	15	11
Managers, officials, and proprietors	4	5
Craftsmen, foremen, and kindred workers	2	2
Clerical and sales workers	47	40
Operatives	17	26
Service workers, farm workers, and laborers	15	16
Total	100	100

Source: U.S. Bureau of the Census

parentage who work are young and single, fewer are found in clerical and sales jobs, where young single women are usually concentrated. Almost all of this difference is made up by the higher percentage working as operatives. Differences among women of recent foreign extraction are greater than the differences between them and women of native parentage. The jobs of German-American women, for instance, are not strikingly different from those of women whose parents were born here. Italian-American working women, on the other hand, are heavily concentrated in factory work.

RESIDENCE AND EMPLOYMENT

The employment of women depends very much on where they live. Urban women are twice as likely to be in the labor force as farm women, and women in some cities twice as likely as women in other cities. Except for the most deprived groups within the Negro population, women rarely work for pay on farms in the United States, and other kinds of paid jobs are scarce in most rural areas. Most women living on family farms, however, contribute directly, in one way or another, to the product of the family enterprise. The Census Bureau seeks to count as members of the labor force those women who perform substantial amounts of unpaid work on family farms, but only a small proportion of the farm women are counted under the definitions and procedures which it is feasible for the Census Bureau to apply.

The proportion of all women who are in the labor force is somewhat higher in the Northeast than in other regions because the Northeast is more urbanized. Within urban areas, however, relatively more women are in the labor force in the South than in any other region, mainly because of the large number of Negro women working as domestic servants. Such differences among regions are insignificant compared to differences among cities. In 1950, for instance, less than 20 percent of the women in Johnstown, Pa., were in the labor force, compared to almost 42 percent in Durham, N. C.

Many circumstances are responsible for the extent to which women work in individual cities, but two seem predominant—the size of the Negro population and the economic character of the area. As has been seen, wherever the Negro population is large, the percent of women in the labor force is above average. Where heavy industry dominates, the proportion of women in the labor force is generally low. This is the case in cities like Pittsburgh, Buffalo, Scranton, Detroit, or Wilmington, Del., where metal refining or fabrication, mining, automobile manufacturing, chemicals, or shipbuilding are important. The proportion of women in the labor force is usually high in cities where the important industries include light manufacturing (particularly clothing, textiles, tobacco, and electrical machinery); public administration; or finance, insurance, and real estate. Thus, the cities with the highest employment of women include most small and medium-sized manufacturing towns in the South and New England, many state capitals, insurance centers such as Hartford, and a number of large cities in which the industrial complex is favorable to the employment of women. The industrial make-up of particular cities influences, but does not determine, the extent to which women are employed. The same job in the same industry may be a "man's" job in one place and a "woman's" job in another. In New York City, for instance, 43 percent of the waiters and waitresses employed in 1950 were men, but in Philadelphia, 85 percent were women.

Perhaps the most striking aspect of the differences among cities in the employment of women is the absence of a clear relationship between the proportions of single and married women in the labor force. There are many cities which are above average in one respect and below in the other. Thus, in Boston, almost 60 percent of the single women but only 18 percent of the married women (living with their husbands) were in the labor force in 1950. In Durham, only 46 percent of the single women but 38 percent of the married women were in the labor force. The national urban average was 54 percent for single women and 25 percent for married women. One reason for this difference is that Durham has a large Negro population, and, as has been seen, Negro wives are much more likely to be working than white wives, while the reverse is true among single women.

Yet, other circumstances are also involved, for, by comparison with the Northeast, there are relatively more married and fewer single women at work among the white as well as the Negro populations of Southern cities. Moreover, in Western cities, the proportion of married women in the labor force is even higher, and that of single women even lower, than in the South. These regional differences in the extent to which single and married women work appear to be closely related to variations in the age of marriage. The percent of all women over 14 who are single may be taken as a convenient measure of differences in the average age of marriage—the fewer single women, the lower the age of marriage.[3] Regional differences in this respect closely parallel differences in the employment of single and married women. In general, as Table 8 shows, the farther south and west a city is located, the lower the age of marriage, and the lower the percent of single women in the labor force. The percent of urban married women working in these regions is slightly above the national average.

Table 8. *Marital Status and Labor Force Participation of Urban Women Aged 14 and Over, by Region, 1950*

| | | Percent in the Labor Force | |
Region	Percent Single	Single	Married[a]
Northeast	24	58	22
North Central	20	55	23
South (White)	19	50	25
West	17	48	25

a Husband present

Source: U.S. Bureau of the Census

One reason for the lower age of marriage in the cities of the South and West is that most of them have been growing rapidly and attracting large numbers of migrants from rural areas, where women generally marry earlier than city women. The age of marriage is higher in the Northeast and North Central regions in part because women of foreign parentage tend to marry at a later age. In the Northeast, almost half, and, in the North Central states, nearly one third of the women were of foreign parentage in 1950. In the South, this was true of only about one tenth of the white

[3] Regional differences in the percent of all women who are single are not significantly affected by differences in the age or sex distribution of the population and thus are a fairly accurate indication of differences in the age of marriage.

women. In the West, women of foreign parentage were as high a percentage of the female population as in the North Central states, but many of these women were of Mexican or Oriental background. The age of marriage is generally much lower among these women than it is for European immigrants.

Where the age of marriage is low, the small proportion of single women in the labor force reflects the fact that many of them are still in school. In the West, almost half the single women over 14 were enrolled in school in 1950, compared to 43 percent in the South, 39 percent in the North Central states, and only 30 percent in the Northeast. The fact that girls tend to remain in school longer in the West also contributes to the very high proportion of single women in school in that region.

The tendency of wives and mothers to return to or begin work when their children are old enough to require less supervision seems to be facilitated in the South and West by the early age of marriage. The proportion of married women in the labor force in these regions is considerably higher among those who are over 30. Indeed, married women under 25 are less likely to work in the South and West than in the North and East. This suggests that in the South and West, where women marry early, they tend to quit the jobs which most of them obtained upon leaving school at an age below the national average. Because they have their children earlier, the mothers are younger when the children enter school, and, consequently, younger when they return to work.

The proportion of single women who work is high where single women represent a high proportion of the population. The same is true for married women. Consequently, there are great variations in the composition of the female labor force in terms of marital status. In both Boston and Los Angeles, 32 percent of all women were employed in 1950. But in Boston over half of the working women were single, compared to less than one fourth in Los Angeles. Most of the single women who constitute the majority of the female labor force in Boston probably expect to work steadily for a considerable number of years after they leave school, but will stop working after they marry and begin to have children. Some will later return to work, but most will not. In Los Angeles, on the other hand, the great majority of working women are already married. Some of the younger ones will drop out of the labor force to have children. Most of them, however, are over 30, and with their children already in school, they will probably remain in the labor force, at least intermittently and part time, for many years.

The description presented in this chapter of the occupations of women workers and of the behavior of different groups of women in relation to paid employment can only suggest the complex interaction of the various circumstances affecting the employment of women. Some important considerations have hardly been touched upon. Among these is the fact that the employment of women, as is indicated elsewhere, is strongly influenced by the attitudes of both men and women towards the appropriate functions of each sex. These attitudes differ vastly from group to group and place to place. Boston and Fall River are separated by only a few miles, but they represent a striking contrast in attitudes toward women's employment. Fall River is one of the few cities where the employment of women, including wives and mothers, has long been taken for granted. Boston is one of the few cities where some employers still require women to leave when they marry.

III. WOMEN IN BUSINESS AND INDUSTRY: AN EMPLOYER APPRAISAL

IN THE COURSE of its womanpower study, the National Manpower Council held seven conferences in different parts of the country to gather from employers a firsthand account of their policies, practices, and problems in dealing with women in paid employment. The conferees were asked to describe the kinds of jobs women held or did not hold in their organizations, the changes which have occurred in recent years in the kinds of jobs women hold and the reasons for these changes, and the criteria used in hiring and in selecting women for training and promotion. At each conference an effort was made to determine whether any distinctive problems arise in connection with the employment of women.

These conferences were held in Boston, New York, Asheville, N.C., St. Louis, Chicago, Los Angeles, and San Francisco. With the exception of the Asheville conference, which was regional in character, most of the participants were drawn from a variety of business and industrial firms located in and around these cities. A small number of conference participants also came from government, placement services, and trade unions. At a special trade union conference held in Washington—which also considered employment policies, practices, and problems—the conferees represented unions accounting for about 40 percent of the organized women workers in the United States.

The seven employer conferences brought together individuals possessing an immediate and intimate knowledge of the stated policies and actual practices affecting the employment of women. No attempt was made to have all the fields of employment open to women within a community or a region covered at each conference. The conferees were, however, selected so as to insure that different kinds of enterprises in which women constitute a significant proportion of the work force were represented. Consequently, information was secured about light and heavy industries, the public utilities, retail establishments, banks, insurance companies, hospitals, the public schools, government, and still other employment fields. Additional experience and insights were provided by conferees in touch with labor-market conditions as a result of work with placement, employment service, and vocational guidance agencies.[1]

The findings of these conferences illuminate many aspects of the current employment of women, but it should not be thought that they are offered here as a definitive account of how employers deal with women workers. Employment policies and practices vary from field to field and from region to region. Substantial differences are to be found among companies in the same field and even among subdivisions of the same enterprise. It is also clear that discrepancies sometimes exist between the declared policies and actual practices pursued by a company. If the conference findings presented warn against the dangers of sweeping generalizations, they nevertheless do indicate the existence of certain employment policies and practices sufficiently common and widespread to establish characteristic patterns. The extent to which conflicting information, viewpoints, and judgments were voiced at each conference emphasizes the changing nature of the current employment scene with respect to women workers. Newer and older attitudes and modes of behavior among women workers, as

[1] The names of the participants in these and the other conferences held by the National Manpower Council in connection with the present study appear in the Acknowledgments.

well as among employers, exist side by side. This situation accounts for the qualifications which could be made, and the exceptions noted, in connection with most general assertions about women in paid employment today.

WHY WOMEN ARE—OR ARE NOT—HIRED

The reasons offered by employers for hiring or refusing to hire women fall into three broad categories. Many employers are strongly influenced by deep-rooted "traditions" according to which the universe of jobs is divided into "men's" and "women's" jobs. The characterization of a job in these terms overrides considerations of its skill requirements and of the qualifications of the individual applying for it. According to the conferees, the classification of jobs as "men's" and "women's" on the basis of tradition is accepted not only by employers, but also by men and women workers alike. Another group of reasons cited by employers for hiring or not hiring women turns on their belief that women possess particular traits or abilities which specially equip them for certain kinds of work or that they have other characteristics which make it undesirable to hire them for many other kinds of work.

There was also a group of reasons offered which involved considerations of labor cost. Thus, employers frequently pointed out that it often costs more to employ women than men because of their qualities as workers, the problems they create, or the special working conditions they require. On the other hand, it was also noted that greater aptitude for certain kinds of work sometimes makes them more desirable employees in terms of production costs. Employers rarely asserted that women are preferred for some jobs because they can be employed at lower rates of pay than men, although this was reported to be the case by other conferees, particularly by some union representatives.

THE INFLUENCE OF "TRADITION"

Many employers reported that the hiring of women is frequently governed by traditional attitudes which establish what jobs are suitable for them. These traditional attitudes, it was emphasized, are operative among workers, as well as at the management level. The distinctions between "men's" and "women's" jobs appear to be particularly sharp in certain manufacturing fields, and in professional, service, and sales work, jobs are often closed to women because it is taken for granted that they should be held by men. It is believed that, if women are placed in such jobs, they are likely to produce negative reactions not only among male supervisors, fellow employees, and customers, but also in the public at large.

Many conferees held that the assignment of most jobs to men or women has been an outgrowth of historical circumstances. Men have usually had first choice of jobs, and certain jobs have remained closed to women simply because men have wanted and succeeded in reserving these jobs for themselves.

Conferees from various manufacturing concerns repeatedly offered examples of occupational fields in which there has been a comparatively rigid, and often arbitrarily determined, division of jobs within a plant, a company, or an industry. In many cases these jobs are considered the exclusive preserve of either men or women out of traditional practice, without any apparent basis in present social attitudes, employee characteristics and competence, or labor costs. In some cases, these considerations originally did operate to determine job assignments, and though they may no longer apply, the traditional divisions continue. The fact that a particular job has customarily been performed by a man or by a woman may exert a stronger influence than any other in determining to whom the job will be assigned when a replacement is made.

According to one point of view, the pattern of assignment of many factory jobs to either men or women is fortuitous. The variety of practices in different parts of the country and the extreme changes which occurred during World War II were cited to support the contention that there had been no logic in the distribution of jobs according to sex. "It depends," it was asserted, "on who gets there first." For example, the aircraft industry considered welding a "man's" job until the war forced the hiring of women. When women demonstrated that they could weld and do other jobs as well as men, they were retained in these occupations and the pattern of job assignments changed. Such changes, however, are not always permanent. When shortages are alleviated, many jobs revert to their former sex classification, even though women have proved their proficiency.

Certain cultural factors, it was suggested, also help determine job patterns. The tradition of male chivalry—the feeling that women should not engage in certain kinds of labor but that they should be given easier and lighter tasks—was said to influence job assignments. Some conferees, however, considered these factors comparatively unimportant, pointing out that women are often found doing hard, dirty jobs, and maintained that when men can choose their assignments, they too look for the cleaner and easier jobs.

Enough exceptions to traditional job classifications were cited to make it clear that some women are found in most "men's" jobs. Although unusual circumstances or unusual capability, or both, may enable a woman to hold a job usually closed to members of her sex, this occurrence may not effect a change in the traditional pattern. Management may want to keep a job a "man's" job for various reasons. On the other hand, it may consciously seek to change the sex label attached to a job. Interestingly enough, little light was shed by employers upon the reasons for the success or failure of such efforts. Most of them were only able to report that the attempt to bring about the change "did work out" or that it "was not accepted."

As a result of prevailing traditional attitudes, it was pointed out, women are usually assigned to lower-paying jobs. Because women can be hired at lower wage rates, some traditional "men's" jobs, when they are mechanized and require less skill, may become "women's" jobs. Tradition, however, may sometimes outweigh developments which would seem to encourage changes in the pattern of job assignments. In the shirtmaking industry, for example, extremely rigid classifications of jobs as either male or female are found. Because of men's greater strength, they would be better than women at certain sewing operations, but even though pay rates are favorable, men refuse to do such work. Especially in factories, it was said, men will avoid jobs they regard as "women's." These are usually the jobs in which a high proportion of the workers, generally over 60 percent, are women.

The strength of conventional attitudes was illustrated by many specific cases cited. Thus, employers in the canning industry, it was noted, will hire men for "women's" jobs, or women for "men's" jobs, only when they are compelled to by prevailing conditions. Currently, shortages of men are resulting in an "invasion" by women of the West Coast fishpacking industry. But this occupation is still considered "men's" work, in spite of the temporary necessity to employ women. A few miles away, in California's Salinas Valley, however, fruitpacking is considered "women's" work. Local traditions with respect to job assignments are inconsistent. In the Midwest, it was pointed out, cornhuskers are traditionally women, while trimmers are almost always men. In the Far West, cornhuskers are men and trimmers are women.

The question of how the public responds when women are employed in jobs customarily held by men was raised in connection with several sales, service, and professional fields. Banks, for example, sometimes do not hire women in their trust departments or as loan interviewers because it is believed that clients would have little confidence in their business judgment. Some insurance companies do not employ women as accident and health underwriters because they believe clients will not accept their decisions. Similarly, a law firm may not hire an otherwise competent woman because it fears clients will not have faith in her judgment, and, if she is hired, she may be permanently assigned to routine work. Even in fields quite open to women, as in retail sales, the weight of tradition is felt. Thus, long-existing preferences of women for certain kinds of sales work are respected by employers, as are the preferences of customers for male or female sales personnel. Women generally, it was stated, prefer jobs with a fixed salary and shrink from the competition of selling on a commission basis. Other factors also determine which sales jobs are considered suitable for women. Women sell women's clothing while men sell not only men's clothing but also women's shoes. Relatively few women sell women's shoes, but it is common for them to sell children's shoes. During World War II, department stores assigned women to sell "big ticket merchandise"—that is, furniture and household equipment. Although no explanations were offered, this experiment was generally considered unsuccessful, and many of the women were later shifted from these sales jobs.

On the whole, it was noted, very few insurance company agents are women. It was suggested that women do not like to sell intangibles and, also, that selling insurance requires the kind of forceful, aggressive, extroverted personality supposedly found infrequently among women. Many selling jobs, it was said, make demands upon women which they do not wish to meet, or require activities which are considered inappropriate for them, such as travelling, night work, or calling on clients in their homes. As adjusters they might face difficult situations in the course of making investigations and arranging settlements.

It was pointed out, however, that employers may be more prejudiced than they presume their customers to be. It was also suggested that women would probably accept many jobs for which they are now considered unsuitable or in which they are thought to be uninterested, if more such jobs were open to them. Almost every generalization ventured at a conference about what women "do" or "do not" like to do was promptly challenged. It is quite clear that many of the judgments about suitable or unsuitable jobs for women grow out of traditional attitudes and highly individual experiences as well as a limited body of tested knowledge.

It should be noted that there are cases where the job-assignment tradition operates with respect to married women rather than women in general. For many years this was true in teaching, but recently the ban against the married woman teacher has almost disappeared. One major public utility company in New England is unwilling to hire married women, and women workers who marry may lose their jobs. Women at the supervisory level who marry can stay on with the company only if they accept demotion to operating jobs. These policies are not pursued by the same company in other parts of the country.

CHARACTERISTICS OF WOMEN WORKERS

For some jobs, the characteristics or abilities displayed by women workers cause employers to favor them over men. Thus, it was frequently said that women are more suitable than men for clerical work or light assembly operations because of their allegedly greater manual dexterity and their demonstrated ability to outperform men in repetitive tasks. These characteristics especially qualify women for work in, for example, powder plants, where they are hired in preference to men. In clerical work, the case was cited of a bank which tested new mechanical record-keeping machines with three men and three women having comparable experience. After a time the women were turning out 10,000 to 12,000 items a day, while the men averaged 7,000 to 9,000 items. Since then only women have been hired to operate these machines.

Other conferees maintained that manual dexterity is about the same for men and women and that other factors are responsible for differences in performance. One of the principal reasons women predominate in clerical work and are more willing to do repetitive jobs in general, it was said, is that they have fewer job alternatives open to them. Also, many young women plan to work for only a short time and are less concerned than men about the limited opportunities for advancement which such jobs usually offer.

The attitudes of women toward work, it was said, often help determine the range of job opportunities open to them. Women were described as usually less willing than men to make sacrifices required to secure the training which would qualify them for advancement. Frequently, it was reported, they are even unwilling to take advantage of chances for immediate promotion. It was suggested that this lack of interest and initiative could be both a cause and an effect of women's restricted opportunities in the working world.

Two of the most widespread complaints against women employees were that, compared to men, they have substantially higher rates of absenteeism and of turnover. Absenteeism was said to be particularly high among married women with young children. When there is illness or some other emergency in the family, the woman is almost always the one who takes time off from her job. A number of conferees pointed out that their companies' experience had shown that, while women's absenteeism and turnover rates were a good deal higher than men's in the first years of employment, they declined for the women who remained in the work force for a number of years. It was suggested, moreover, that turnover rates can be meaningfully compared only between men and women holding similar jobs, rather than between men and women in general. An important factor contributing to the high rate of turnover among office workers, it was pointed out, is the fact that they are often selected partly on the basis of youth and attractiveness. Such women are likely to marry comparatively soon after they begin to work.

Generally, it was noted, a woman may stop working for any one of a number of reasons—in order to marry, to have a child, because the financial need that required her to work has been met, or simply because she wants to stop working for a while. Consequently, it was reported, employers often do not allow women, especially younger ones, to hold jobs for which a sizable training investment is required. Companies interested in developing female

career personnel often have a shakedown period of several years
for new employees so they can determine which young women
intend to stay on the job and may, therefore, be interested in
training and advancement. Several conferees distinguished between older and younger women workers with respect to work
performance and stability. Some industries—glovemaking among
them—were said to prefer older women because they find them
more efficient and stable.

Some conferees contended that employers exaggerate the alleged failings of women workers and are more tolerant of the
failings of men employees merely because they are accustomed
to them. It was pointed out that employers had learned to live
with excessive drinking and irresponsibility about finances
among men workers, even though these conditions have some
consequence for job performance and, therefore, production costs.
Cases were cited of women whose competence and interest in
their work equal that of outstanding men workers. Women with all
sorts of qualities, it was pointed out, can be found in paid employment. There are emotional and intuitive women, but also highly
rational, calculating, and analytical women. There are women
with the strongest attachments to work and to their jobs, and
those who are very tenuously tied to paid employment. Because
of the wide range of characteristics displayed by women workers,
it was said, generalizations about feminine traits and employment
policies based on stereotypes of women's behavior could be costly
to employers and wasteful of the abilities of potentially valuable
individuals.

Women's physical limitations play an important role in restrict-
ing the opportunities open to them in industry. Women generally
cannot handle heavy objects as well as men, and state laws often
set limits on the weight of objects which a woman is permitted to
lift. Thus, quite frequently, employers must make special provisions, such as assigning a man to do the lifting, although the
weights involved might be light enough for a woman to handle

without difficulty. Some occupations require heavy lifting only in beginner's jobs, and women cannot reach the more advanced, lighter jobs because they are denied the necessary beginner's experience.

Employers are sometimes reluctant to hire women because mixed groups may produce problems. It was reported that young women working together with men sometimes take advantage of their sex to secure privileges on the job, and that even without making any effort an attractive girl is likely to receive attention which her co-workers will resent. Some employers said that such situations contributed to poor morale, but others thought that there was a tendency to exaggerate their significance. Specific cases were also cited where the existence of mixed work groups led husbands or wives to complain about the "social" relationships that developed on the job. It was pointed out that management may seek to avoid such problems by not hiring women at all or by keeping the number of women employees at a minimum and within a restricted group of jobs. Some conferees, maintaining that these problems are not as serious as they were alleged to be, asserted that at worst such difficulties as might arise with mixed work groups can be anticipated and handled in the normal course of events. It was also observed that patterns of job differentiation according to sex often are not intended to prevent men and women from working in close proximity. In the garment industry, in millinery, in shoe factories, in packing houses, in auto plants, and elsewhere, men and women may work on different jobs, but they frequently work alongside each other.

THE INFLUENCE OF COSTS ON JOB OPPORTUNITIES

In some cases, lower prevailing wage rates for women, as compared to men—or, more commonly, the availability of better qualified women at the same wage rates as men—lead employers to prefer the former for certain jobs. One of the reasons an increasing number of women are being employed in banks, some conferees said, is that it is often difficult to hire able young men at the salaries offered. In some industries and occupations, separate salary schedules may exist for men and women in the same job. Quite often, a man is preferred for a particular job, but if he is not available, a woman may get it at lower pay.

Some evidence was presented which indicated that the establishment of equal wage rates where differentials had previously existed in favor of men may have the effect of reducing employment opportunities for women. This occurred in a metalworking plant on the West Coast, where management stopped hiring women, after their rates were brought up to the men's, on the ground that men were more efficient and, consequently, more economical. In order to preserve the jobs for women, it was reported, the differential in favor of the men was restored.

Many conferees expressed concern about the factors which, they claimed, often make it more expensive to employ women. It was generally maintained that the interruptions which occur in most women's working lives usually make it uneconomical to select women for jobs requiring a substantial investment in training. Other factors which were said to make it frequently more expensive to employ women than men on many jobs were their absenteeism and the fact that they often could not be completely integrated into the job-promotion ladder, since there are certain jobs to which they cannot be assigned.

Women require special accommodations, it was noted, and this can contribute to higher labor costs. Employers who might otherwise be willing to introduce women into certain jobs may be deterred from doing so by the cost of providing the necessary separate facilities for them, such as locker and rest rooms. There are legislative restrictions on the hours women can work. Employing women on the night shift may require special provisions for their transportation, such as arranging bus service at the end of the shift or providing a taxi when a woman has to leave before the shift is over.

LABOR SHORTAGES AND JOB OPPORTUNITIES

Tradition, cost considerations, and the special characteristics of women workers were cited as important determinants of their job opportunities. Somewhat different factors were cited, however, when the conferees were explaining why most of the companies represented employed more women now than formerly and why women were found in jobs once closed to them. Many conferees warned against general explanations of these developments. Changes in employment patterns, they pointed out, occur in varying ways and at varying rates in different situations.

It was generally agreed, however, that one of the most important factors had been World War II and the consequent shortage of male workers, which brought about many rapid and far-reaching changes in women's job opportunities. The development of a wider range of both opportunities and skills was also seen to be dependent upon what might be termed a "snowballing" effect. Gradually, as more jobs calling for a wider range of skills are opened to women and are successfully filled, management's attitudes change and still more places are opened. And as women see increased opportunities becoming available, more of them prepare themselves to be eligible for such jobs. The break-through in the jobs open to women during World War II was most notable in factory and other industrial or "blue-collar" occupations from which women had been rigidly excluded. Wartime opportunities enabled women to prove they could handle many jobs as well as men, if not better, and they often were retained even after the war, when men might have been found to replace them.

The increase in job opportunities during the postwar period was attributed to several causes, among them the general expansion of industry and the Korean conflict. Business and industry often had to hire women to fill places in "men's" fields. Shortages in scientific and technical fields usually dominated by men led to the greater utilization of women, and a willingness to hire women engineers and female technicians of many kinds is now common throughout industry.

The expansion of the clerical and service fields also provided increased opportunities during the postwar period in areas already dominated by women. In the clerical field, the constantly growing stress on record-keeping for a variety of purposes has enormously increased the number of job openings. For example, a conferee from a small manufacturing company pointed out that 50 percent of all his company's employees are in the office force today compared to 20 percent in 1945.

When women were found capable of doing certain production-line jobs if heavy physical demands were eliminated, many companies consciously redesigned such jobs so that heavy duties were assigned to men. On one company's production line, it was noted, the removal of heavy duties from most jobs and their assignment to men have permitted women to be employed in over three fourths of the production-line jobs. These "light" jobs, however, usually require less skill. Also, it was said, in many cases the job evaluation system considers physical effort as one of the factors determining job classification and the consequent wage rate. As a result, this redesigning of jobs has often served to reduce labor costs.

Women have not always held on to their new opportunities in industry. During World War II, many jobs had been broken down into simpler tasks requiring less skill, and women had a wide range of employment opportunities. In the face of postwar competition from skilled men, many women failed to retain their jobs, as in machine work, because employers could hire men with a wider range of skills. Similarly, postwar technological changes, or changes in the company's products, have displaced women whose skills were found to be inadequate. In some cases, however, as in the manufacture and assembly of delicate, precision electronic equipment, women proved they were more capable as a group than men, and the women stayed on.

The expanded need in certain fields for part-time or intermittent workers for seasonal or peak-hour periods has also helped to increase total job opportunities for women. Department stores, for example, now rely heavily on part-time workers. Sometimes, it was pointed out, it is difficult to find applicants for part-time jobs, in spite of desirable working conditions, because of the lack of child-care facilities. Business and industry have been reluctant to provide such facilities because of the problems and responsibilities entailed. But this difficulty no longer exists in the case of older women, who are a major, and sometimes almost the sole, source of part-time labor.

Negro women have far more limited job opportunities than white women, it was acknowledged. The expansion in the range of jobs open to them, especially in the larger urban centers, has enabled a growing number to leave domestic and similar service work, but they still suffer marked discrimination both in and outside the South. This has taken the form not only of limited opportunities but also of unequal treatment as compared with white women in the same industry, company, or plant.

In the South as well as in the North, the number of Negro women in private domestic service is decreasing. Many are finding new job opportunities and higher wage levels in Federal institutions, such as veterans' hospitals, and an increasing number are obtaining clerical jobs with Federal agencies. It was reported that relatively few Negro women are working in factories in the South, and that the number employed there in textile plants has declined. Most garment factories in the South employ Negro women only to press garments, although an Alabama factory was mentioned where the entire work force is Negro, most of them women. Instances were cited of the appearance of Negro women in occupational areas previously closed to them in the South. A few Negro nurses and technicians are being employed in the care of white patients, and more Negro women are employed as social workers.

It was stated that the surplus of manpower in the South is

one reason for the relatively slow growth in the employment of women, white as well as Negro. It was suggested that, if the South experiences manpower shortages in the future, there will be an even greater willingness than there has been to employ white women in factories, but not Negro men. If the supply of white men and women is inadequate, however, it was anticipated that some factories would hire Negro women in preference to Negro men, especially where white women are already working.

MANAGEMENT POLICIES AND JOB OPPORTUNITIES

As a result of women's demonstrated ability to do many jobs formerly considered beyond their capacities, it was said, management policies specifically designed to expand the opportunities open to women have become increasingly common. It was noted that the original opportunities may have been offered out of necessity, but that the consequent success of women in many fields previously closed to them has served to change the attitudes of a substantial number of employers with respect to the capabilities of women workers.

This view was challenged by many conferees who doubted that employer attitudes have actually changed to any significant extent. The expansion of job openings, it was suggested, represents only a necessary accommodation to labor shortages rather than a fundamental change in attitude and policy. A serious recession, it was claimed, would quickly lead many employers to abandon policies favorable to the employment of women.

In this context it may be noted that at the special conference with trade union representatives, the participants were asked how unions view job differentiation on the basis of sex. Some unions oppose this practice, but in many cases, it was said, tradition is accepted and allowed to take its course. Even where there is a national policy opposing such differentiation, locals are frequently allowed considerable leeway in modifying or implementing it. The elimination of differential treatment, it was suggested, is often comparable to the problems of integrating whites and Negroes, and its achievement moves at a pace and in a manner that varies with local conditions.

It was the judgment of many employers that business and industry are still a long way from thinking of ability to perform as the sole criterion for job assignment and that jobs at all levels are still usually designated as belonging to either men or women. It was reported that in many instances top-level management may establish a policy of equal eligibility for jobs, but lower-level executives and supervisors continue to limit the opportunities available to women. Even in companies where women hold a wide range of jobs, opportunities usually remain very restricted when higher-level jobs are involved. This situation is often reinforced by the policies that govern training and promotion. For example, it was pointed out that, of the four graduate schools of banking maintained by the bankers' associations, three are closed to women, even though three fourths of all bank employees are women. Individuals receiving this advanced training are generally older and already advanced in position and salary level, which minimizes the loss of training investment due to turnover.

HIRING STANDARDS AND PRACTICES

It was generally agreed that employers have been tending to set higher educational requirements for their new employees. In the past, most employers apparently assumed that a high school education was unnecessary and perhaps even undesirable for a woman in an industrial job. Now high school graduates are preferred. The conferees from industry asserted, almost unanimously, that in selecting high school graduates they are more concerned that they have a good general education than that they have specialized vocational skills. Employers do, of course, expect that girls applying for secretarial work have some knowledge of typing and stenography. In some places, the market is so tight for these skills that a few companies conduct free evening classes in typing and shorthand for interested employees.

Women with college degrees, it was reported, are actively recruited by many department stores, by some manufacturers and utilities, and for civil service employment. Many firms which recruit male college graduates were reported to have no particular interest in hiring women college graduates. College women constitute only a small proportion of all women employed by the firms represented at the conferences.

Many employers set a limit on the age of the women they are willing to hire. Some establish a maximum age of 30 or 35, and a few will not hire young women above 26 or, in some cases, even over 21. Pension considerations were said to be an important reason why companies prefer to hire young workers. In recent years, however, employers have been hiring older women to an increasingly greater extent. Several conferees observed that employers who insist on hiring young women would often fare better by hiring women between 35 and 45, for they would be more likely to remain on the job longer.

Some employers, however, asserted that older women are likely to have characteristics which make them unsuitable as employees. They frequently become inflexible, set in their ways, and find it difficult to get along with their superiors and fellow workers. It was noted, however, that when firms need workers badly they change their age standards for hiring with more success than had been anticipated. One conferee observed that older women were being hired for clerical jobs in his field and that, while some inflexibility has been encountered among them, their stability, loyalty, and capacity for steady work were felt to outweigh by far any undesirable qualities shown. One of the major problems in hiring older women as beginners, it was said, is that they often become dissatisfied because their lack of skills forces them to work at the less interesting, "blind alley" jobs. However, when older women with previous experience return to work, employers usually find that their old skills, though rusty, are of value.

OPPORTUNITIES FOR PROMOTION

The conferees assigned major weight to three kinds of reasons in explaining the limited opportunities open to women for advancement to supervisory and executive positions: general traits attributed to them which are considered inimical to successful functioning as supervisors and executives; attitudes—held by men and women workers and by employers—or social customs, which make it difficult to integrate women into male executive staffs; commitments as wives and mothers resulting in attitudes toward work and in behavior on the job that, compared to men, make it less desirable to utilize them in supervisory or executive positions. The conferees made it clear that a complex interplay of reasons is frequently responsible for the lack of opportunities for promotion. They indicated that it is sometimes difficult to discern whether the traits alleged to make women unsuitable for promotion simply reflect the prevailing employment situation or express bias on the part of management. Several conferees specifically said that management is primarily responsible for blocking the advancement of qualified women who are eager to move ahead.

It was frequently stated that most women dislike assuming responsibility and many seem satisfied with repetitive jobs. They often seem to have comparatively limited interest in their jobs. The reason for this was said to be that they are concerned with supplementing family income rather than with a career. However, several conferees noted that most workers, men as well as women, dislike undertaking responsibilities and additional duties and are interested in doing no more than the immediate job requires.

It was contended that women are often not so much unwilling to accept the responsibilities of higher-level positions as unable to give their work the priority in their lives that such jobs require.

Too frequently, their home and family responsibilities force them to give secondary attention to their jobs. Even the professional woman who is married usually recognizes a primary responsibility to her home and family, however eager she may be to pursue a career outside the home. In the selection of women for higher-level positions, it was suggested that it is important to distinguish among three groups of workers: those who are clearly "career" women; the younger women whose employment goals have not yet been set; and the women whose job aspirations are limited, though they, too, may look forward to varying degrees of advancement. It was also noted that employers should bear in mind the fact that employment goals may change with alterations in the personal circumstances of their women workers. Many women whose homemaking duties are no longer burdensome could be successfully utilized in responsible positions.

The general reluctance of management to advance women was said to result in the loss of incentive to seek promotion among capable women workers. It was maintained that women present special problems to management and that they often cannot be utilized as fully as men. For example, they usually are not willing or able to move geographically, if the company requires it, and many are reluctant to travel in connection with their work. More important is the fact that women often leave paid employment for intervals of from two to five years. An older woman, therefore, is likely to have had less experience than a man of the same age and, as a result, may be less qualified for promotion. An employer will hesitate to make a significant training investment in a woman in order to qualify her for promotion, if he thinks that she may withdraw from paid employment for any one of a series of reasons which lie outside the work situation. Considerations of cost related to work continuity, rather than prejudicial attitudes against women as such, were said to be particularly responsible for the reluctance to promote women to higher-level posts.

WOMEN AS SUPERVISORS

An outgrowth of the discussion of promotion opportunities in general was an extensive consideration of the problems that result from the employment of women as supervisors, particularly in manufacturing concerns. The conferees were concerned with the traits and capacities displayed by women supervisors and with problems involving their relationships to male and female subordinates and superiors.

Most of the conferees maintained that women as well as men generally prefer male supervisors. It was asserted that women are more likely to accept instructions from a man than from a woman, but also that some women prefer to work for men because they can "get away with more." It was reported that the preference for men supervisors appears to be stronger among older women. Women supervisors were said to be more demanding of their subordinates than men and usually give them more detailed instructions. One of the criticisms which workers most frequently level against women supervisors is that they are guilty of "discrimination and partiality." The point was also made, however, that employees are accustomed to find men in positions of authority and, therefore, are less likely to express resentment against an incompetent male supervisor than an incompetent woman supervisor.

Many women are reluctant to accept promotion to supervisory positions, it was said, because they are not sure they will receive the support of the women working under them. When a woman is put in a position of authority, it was noted, she has the burden not only of proving herself to the group she supervises, but also of proving herself so capable to her superiors that a woman will be readily acceptable as her successor.

Several examples were cited to indicate that tradition plays an important role in the acceptance of women supervisors. The telephone companies, it was pointed out, have long used women to supervise operators. According to surveys, operators' attitudes toward their supervisors are no different from those of women in other departments who have male supervisors. In department stores, most supervisors and many department managers are women, and no special problems are encountered.

OPPORTUNITIES TO BECOME EXECUTIVES

The comments of the conferees indicated that the same kind of considerations which determine whether women will be hired in general and whether they will be promoted to low-level supervisory positions apply with particular force when women are considered as potential executives. In competing for positions at higher levels, women usually face an extremely critical scrutiny from management. Few women now hold top executive posts in large corporations, but it was evident from many comments that an increasing number of women are assuming quite responsible positions.

Some of the reasons given for the limited executive opportunities open to women have already been noted, such as high turnover and the fact that certain working conditions are considered either too difficult or demanding for women. Certain executive jobs, moreover, require travel or entertainment activities which may be a source of embarrassment. Much emphasis was placed on the importance of technical knowledge for executive posts, particularly in manufacturing, which most women lacked. One reason that difficulties are sometimes encountered when women are placed in high-level positions, a conferee declared, is poor initial selection. In considering a woman for an important position an executive's judgment is often affected by his attitudes toward women in general. It was pointed out that he would make sounder decisions if they were based upon the same criteria used in selecting a potential male executive.

Few women will rise to high-level posts, it was agreed, until a substantial number hold jobs at intermediate levels and a regular promotion ladder is thus established. Many of the better jobs now open to women are highly specialized, and the opportunities for further promotion are, consequently, limited by the nature of the work. Now that more women are reaching higher posts and are doing well in them, however, it was felt that additional opportunities will open up with greater rapidity. Their accomplishments are changing management attitudes, and it was suggested that a key problem in the future will be the availability of enough women qualified for and willing to accept more responsible duties.

FUTURE PROSPECTS

The conference participants were generally confident that in the future a larger number of women would be found in paid employment, and an increasing proportion of women would be occupying supervisory and higher-level executive posts. There was widespread agreement that, as management acted to implement already stated policies favorable to the employment of women, and as women themselves took it for granted that they would be likely to spend an increasing number of years in work outside of the home, the range of job opportunities open to women would inevitably expand.

Some conferees believed that the future would bring an even more rapid growth in the participation of women in paid employment than that which has occurred since 1940. Others thought that such an acceleration would be unlikely, and still others pointed to certain fields of employment, notably in heavy manufacturing, where a contraction of job opportunities could occur. Moreover, some doubt was voiced about the strength and permanence of the newer and more positive attitudes displayed by management toward women workers. There emerged in the course of the conferences the feeling among the participants from industry that a continued growth in the paid employment of women, at whatever rate it proceeds, would contribute to the vigor of the economy and the well-being of women themselves.

The point was also made that women are not going to abandon their primary functions as wives and mothers and that the greater willingness they have been displaying to work outside the home must be read against this stubborn fact. Considerable uncertainty was also expressed about what is likely to transpire in the event of heavy unemployment. Trade union conferees representing certain manufacturing fields felt that there were employment developments now under way which warned against overly optimistic views of the total employment situation for women in the future. The point was repeatedly made that it is at least as risky to venture grand generalizations about future developments as it is about the present situation with respect to women in paid employment.

It was the general feeling of the conferees that the major factors conditioning both the extent to which women worked outside the home and the occupations and job levels open to them are operating to effect further changes in line with those of recent years. The age of marriage and the pattern of childbearing, the rise in life expectancy, the shift in attitudes on the part of management toward women workers and on the part of women themselves toward paid employment, the pressure for larger family incomes to satisfy ever-rising consumption aspirations, the manpower requirements of an expanding economy, current and impending technological developments, the expansion of service functions of all sorts—these and still other considerations were thought by many to indicate that past trends were likely to continue into the near future.

iv. TRENDS IN THE EMPLOYMENT
OF WOMEN

In 1890, when the outlines of today's economy were becoming clear, the Census counted 4 million working women, who constituted about one sixth of the working population. Of all the women in the United States, about one sixth were in the labor force. Since then, the number of working women has increased steadily. There are now about 22 million women in the labor force, as has been seen, and they constitute over one third of all women and nearly one third of the nation's workers.

These increases, as Tables 9 and 10 show, have been most rapid since 1940. World War II brought millions of women into employment. While many of them withdrew from the labor market in 1946 and 1947, the proportion in paid employment remained well above what it had been in 1940. After 1947, moreover, the number and proportion of women in the labor force began to increase once more, and by 1954 more women were working than during the war.

In 1890, paid work was much more peripheral to the lives of most women than it is today, and women workers were even more heavily concentrated in the poorer-paid, routine, unskilled jobs. Before World War II, changes in the character of women's work, in the kinds of women who worked, and in the place of work in women's lives were far more important than increases in the proportion of women in paid employment. In the half century before the war, the proportion of women in the labor force increased at the rate of about 0.15 percentage points a year. But since 1940 this proportion has increased at the rate of almost 0.5 percentage points a year. There is, therefore, good reason to concentrate, for the period before 1940, on changes in the character of women's work and in the kinds of women who worked, rather than on the number and proportion of women in the labor force.

Table 9. The Female Labor Force, 1890-1950

Year	Thousands	Percent of Women
	Gainful Workers Aged 10 and Over	
1890	4,006	17.4
1900	5,319	18.8
1910	7,445	21.5
1920	8,637	21.4
1930	10,752	22.0
	Labor Force Aged 14 and Over	
1930[a]	10,396	23.6
1940	13,015	25.7
1950	16,552	29.0

[a] Up to and including 1930, the Census counted "gainful workers" aged 10 and over. In 1940 and 1950 it counted persons "in the labor force" aged 14 and over. Basically, "gainful workers" were individuals who regarded themselves as having a regular occupation producing an income, regardless of what they were doing at the time of the Census. Persons in the "labor force" are those who worked or sought work for pay or profit during the week preceding the Census. Under both definitions, some women who worked without pay on family farms or in family businesses were also included. The labor force figures for 1930 were estimated by the Census from the gainful worker figures.

Source: U.S. Bureau of the Census, Decennial Census Reports

OCCUPATIONAL TRENDS AMONG WOMEN WORKERS

Since the end of the last century the United States has been transformed from an agricultural to an urban society. In 1890, almost two thirds of the population lived in rural areas. By 1950, the proportion was reversed; about two thirds were living in

Table 10. The Female Labor Force, 1940-56

Year	Thousands	Percent of Women Aged 14 and Over	Percent of All Workers
1940[a]	13,840	27.6	25.4
1941	13,930	27.4	25.3
1942	15,460	30.1	27.7
1943	18,100	34.9	33.0
1944	18,450	35.2	34.0
1945	19,570	37.0	36.1
1946	16,590	30.9	29.4
1947	16,320	30.0	27.6
1948	17,155	31.2	28.3
1949	17,167	30.9	28.2
1950[a]	18,063	32.1	29.0
1951	18,607	32.7	30.1
1952	18,798	32.7	30.4
1953	19,296	33.1	30.6
1954	19,726	33.4	30.8
1955	20,154	33.8	31.2
1956	21,194	35.1	31.8

[a] Figures for 1940 and 1950 are higher than those shown in Table 9, which are derived from the Decennial Census. It is believed that the current survey figures are more accurate but that Decennial Census figures are more comparable with those for earlier Census years. All data are for April, except 1940, where they are for March. Data do not include women in the armed forces.

Source: U.S. Bureau of the Census, Current Population Survey

urban areas. For women as for men, this change has meant greater opportunities for employment in an ever-growing variety of jobs in industry, commerce, and in professional, personal, and governmental service.

Of the 4 million working women reported by the 1890 Census, about 20 percent were agricultural workers. By 1950, mainly as a result of the decline in the number of men and women in the farm population, only 5 percent of the employed women worked on farms. It is extremely difficult, however, to distinguish between women who only live on farms and those who also "work" on them. Because of inadequacies in the data on women farmers and farm workers, the discussion of changes in the occupations of women workers which follows is confined to nonfarm work.

By far the most striking change in the work of women since the close of the nineteenth century involves the shift from unskilled and semiskilled manual work to clerical and sales employment. In 1890, as Table 11 indicates, almost 85 percent of all women in nonfarm work were employed in domestic and personal service or in "manufacturing and mechanical industries," and only about 5 percent were clerical or sales workers. Table 12 shows that by 1950 semiskilled and unskilled manual workers accounted for only 44 percent of the total number of women in

Table 11. Principal Occupations of Women in Nonfarm Work, 1890

	Thousands	*Percent Distribution*
Professional Workers	312	9.6
Teachers	246	7.6
Musicians, artists, and teachers of music and art	45	1.4
Physicians and surgeons	5 ⎫	
Actresses and entertainers	4 ⎬	.6
All other occupations	12 ⎭	
Trade and Transportation	228	7.0
Clerical workers [a]	113	3.5
Saleswomen	59	1.8
Retail merchants	22	.7
All other occupations	34	1.0
Domestic and Personal Service	1,668	51.6
Servants	1,217	37.6
Laundresses	217	6.7
Laborers, not specified [b]	55	1.7
All other occupations	179	5.6
Manufacturing and Mechanical Industries	1,027	31.8
Needle trades	580	17.9
Textile mills	224	6.9
Boots and shoes	34	1.1
Tobacco and cigars	28	.9
All other industries	161	5.0
Total, nonfarm	3,235	100.0

[a] Includes all clerical workers, whether employed in trade and transportation or elsewhere.
[b] Includes all female laborers, except farm laborers, whether employed in service fields or elsewhere. This figure is also believed to include many farm laborers.

Source: U.S. Census Reports, 1890, unadjusted data

nonfarm employment, while the rapidly growing number of clerical and sales workers had reached 37 percent of the total.[1]

*Table 12. Major Occupational Groups of Men and Women in
Nonfarm Employment, 1910-50*

	Women: Percent Distribution				
	1910	1920	1930	1940	1950
Professional workers	12	13	15	13	12
Proprietors, managers and officials	2	2	2	3	6
Clerical and sales workers	17	30	31	30	37
Skilled workers and foremen	2	1	1	1	1
Semiskilled and unskilled workers	67	54	51	53	44
Total	100	100	100	100	100

	Men: Percent Distribution				
	1910	1920	1930	1940	1950
Professional workers	5	5	5	6	7
Proprietors, managers and officials	12	11	12	12	15
Clerical and sales workers	14	15	17	17	16
Skilled workers and foremen	22	23	22	19	21
Semiskilled and unskilled workers	47	46	44	46	41
Total	100	100	100	100	100

	Women Workers as Percent of Total Workers in Occupational Group				
	1910	1920	1930	1940	1950
Professional workers	44	48	49	45	42
Proprietors, managers and officials	5	6	7	10	15
Clerical and sales workers	28	39	39	41	52
Skilled workers and foremen	2	2	1	2	2
Semiskilled and unskilled workers	31	27	28	31	33
Total	24	24	26	28	31

Source: A. J. Jaffe and Charles D. Stewart, *Manpower Resources and Utilization,*
New York, 1951. Based on U.S. Census Reports.

Even today, as Chapter II indicates, women workers are concentrated in a few occupational fields, many of which involve the
functions traditionally performed by women. This was far more

[1] The occupational classifications used in Tables 11 and 12 are not strictly
comparable. Nevertheless, the categories of "Domestic and Personal Service"
and "Manufacturing and Mechanical Industries" in Table 11 are roughly equivalent to "Semiskilled and Unskilled Workers" in Table 12.

true in 1890, when, as Table 11 shows, almost 85 percent of all women in nonfarm employment were found in domestic or personal service, teaching, or in the clothing and textile industries. These occupational fields accounted for only about one third of all women workers in 1950.

One important characteristic of the jobs held by women in 1890 is not revealed by the names of their occupations. Perhaps half of the women in nonfarm employment before the turn of the century were not employed in offices, shops, or factories, but in private homes—either their own or their employers'. This situation held for the great majority in the service occupations and for a high proportion of the women in manufacturing and mechanical industries. In 1910, the earliest date for which such information is available, about three fifths of the women in the clothing manufacturing industry worked directly for their customers or were paid by manufacturers for piecework done at home. In addition, many of the art and music teachers, storekeepers, cigar makers, and boarding and lodginghouse keepers also worked in private homes. Today, this is true of only a small fraction of the women in nonfarm employment. Service workers in private households were less than 10 percent of the total in 1950, and dressmakers and seamstresses not working in factories were well under 1 percent.

The women employed in private homes in 1890 had a relatively tenuous attachment to their jobs. They constituted a large reserve who worked when they were needed and when they themselves desired employment. The majority of women workers today do not work full time over the course of a whole year, but women's work was probably more intermittent before the turn of the century.

MANUFACTURING AND SERVICE OCCUPATIONS

Although the growing employment of women in manufacturing has received wide attention, the role of women has actually changed less in this than in many other sectors of the economy. Women played a major role in the manufacture of commodities when production was concentrated in private homes and small shops, and they continued to do so as the factory became increasingly important. During the first half of the nineteenth century, factory employment was widely regarded as "women's and children's," rather than "men's" work. One reason was that the first large factories were textile mills. Spinning had always been a woman's job, and weaving had early been preempted by women. Throughout the nineteenth century employment of women in manufacturing was facilitated by the fact that light, nondurable goods made up a high proportion of all manufactured products. To this day, the manufacture of such goods depends on women workers to a far greater extent than do the heavy durable goods industries which have developed very rapidly in the last half century.

There have, however, been important changes in the kinds of work done by women in manufacturing. In 1890, about 80 percent of all women in the Census grouping of "manufacturing and mechanical industries" were textile or apparel workers. Today, textiles and apparel account for only about one third of the total number of women in manufacturing. Another one third are employed in various metal fabricating industries which provided employment for very few women in 1890. These and other changes reflect transformations in manufacturing as a result of the development of new industries, the expansion or decline of old industries, and alterations in the extent to which particular industries rely on women workers.

In most industries which relied heavily on women workers, and had the largest numbers of women workers in 1890, women have just held their own or have lost ground relative to the number of male workers. Thus in both 1890 and 1950, women were about 80 percent of all operatives and laborers in the clothing industry and about half in the textile industry. In a few of the industries which relied heavily on women, notably in paper and rubber, the ratio of women to men workers has declined sharply. In most industries where few women were employed at the close of the nineteenth century, they have gained substantial ground, even where they are still greatly outnumbered by men. In 1910, for instance, when the automobile industry was in its infancy, only 2 percent of the operatives and laborers were women; by 1950, however, 15 percent were women.[2]

The reasons for changes in the extent to which women are utilized in particular manufacturing occupations and industries are still far from clear. There is little question, of course, that the manner in which an industry grows affects the extent to which women are employed. In the clothing, textile, and most other industries in which the total number of workers has remained relatively stable, the ratio of women to men has not increased. This ratio has gone up, for the most part, when and where the total number of workers in an industry has also increased rapidly. The beverage industry after the end of prohibition and the aircraft and ordnance industries during World War II and the Korean conflict provide striking instances of rapid expansion accompanied by substantial increases in the proportion of women workers.

Innovations in technology, frequently accompanied by changes in an industry's products, also influence the degree of reliance upon women workers. Particular jobs have almost always been rigidly classified as "women's" or "men's" jobs, and only rarely have men and women worked side by side doing the same tasks. Work requiring great skill or physical strength has virtually been monopolized by men, and the women production workers have generally been semiskilled machine operators, or sorters, assemblers, and packers of small light objects. By altering the physical or skill requirements of particular tasks, technological changes

[2] This and subsequent sections of this chapter dealing with changes in the detailed occupations of women are based in large part on the data presented in Bulletins 218 and 253 of the Women's Bureau, U.S. Department of Labor.

have influenced the decision to hire men or women for these jobs.

Some changes have made the work in an industry lighter, cleaner, or easier and have thus encouraged the employment of women. For example, the switch in popular taste from the cigar to the cigarette, together with the development of increasingly automatic machinery, led to the replacement of skilled male cigar makers by female machine tenders. Other changes in product or technology, however, have had quite different effects. The replacement of inefficient hand operations by high-speed machine operations has frequently led to the displacement of semiskilled, low-paid women workers. The introduction of machines for making paper boxes and other paper products eliminated the work of women pasters, folders, and cutters. In the cotton textile industry, the steady development of ever larger, faster, and more complex spinning machines and looms increased the physical demands of the work and contributed to the gradual decline over the past century or more in the ratio of women to men workers.

Technological change has often provided the occasion for hiring women in manufacturing even when it has not provided the reason. The significance of this fact should not be underestimated for, once made, the assignment of a job to one sex or the other tends to persist as long as the job remains essentially unchanged. When new kinds of jobs are created, some of them are assigned to men and others to women on the basis of a variety of considerations. In many instances, the objective characteristics of the job provide no clue to its sex classification. The important point that emerges from an examination of the changes in women's industrial employment in the past is that significant new job opportunities were usually made available to women when new kinds of work appeared as the result of changes in processes, machines, or products.

Service workers were shown as the largest group of employed women in every census until 1950, when clerical work assumed first place. The great majority of women service workers have been employed as household servants, cleaning women, janitresses, laundresses, waitresses, and in similar unskilled, poorly paid, low prestige occupations. Service work has always employed disproportionately high numbers of the very young and the old, of widows, immigrants, and Negroes.

Since 1890, the proportion of all women workers in service jobs has dropped sharply and the proportion of the total female population so employed has declined slightly. By 1950, service occupations accounted for only a little more than one fifth of the women in the nonfarm labor force, compared to about half sixty years earlier. Between 1940 and 1950 the number of women in private household employment fell from almost 2 million to about 1.3 million. In 1890, when the population was less than half as large as in 1950, about the same number were probably in private household employment. Service employment outside private homes has been rising since 1890, reaching over a million by 1940, and almost 2 million by 1950. The restaurant and health fields accounted for most of the increase between 1940 and 1950.

Women have always constituted the overwhelming majority of private servants, but they have been a minority of other service workers. In nonhousehold service fields, however, the ratio of women to men has been increasing. Women constituted about 45 percent of all nonhousehold service workers in 1950, compared to 38 percent in 1940. The primary reason for this increase has and 12 percent of the sales jobs. By 1950, over three fifths of the in finding men willing to take such work.

CLERICAL AND SALES OCCUPATIONS

Throughout most of the nineteenth century, stores and business offices, unlike factories, were almost exclusively masculine preserves. Before 1880 almost all clerical and sales workers were probably been the growing difficulty employers have encountered men. By 1890, women held about 15 percent of the clerical jobs office workers and over one third of the sales workers were women.

Several explanations have been offered for the spectacular growth of women's employment in clerical work. The beginning of this growth coincided with the invention of the typewriter and the telephone — the characteristic equipment of the clerical worker. The changing technology of offices, however, was not, by itself, responsible for the shift from men to women. Hand bookkeeping remained the rule until after World War I, and sales work has still to be significantly affected by technological developments. Yet the rapid growth of women's employment began simultaneously, not only in typing occupations and telephone offices, but also in bookkeeping and sales work. The typewriter, the telephone, and women clerical and sales workers all made their appearance at the same time largely in response to more basic changes in the economy.

Since the close of the nineteenth century, the corporate form of business has achieved dominance, and giant companies have spread their operations across the continent. The nation has become the world's foremost industrial power and has assumed a major role in world trade. These and related developments, including rapid urbanization, enormously expanded the need for communication and record keeping. In recent decades, this need has continued to rise because of the constantly growing size and complexity of business units, the trend toward fuller record keeping in order to improve control over business costs and to meet government requirements, the expansion of governmental activities and employment, and the apparently universal tendency of administrators to increase paper work.

The demand for clerical workers has grown so rapidly that it could not have been met if employers had insisted on hiring only men. Most clerical work requires an education well above the average that prevailed at the end of the last century. The supply of young people who were qualified and available for clerical employment included many more girls than young men. More girls than boys attended and graduated from high school but, as will be seen, fewer went on to college. Moreover, aside from teaching, there were few other fields of employment open to a reasonably well-educated young woman, and marriage generally came later than it does today. At first, the propriety of office work for women was questioned, but it was always held to be more respectable than employment in a factory or as a servant.

Since women were willing to take clerical jobs for lower wages than men, hiring them kept down the cost of the rapidly growing volume of paper work. At the same time, the greater volume of administrative work facilitated specialization and subdivision of tasks. Specialization, while helping to cut costs directly, also contributed to the employment of young women, most of whom did not intend to stay at work for many years and had little interest in learning to perform a wide range of clerical functions.

Women did not often take over jobs formerly held by men. As in manufacturing, new jobs were created, which from the beginning were allocated to women. Most of the new jobs involved less skill, knowledge, responsibility, prestige, and pay than the old clerical occupations. Indeed, the titles were among the few things about the clerical occupations which did not change. The old meanings of the terms "clerk" and "secretary" are preserved today only in such special titles as "County Clerk" and "Secretary and Treasurer." Although in recent years many women have advanced from the routine work and relatively low wages typical of most clerical jobs to better paid and responsible positions, their progress is generally not reflected in the names of their jobs. For Census purposes, those holding better jobs are grouped together with other clerical workers.

Very early in the history of the woman office worker, the opinion developed that she was especially suited to clerical work because she was tolerant of routine, meticulous, conscientious, and possessed a degree of manual dexterity which made her the natural operator of the typewriter, adding machine, and switchboard. In spite of the dubiousness of some of these propositions, their widespread acceptance undoubtedly contributed to women's virtual monopoly of this kind of work. There is also reason to believe that the growing use of women in clerical work was encouraged because many employers found it pleasant to have their offices graced by bright, attractive young women.

The steady growth of an ever-larger and more complex market economy also created a rising demand for sales workers. Women have not achieved as large a role in selling as in clerical work, however, partly because the demand for workers has not increased as rapidly. Moreover, it has not generally been possible to subdivide the selling job, giving some functions to women, and leaving others for men. Sales personnel have been relieved of some of their functions by stock clerks, cashiers, bookkeepers, package wrappers, etc., but these assistants have not usually been classified as sales workers. Women have directly replaced men in many less desirable sales jobs, leaving men in most of the positions where high earnings are possible.

THE PROFESSIONS AND MANAGEMENT

Like clerical and sales work, the professions were once a male preserve. Most of the increases in the employment of women in the professions did not involve the entrance of women into professions formerly monopolized by men, but reflected rather the acquisition of professional status by occupations traditionally held by women.

By the Civil War, if not before, public school teaching was already a woman's job in the United States. It was not, at first, a profession, but a job which could be held by any reasonably literate person. In 1870, when the first complete occupational count was made by the Census, teachers were classified as professional workers, even though the standards for the occupation were not very high. Around the turn of the century, nursing also began to achieve professional status. The Census of 1900 was the first which distinguished a small group of "trained nurses" from the much larger group of "nurses and midwives."

Teaching and nursing have accounted for most of the growth in the professional employment of women. In most other professional occupations they have not made spectacular gains since 1890. In that year, 10 percent of the women nonfarm workers were professionals. The figure reached 15 percent by 1930, but declined to 12 percent by 1950 because of the much more rapid growth of clerical employment. In 1890, women constituted about 36 percent of all professional workers. By 1930, they were nearly half, but by 1950 the figure had fallen to about 40 percent, mainly because of the rapid growth of male employment in engineering and technical fields.

The employment of women in the professions has changed, however, in one important respect. In 1870, 90 percent of the professional women were teachers. By 1950, only 43 percent were teachers, and one fourth were nurses. The remaining one third were widely distributed among other professional occupations. The growing number of women in these other professions resulted mainly from the appearance of new occupations and the expansion of older ones in which women were employed from the beginning. It was not due to the replacement of men by women in particular professional fields. The great majority of teachers, nurses, social workers, and librarians have been women since data were first collected. In a second group of occupations—which includes music, art, entertainment, writing, and college teaching —women constituted a substantial minority even before the turn of the century. In none of these occupations has there been any consistent growth in the ratio of women to men.

In most of the traditionally male professions, however, women have gained on men, but very slowly. During the last quarter of the nineteenth century a small, determined group of women literally fought their way into medicine, the law, dentistry, and other such professional occupations. But their victory was mainly symbolic, at least until 1940, when men still constituted 97 percent or more of the lawyers, dentists, architects, natural scientists, and engineers, and 95 percent of the doctors. Although there have been increases in the number and proportion of women employed in almost all of the "male professions" since 1940, men still constitute at least 95 percent of the workers in most of these occupations. Women have made consistent and substantial gains on men in only one profession. In 1870, 99 percent of the editors and reporters were men, but by 1950, nearly one third were women. Even here, however, women have been hired mainly to write and edit the increasing volume of material dealing with fashions, homemaking, social news, and other subjects published specifically for women readers.

Although women have played a minor role in management, the proportion which women constitute of all managerial personnel and proprietors has steadily increased since the beginning of the century. As in professional employment, substantial gains have come only since 1940. The majority of women managers and proprietors are found in retailing, eating and drinking, and personal-service establishments, but they have also been gaining on men in other sectors of the economy. In banking and finance, women constituted about 10 percent of the managers and proprietors in 1950, compared to less than 4 percent in 1920. In industry, including manufacturing, mining, construction, transportation, and communications, the percentage rose from less than one half of 1 percent in 1890 to about 5 percent in 1950. In government, the increase was from 4 percent in 1910 to about 15 percent in 1950.

More women are found in managerial employment in part because of the enormous increase in the number of women working in the lower-level white collar jobs. As the number of women clerks, secretaries, sales personnel, cashiers, and bookkeepers increased, more of them demonstrated the will and ability to become supervisors and managers. At the same time, as attitudes changed, it became possible for both men and women to think of women as executives. As has been seen, however, most of these gains have been in small organizations or in the lower levels of management.

THE AGE OF WOMEN WORKERS

In 1890, 70 percent of all women workers were single, and over half were under 25. Only about 2.5 percent of the white wives in the country worked. If a woman worked at all, it was usually before she was married. Perhaps half of the women in the country never worked for pay. Most of the other half stopped working for pay when they married and did not return to work unless their husbands died or were incapacitated. Most of the women who followed a different pattern were immigrants, the daughters of immigrants, or Negroes, and a high proportion of them were concentrated in a few localities.

Today, on the other hand, over half of the working women are married and almost half are over 40. With nearly 30 percent of the married women of the nation in the labor force, the working wife is found in all parts of the country and among all social, racial, and ethnic groups. More and more women are remaining in the labor force for most of their adult lives, except for longer or shorter periods when their children are young. For the first time in the history of the United States there is a substantial group of women for whom paid employment constitutes far more than an experience in youth or a necessity imposed by misfortune.

The new significance of paid work in the lives of American women is largely a development of the last fifteen years. Its revolutionary character is illustrated by Figure 2, which shows the relationship between the age and the percentage of women in the labor force in 1890, 1940, and 1956. The proportion of women in the labor force in 1940 was substantially higher than in 1890 among all age groups except the very young and the very old,

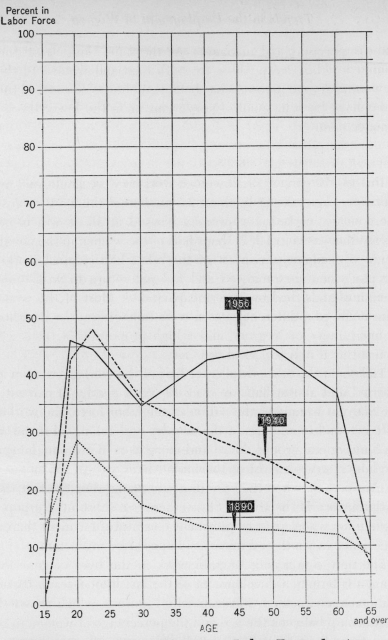

Figure 2. Percent of Women in Labor Force, by Age,
1890, 1940, 1956

Data for 1890 are from the 1890 Census Report and are for age groups 10-14, 15-24, 25-34, 45-54, and 65 and over. Data for 1940 and 1956 are from the Census Current Population Reports and are for age groups 14-15, 16-17, 18-19, 20-24, 25-34, 35-44, 45-54, 55-64, and 65 and over.

but the general pattern of participation in paid employment was similar for both years. Thus, the highest percentage of women in paid employment was reached around the age of 20, and the proportion in the labor force fell off sharply for successively older groups of women. Since 1940, this pattern has been transformed. Today, the proportion working stops declining at around age 30, begins to rise sharply, and continues to grow until about age 50. Although the proportion in paid employment drops quickly with advancing age among women over 50, there are now substantially more women in the labor force at all ages over 30 than there were in 1940, or even in 1950. During the last sixteen years, the percentage employed among women 45 to 54 years old has nearly doubled, from under 25 percent to nearly 45 percent. The same is true even of women between 55 and 64 years of age, among whom the proportion employed has gone up from 18 to over 36 percent.

But this is only a part of the story. Figure 2 might seem to indicate that women tend to leave the labor force rapidly after the age of 50. A second look shows that of the women who were 60 in 1950, for instance, more were actually working than had been in 1940, when these same women were 10 years younger. Instead of focusing on women of different ages at one point in time, Figure 3 indicates the labor force participation at successive points in time of women born in specified decades. It shows that the women who were born before 1886—and who consequently were entering the labor market up to about the end of the century—worked in largest numbers when they were young, and the proportion in the labor force declined steadily with age, except for a slight increase as they passed from about 40 to about 50. This increase appears to be accounted for mainly by the growing number of widows during this age span.

Women born since 1886—and this means almost all women who are now working—have followed a strikingly different pattern, which began to emerge during the 1930's. Within each of

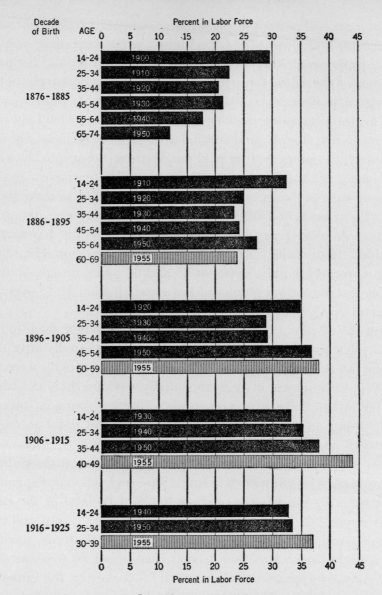

Figure 3. *Changing Labor Force Participation Rates of Women Born in Specified Decades as They Grew Older, 1900-55*

Rates are estimates based on published and unpublished data from the U.S. Bureau of the Census.

the groups of women born after 1886, the proportion in the labor force was higher in 1940 than it had been in 1930, higher in 1950 than in 1940, and, with the exception of the oldest women, higher in 1955 than in 1950. Instead of dropping out of the labor force as they grew older, more and more of these women were entering paid employment.

Today, the lifetime pattern of women's participation in the labor force is taking the following shape: An increasing number of girls go to work during their teens, with a temporary peak of nearly 50 percent participation in the labor force being reached at around 18 or 19. As they marry and begin to have children, more and more of them stop working. At the low point, around the age of 30 or slightly before, about one third of the women are in the labor force. After this point, more women return to work or go to work for the first time than stop working. The proportion in the labor force continues to rise to about age 60.[3]

These developments must be seen in relation to the aging of the population as a whole. The decline in the birth rate between 1890 and the late 1930's, the rising life expectancy since 1890, and the curtailment of immigration since World War I have substantially increased the ratio of old to young people in the population. The declining role of young women in the labor force and the growing importance of older women are illustrated by Figure 4. In 1890, women under 25 constituted over half of all working women; in 1940 they were only a third; today, they constitute less than one fifth. Women over 45 were only 15 percent of the female labor force in 1890, and in 1940, they were about 22 percent. But by 1956, they made up 37 percent of the female labor force.

---

[3] At all ages, many women are entering and many other women are leaving the labor force. Because of limitations in the data, it is possible to describe only net changes.

WORK IN RELATION TO SCHOOL, MARRIAGE, AND CHILDREN

Whether or not a woman works at different ages depends not so much on her age alone as on her background and on her circumstances, including those which change as she grows older—such as school attendance, marital status, whether or not she has children, and the age of the children. Since the close of the last century there have been major changes in the relationships be-

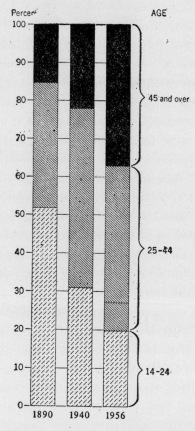

Figure 4. Distribution of Female Labor Force by Age, 1890, 1940, 1956

Data for 1890 are from John D. Durand, *Labor Force in the United States, 1890-1960*, New York, 1948. Data for 1940 and 1956 are from the Census' Current Population Reports.

tween these circumstances and both the age and the employment of women.

The highest proportion of women in the labor force has always been found among those who have finished or left school, but are not yet married. Before the turn of the century, the period between leaving school and starting marriage was much longer than it is today. Some girls went to work even before they reached their teens, and a government study of 17,000 urban working women conducted in 1887 found that on the average they had obtained their first jobs at the age of 15. Since the average marriage age for women was then about 22, the girls who entered paid employment were likely to stay at work for about seven years before marrying.

During this century, the ages at which girls and boys leave school and go to work have steadily advanced. Today the great majority of girls do not have regular full-time jobs much before the age of seventeen or eighteen. Two other developments, however, have tended to increase the supply of young women available for employment. In the first place, it has become customary for young women to go to work when they leave school. In 1890, perhaps half of all young women stayed home after they finished school until they married, but by 1940 the overwhelming majority were spending the time between school and marriage in the labor force. In the second place, continuing high employment has made it possible for many boys and girls to combine school attendance with part-time work. Consequently, although the average age at which girls leave school and take full-time jobs has continued to rise slowly, the proportion in the labor force among teen-aged girls has changed very little in recent years.

Since 1940, a sharp increase in the number of early marriages has still further reduced the period between school completion and marriage. As many women were married by age 21 in 1950 as were married by 23 in 1940. In 1940, about 10 percent of the women who would probably marry eventually were still single when they reached 30. But by 1950, virtually all of those who would marry were already married by this age.

The recent lowering of the age of marriage has been accompanied by a sharp increase in the birth rate among young women. Since 1940, for instance, the birth rate has risen by 70 percent for women aged 20 to 24. In spite of these changes in the timing of marriages and births, the employment of women in their twenties has not declined significantly. A growing majority of young women are staying at work until shortly before their first child is born, and more mothers of young children are also working. Since 1940, the proportion in the labor force among mothers of preschool children has probably more than doubled, and is now 18 percent.

The most spectacular development of recent years, however, has been the rise in the employment of women over 30, most of whom are wives and mothers. Among married women aged 35 to 44 and living with their husbands, the proportion in the labor force more than doubled between 1940 and 1955, from 16 percent to 34 percent. Among wives between the ages of 45 and 64, the proportion nearly tripled in the same period, from 10 percent to 29 percent.

A number of causes brought about the sharp increase in paid employment among married women over 30. The cultural and economic forces which had earlier led to a steady increase in the employment of women were enormously strengthened after 1940, and employment has increased significantly since then among all groups of women: schoolgirls, young mothers, elderly widows, etc. Older married women, however, were in a much better position than any other group to respond to the steady high demand for workers and the weakening of cultural attitudes opposing women's employment. Most older women who were not married were already employed. Among young women, increasing proportions were still in school, married, or caring for young children; of those who were not, almost all were already working. Moreover, because of the declining birth rate in previous decades, the number of young men and women reaching working age fell sharply during the 1940's and only recently has begun to increase again. In the face of a growing demand for workers and the limited availability of other groups, many employers found it convenient to fill their needs by hiring older married women.

Not only were relatively few of the older married women already employed, but most of them were also free from responsibility for the care of young children. The growing employment of older women, as has been noted, is largely a reflection of a greater tendency to enter paid employment on the part of those wives who do not have young children requiring constant care. There has also been a substantial increase in employment among young mothers since 1940, but the proportion in the labor force among mothers of school-age children is more than twice as high as it is among mothers of preschool children. In 1940, probably some 10 to 15 percent of the mothers whose children were between 6 and 17 were working, compared to 38 percent in 1955.

It is clear, therefore, that changes in the employment of older wives are significantly related to changes in the patterns of family formation. Because of the steady decline in the birth rate up to shortly before the beginning of World War II, women who had reached or were then approaching the end of their childbearing period had fewer children than any preceding generation of American women. This circumstance undoubtedly contributed to their readiness to enter the labor force in the following years. The long-run decline in births, moreover, reflected mainly the gradual disappearance of large families which were not completed until late in the mother's period of fertility. As the period during which women were bearing children was progressively shortened, the average age of women when their children reached an age of relative independence fell.

The sharp increase in the birth rate since the beginning of

World War II has been most pronounced among women in their teens and early twenties, who are now bearing children at record rates. Many population experts believe that, in spite of the increase in the birth rate, the average size of the family is not rising substantially, and that the age at which most women have their last child is not going up. On the basis of such assumptions it has been estimated that half of the women who married in 1950 would have borne their last child during 1956 or earlier. Since the median age of women who married in 1950 was 20 years, this means that the median age of the mother at the birth of her last child may now be only 26, a drop of 6 years since the end of the last century.

Still another development has facilitated the increase in the employment of older women. Improvements in medical care, especially in childbirth, together with the fact that women are having fewer children than previous generations, and having them earlier, have resulted in a steady improvement in the health of older women. Moreover, fewer women now seem to be seriously affected by the psychological and physical disabilities associated with the menopause.

These developments have great significance for the employment of married women. Since 1940, labor market conditions and changes in attitudes and values have opened a new range of opportunities in paid employment to wives and mothers. Most mothers wait until their children are at least of school age before they take jobs. Today this point is often reached when mothers are still relatively young, while their health is good, and before such skills as they had acquired in school or early work experience become rusty or outmoded.

Women who were formerly married—widows and divorcees together—constitute about 16 percent of all women workers today, as they did in 1890. Then, almost all in this group were widows. Today, the number of divorced women in the labor force is more than half as great as the number of widows.

Labor force participation has always been higher among widows and divorcees than among married women. Today, there are relatively fewer widows than there were a half century ago in every age group but the very oldest, because the men, like the women, are living longer. Widows, however, are now much older than they were in 1890, when nearly half were under 55. In 1954, almost 80 percent were over 55, and over half were over 65. This age increase has not served to reduce the proportion of widows working. Of some 7 million widows in the United States in 1954, over 2 million, or about 28 percent, were working, almost exactly the same percentage as in 1890. Among those over 65, fewer are working, but among younger widows there have been substantial increases. While 37 percent of the widows aged 45 to 54 worked in 1890, 60 percent were working in 1954.

It appears likely that increasing numbers of widows in middle and late middle age have been drawn into the labor force by the same influences affecting wives in the same age groups rather than by more compelling economic reasons. It is true that the decline in family size, the extension of schooling, and the lower average age of marriage have tended to make it less likely that a widowed mother will be able to count upon being supported by her children. But these circumstances are undoubtedly outweighed by the development of social security legislation and public assistance programs, combined with the increase in family income and the growth of life insurance and private savings.

Divorced women have always been more likely to work than any other group except single women not in school. Even in 1890, half were in the labor force. But divorce was rare then, and less than one half of 1 percent of the women aged 14 or older were divorcees, compared with almost 2½ percent today. In 1954, of nearly 1.4 million women who had been divorced and were not remarried, over 1 million were in the labor force.

WOMEN'S EMPLOYMENT AND THE ECONOMIC STATUS OF FAMILIES

At the close of the nineteenth century the great majority of the women in the labor force were members of families in which the earnings of the male breadwinner were quite low. The employment of substantial proportions of married women was taken for granted in several low-income groups in the population—such as Negroes in the South, French Canadians in the New England cotton mill towns, and Bohemian immigrants in New York where married women worked as skilled cigar makers. The dominant social practice, however, was that the wife worked only when the husband was incapable of supporting the family. Even among the single women who worked—and they constituted about three fourths of the women in the labor force—almost all were daughters of farmers, laborers, or factory workers. Two thirds of them, moreover, were Negroes or the daughters of immigrants.

The proportion of women compelled to work by sheer necessity was greater in 1890 than today, but many worked for other reasons. Some working class families enjoyed comfortable total incomes from the employment of the father, several children, and even the mother, each of whom may have earned little. Thrift-minded observers of the 1890 scene frequently lamented the extent to which working girls squandered their money on personal finery and large wardrobes. More objective contemporary surveys of the budgets of working girls also indicated that they did not stint on such expenditures.

In 1890, as today, therefore, a great many young women and girls went to work so that they and their families could enjoy more of the comforts and luxuries of life. The great difference between the two periods is that in 1890 the improvement of the standard of living through the earnings of women was confined mainly to families near the bottom of the socio-economic scale. In typical middle class families, the wife and unmarried daughters were not gainfully employed. Today, on the other hand, in such families the employment of the wife appears to be a characteristic way of achieving higher consumption levels and social status simultaneously.

In spite of the rapidly growing employment of wives, the ratio of workers to nonworkers in the American family today is probably roughly what it was in 1890. As more and more women have been going to work, children, adolescents, and old people have been withdrawing from the labor force. The number of old people, moreover, has been increasing. These changes in the age composition of the family and the labor-force status of family members have affected different groups of families in different ways. Families in which the father has a low-paying job do not receive nearly as much income, proportionately, from the employment of sons and daughters as such families did in the past. Nor does the employment of the wife make up for the income which formerly might have been earned by several sons and daughters. On the other hand, most middle and upper class families had only one working member in the past, but now an increasing number have income from two workers. There may be relatively fewer families with three or more members in the labor force, but substantially more with two. Consequently, the financial gains secured from having family members other than the father employed are now spread more widely throughout the population.

TRENDS IN THE EMPLOYMENT OF MINORITY GROUPS

Changes in the patterns of employment within families are an integral part of a transformation which has reduced many of the sharp socio-economic differences earlier found in American life. From this point of view, for example, most of the 1890 population could be divided into three groups, each following a distinctive way of life. One group, accounting for about 55 percent of the population, were native-born whites of native parentage, most of whom lived and worked on farms. They constituted the great majority of the population in most rural areas and in most of the towns and villages of the nation. Those who lived in urban centers were likely to be found in the more desirable occupations and jobs. Their wives were rarely found in paid employment, and although many of their unmarried daughters were employed, most of them married without ever having worked for pay.

A second group, making up one third of the population in 1890, were immigrants or the children of immigrants. Most of them lived in the large cities and smaller manufacturing and mining towns of the Northeast and Midwest, where they often accounted for 65 to 90 percent of the inhabitants. Only one fourth of the men worked on farms, and four fifths of those who did not were manual workers. The wives in the immigrant population were employed in only slightly higher proportion than other married white women, but probably two thirds of the girls and young women worked before marriage, all but a few as domestic servants or manufacturing operatives.

Negroes, constituting about one eighth of the population in 1890, made up the third group. More than 90 percent of them lived in the South, and more than three fourths in the rural South, where they earned the poorest livelihood of any large group in the country. For many Negro women, emancipation brought little change in the pattern of their daily lives. They had worked as slaves, and they continued to work out of economic necessity. At the close of the nineteenth century, almost all Negro girls worked before marriage, and at least one fourth continued to work after marriage. Of the large group of widows, more than 60 percent were working, compared to less than 25 percent among white widows.

In the course of the present century, these differences among the three groups—native whites, immigrants, and Negroes—have become less clear-cut. The descendants of the earlier immigrants have been quite thoroughly integrated into the society, and restrictions on immigration since World War I have reduced the foreign-born and first-generation group to less than one fourth of the total population. Immigrants and their children today differ much less from other groups than they did in 1890, and women of foreign parentage no longer make up a grossly disproportionate share of the female labor force.

Negroes still constitute a handicapped group in terms of educational and occupational opportunities, but the patterns of their lives are moving increasingly closer to those of the larger society. One third of the Negroes now live in cities outside the South, and half of those who remain in the South are also urban residents. Particularly since the beginning of World War II, the opportunities for Negroes to gain entrance into a wide variety of jobs have increased greatly in Northern cities, and, to some extent, even in the South. Since 1890, there has been a substantial decline in the proportion of Negro women in the labor force. In 1890 the percentage was more than twice as high for Negro as for white women, but today, about 45 percent of the Negro women are in the labor force compared to 35 percent of the white women.

The long-run decline in the employment of Negro women is mainly the result of a sharp reduction in the employment of girls under 20 and women over 65. This has been made possible largely by the steadily improving economic status of Negro families and by improved educational opportunities. Today the proportion of single girls and women in the labor force is actually lower among Negroes than among whites. Among elderly women, there is now little difference between the races. While employment was decreasing among young and old Negro women, it was increasing moderately among those in the intermediate age groups, most of whom are wives and mothers. The proportion of Negro wives in the labor force is still considerably higher than that of white wives, largely because of the heavy responsibility Negro women continue to carry for the support of children and other dependents.

Negro women have made substantial occupational gains since

1890, but are still concentrated in the least desirable jobs. In that year, about 95 percent of the Negro working women were farm workers or domestics, as they had been under slavery. In 1940, 75 percent were still in these two categories, but by 1950, the figure had fallen to about 53 percent. As Negro women moved out of farm and domestic-service employment, more of them found work in all other occupations. The largest increases were in nonhousehold-service work; in operative occupations in factories, laundries, etc.; and, particularly in the North, in clerical and sales work.

WOMEN'S EMPLOYMENT IN THE FUTURE

Prediction is always hazardous, and with so complex a phenomenon as the employment of women detailed forecasts are especially risky. The past, however, does provide important clues to the probable character of future developments. For the whole period for which there are reliable data, the number and proportion of women in the labor force of the United States have been growing; work for pay has come to occupy more of their time and interest; and it has become increasingly common among many different groups of women.

These trends have resulted from a number of historical circumstances. A dynamic, expanding economy has resulted in a strong and continuing demand for labor. The high value which Americans have placed upon work and their striving for a constantly rising standard of living have motivated increasing numbers of women to seek employment. Technological changes have reduced the physical demands of many kinds of work and led to the emergence of new occupations. The shrinking work day and work week, together with changes in the technology of housekeeping, have steadily increased the opportunity for women to combine paid work and household functions. A constantly changing cultural and economic environment has facilitated the acceptance of new functions for women. Finally, two world wars not only resulted in temporary increases in the demand for workers, but also had the more lasting effect of quickening the erosion of attitudinal barriers to women's employment.

It seems reasonable to assume that most of these long-run influences will continue to prevail, and that the proportion of women in the labor force will continue to increase, particularly among those who are over 30 years old. The rate of increase in the female labor force will depend heavily on the rate of expansion of the economy, but the experience of the 1930's suggests that even a prolonged depression would not reverse the long-run trend. That complex of technological developments currently spoken of as automation, however, introduces an element of uncertainty. Some experts anticipate a wave of technological unemployment which will affect women particularly, because employers, if they have a choice, may be inclined to release women first should a reduction in the work force be necessary. It is expected, moreover, that automation will have its greatest impact on semi-skilled and routine work in offices and factories, which are among the most important fields of employment for women.

There is reason to expect, however, that automation will not appear so quickly as to preclude the kinds of adjustments that the labor market has made to increasing productivity in the past, and that women will not be displaced in significant numbers. Moreover, there seems to be little prospect that automation will soon affect such major fields of women's employment as the apparel industry, nursing, teaching, retail sales, the service occupations, or secretarial and stenographic work. While some women will be squeezed out of semiskilled factory jobs, automation will also result in the expansion of some industries, such as the electronics industry, which is staffed mainly by women. Some of the increased productivity resulting from further automation may be balanced by a reduction in the hours of work, which would facilitate the employment of women. In short, for women as for men, automation is likely to have essentially the same results that technological changes have had in the past—the temporary displacement of some workers; the appearance of new jobs and skills; considerable personal hardship for a certain number of workers; but no destructive effect on the over-all demand for labor.

The employment of women is related, not only to such broad social and economic forces as have been discussed, but also, as has been emphasized, to the changing characteristics and circumstances of individual women. Changes in these relationships suggest that paid employment is rapidly assuming a new place in the lives of women. The likely pattern of the future, the outlines of which are already clearly visible, is one in which adolescence and early adulthood are devoted mainly to school. The following decade is devoted mainly to marriage and motherhood. In the next and longest stage, work becomes increasingly important.

The significance of low income and social status for the employment of women will probably continue to decline. The number of middle income families has been growing and women in the middle and upper income groups have been going to work in steadily increasing numbers. To the extent that these developments continue, fewer women will be working because of sheer economic necessity, and more and more because they choose to.

Women are gaining increasing freedom to choose for themselves the particular pattern of employment which best meets their own needs and preferences and those of their families. This greater freedom is bringing more and more of them into the labor market for longer periods of their lives. For women as for men, access to the most desirable jobs is generally gained through the acquisition of knowledge, skill, and capacity during years of work experience. Consequently, the fact that women are working for longer periods in their lives in itself is likely to bring more of them into the better jobs.

v. THE IMPACT OF WORLD WAR II ON WOMEN'S EMPLOYMENT

THE SIGNIFICANT increases in the number and proportion of women in paid employment have not been uniform from decade to decade. These increases have in considerable measure resulted, moreover, from exceptional developments affecting the American economy. World War II is, perhaps, the most important of these. The alterations it brought about in the utilization of womanpower warrant examination because of the light they cast both on the behavior of women in the labor market under conditions of full employment and on planning for possible future mobilization.

The manpower policies of the United States during World War II were very greatly influenced by conditions that prevailed during the 1930's—a decade characterized by the most extended period of severe unemployment in the history of the country. When the United States entered the war, there were still some 4 million men and 2 million women unemployed. It appeared that additional millions would soon be dislocated as essential raw materials were redirected from civilian to war industry. Consequently, there was little initial interest in plans for the recruiting, training, and utilization of large numbers of women.

Even those whose memories went back to World War I found little to support the belief that the country would have to dip very far into its reserves of womanpower. In 1917 and 1918 some communities with war production facilities experienced such heavy calls upon men for the armed services, coincidental with their need for additional labor for expanding war industries, that it was necessary to turn to women to help meet the demands of the new situation. Women held jobs as ticket collectors in local transportation, previously an exclusive male domain; in high school teaching, also previously dominated by men; in new powder and ordnance plants; and in a host of other fields. A great many women were employed in unskilled manual jobs under disagreeable working conditions. It must be remembered, however, that the United States was in World War I for something less than twenty months. This period was long enough to modify traditional patterns of "men's" and "women's" work, but too short to produce permanent changes in women's employment. Many wartime innovations, such as the use of women in some manual occupations, did not survive the return to "normalcy." A few changes, such as the altered sex composition of high school faculties, persisted.

The manpower shortages of World War I did not lead to a heavy reliance on womanpower. Nor was there any pressure to relieve shortages by using women during the prosperous 1920's. The overwhelming problem of the depressed thirties, on the other hand, was the shortage of jobs. In retrospect, it is easy to understand why early in World War II the recommendation discussed by the Young Committee on Wartime Requirements for Scientific and Specialized Personnel, to undertake a registration of the trained women of the country, did not meet with favor. Even as late as the spring of 1942, there was little basis for anticipating that in the near future war production might be limited by the effectiveness with which women could be drawn into the war effort.

POLICIES AND AGENCIES

The policies that guided manpower mobilization at the beginning of World War II were shaped by optimistic assumptions about the adequacy of the nation's labor force. These policies placed primary reliance on voluntary means for attracting people to, and allocating them in, the labor force, and gave the states and communities responsibility for resolving urgent manpower problems.

The determination of policies and procedures governing womanpower in World War II was shared by such older agencies as the Women's Bureau of the Department of Labor and the Children's Bureau, and by such major emergency organizations as the War Production Board, the War Manpower Commission, and the War Labor Board. Much of the decision-making with respect to manpower policies remained in the hands of employers and trade unions, who, individually and through collective bargaining, continued to determine the basic character of the labor market.

After its establishment in 1920, the Women's Bureau had major responsibility within the Federal government for advancing the well-being of the working woman, and its efforts were strongly supported by social welfare and labor organizations. From the start of the war, the Women's Bureau sought to facilitate the employment of women. It recognized the contribution that women could make and hoped that the emergency would contribute to advancing the position of women in the American economy. Championing the large-scale use of women, it held that the best and most effective way to utilize them was to take cognizance of their sex but not to discriminate against them because of it.

Early in the war, the Women's Bureau, reviewing the experience of World War I, urged employers to introduce special health and safety provisions; adjust jobs to meet the physical limitations of women; provide appropriate facilities, including dressing and rest rooms; and establish a moderate work schedule, preferably not to exceed eight hours per day or forty hours per week. The Bureau also stressed the importance of setting rates of pay on the basis of the occupation rather than on the basis of the sex of the worker—equal pay for equal work having been one of its major objectives for many years.

The Women's Bureau exercised a significant influence on other policy-forming agencies of government. Its field investigations shed light on problems with respect to women workers. Early in the war, the key problem was the failure of many employers, such as the aircraft companies, to hire women. Later on, it was the failure to assign them to suitable work, as in the shipyards. Still later, attention was focused on the failure to upgrade them so that they might assume supervisory responsibilities commensurate with their demonstrated ability.

The Children's Bureau had an indirect concern with womanpower in World War II. Its interest derived from the repercussions upon the health and welfare of children—especially of younger children—of mothers being drawn into paid employment. The Bureau had long been concerned with children who suffered physical and emotional neglect because of the absence of the mother or an insufficient income in the home. World War II, moreover, drew increasingly large numbers of mothers of younger children into employment. At the beginning, less than one out of every ten mothers was at work; at the end of the war, the figure was nearly one out of five in families with children under 18 years of age and nearly one out of eight in families with children under 6.

Early in the war the interested government agencies agreed to recommend to employers that they avoid recruiting women with children under 14 years of age until all other sources of workers had been exhausted. At the same time, they made it clear that this criterion should not prevent the hiring of those mothers who could make arrangements for the proper care of their children. Closely related was the recommendation that the assignments of women with younger children be planned so as to disrupt family life as little as possible. In many instances wives and husbands planned their work in order to insure that one or the other would always be at home with the children. For example, in the Kenosha, Wis., area this dovetailing of shifts was followed by two out of every five working mothers; in Detroit and in Springfield, Mass., by one out of every five or six.

The Children's Bureau was largely instrumental in securing the use of Federal funds under the Community Facilities Act—the Lanham Act—to help finance over 3,000 child care centers, which at peak cared for approximately 130,000 children. But this effort must be measured against the fact that some 1.5 million mothers with children under 6 were employed during the later stages of the war. A survey of ten war production areas at the close of the war indicated that in none of them did more than 11 percent of the mothers rely on day care centers. Aside from receiving assistance from their husbands and older children, most mothers relied primarily on relatives and others living in the household to care for their children while they were at work. Many mothers were reluctant to turn over responsibility for their children to day care centers, and many were also aware that such centers had great difficulty in securing competent personnel. Informed observers were distressed at the inadequate care that many children received at these centers, particularly because they were left there frequently as early as 8 A.M. and were not picked up by their mothers until 6 P.M.

The Children's Bureau advocated that employers adopt liberal maternity policies. Unlike most Western European countries, the United States had not adopted legislation to assist prospective mothers by protecting their jobs and offering them financial assistance at the time of delivery. The unions were unable to secure alterations in their basic contracts because of wage stabilization policies, but they frequently pressed for such fringe benefits as maternity leaves.

The United States had not been in the war many months before employers experienced delays in meeting urgent military schedules because of an inability to expand their work forces as rapidly as required. The War Production Board sought at first to use its influence to slow withdrawals of men from industry to the armed forces, but it soon became clear that, if the services were to meet their commitments, they could not long be denied any sizable proportion of the younger men of the country. At best, Selective Service Boards would agree to delay the induction of a small number of highly skilled men, thereby providing a little time for the training of their replacements.

As the War Production Board and its associated bodies—the procurement services of the Army and the Navy—came to appreciate more clearly the strategic importance of manpower in war production, labor surpluses were taken into account in awarding contracts. Government officials soon recognized that scarce materials could be saved by drawing on available reserves of women in existing industrial centers to expand production, instead of awarding additional contracts in localities where new housing and other facilities would have to be provided in order to bring in new workers.

In April, 1942, the War Manpower Commission was established to formulate policies and procedures to achieve the most rapid and efficient use of the nation's manpower. In August of that year, a Women's Advisory Committee was appointed to assist the Commission in developing appropriate policies with respect to womanpower. In line with the over-all approach of the Commission, emphasis was placed on finding appropriate local solutions to problems involving the recruitment, training, and utilization of women workers. Every effort was made to meet pressing labor requirements within a region before seeking to encourage workers to move from one area to another. The War Manpower Commission urged each locality to exercise caution in recruiting women with young children and to provide adequate day care centers if large numbers of young mothers were to be employed. On the crucial question of training, the Commission advocated that women be given the opportunity to enter preemployment courses conducted under public auspices, so that they would not be compelled, as many originally had been, to secure such training through private schools. Further, the Commission emphasized that women should be permitted to enroll in supplementary war training courses, in plants and outside, so that they might qualify for more responsible positions. Finally, the Commission specifically recommended that women be admitted on an equal basis with men into the engineering, science, and management courses sponsored by the Federal government. The graduates of these courses found employment in industry in staff and managerial positions.

To speed the absorption and to support the morale of women workers, the Commission recommended that employers review their work assignments with an eye to determining how, through technological changes, more women might be utilized in place of men. The redesigning of jobs in the shipyards is an outstanding illustration of such a change. In the shift from custom to mass production techniques in shipbuilding it was possible to find two hundred new jobs that women could do. The Commission recommended that women be used in all jobs that they could perform. It was anticipated that some men might not be able to move up to better jobs to which they were entitled by seniority because women were entering them. If this occurred, and the men were kept in lower-paid work from which women were barred because it was physically demanding or otherwise unsuitable, the Commission recommended that men get the wages they would have received in the better jobs. In general, the Commission supported the principle of equal pay for equal work. The

Commission also urged that women be given special consideration in work-shift assignments because of their responsibilities at home.

The National War Labor Board played a crucial role in furthering the principle of equal pay for equal work. The Board held that women who worked on jobs previously performed by men or on jobs currently performed by both men and women should receive the same rate of pay as men, unless their output was less or unless their employment entailed additional costs. But, since the Board preferred not to abrogate existing collective bargaining agreements, it frequently could not act to equalize rates of pay for men and women.

As the war progressed, the principle of equal pay was more widely accepted, at least as far as entrance jobs were concerned. But inequities were common. In one Navy Yard all women, regardless of previous experience, were hired as "mechanic learners" at 58 cents an hour, while men with no experience were taken on as "classified laborers" at 74 cents an hour. As early as 1942, it was found that women usually entered aircraft plants at the same pay scale as men. In a survey of twenty-three plants only three had different scales for men and women. Differential treatment was more marked in the case of upgrading. Women were less likely to be promoted, and, even when they were, they frequently failed to get the same wages that men were paid for the job. So many women, however, were earning so much more than they had ever earned before, that they frequently did not press for equality in pay. In many instances, employers or local unions showed little interest in implementing the principle of equal pay. On the other hand, many women appeared to be more interested in securing better working conditions in the form of maternity leaves, time off for personal needs, and improved luncheon and rest room facilities.

Late in the war, in 1944, the issue of a National Service Act arose, in part because key officials in the War Department became greatly concerned over delays in essential war production and over a threatened insufficiency of nurses to care for battle casualties. Some who favored a measure extending the principle of compulsory service to women held that it would give women a greater sense of involvement in the war effort. There was, however, little overt support for it either in the government or among the public at large. Yet such a measure did win majority approval from the Women's Advisory Committee, though not from the War Manpower Commission itself. The majority of the Women's Advisory Committee urged that the duty of serving the war effort, whether in or out of uniform, should be imposed on men and women alike by law—exempting, however, women with children below the age of 16. They also believed that legislation which would obligate employers to accept, upon the referral of the appropriate agency, all qualified persons, regardless of sex, would strike a blow against such discrimination as still prevailed.

THE ATTITUDES OF EMPLOYERS AND TRADE UNIONS

Because of the largely voluntary approach followed by the United States in its manpower policies, the attitudes and behavior of employers and trade unions were of overwhelming importance throughout the war. They exercised great influence over the employment and utilization of women workers, both during the war and after.

In 1940, about 800,000 women were union members, most of them employees in the textile, apparel, food products, and electrical manufacturing industries. The unions had never had much success in organizing other occupations where women were heavily concentrated, such as clerical work, wholesale and retail sales, domestic service, and the professions of teaching and nursing. When women flocked into war jobs, many found work in plants covered by collective bargaining agreements. Others became union members, as did many men, when the plants in which they worked were organized. By 1944, it was estimated, union membership among women totaled over 3 million and accounted for about 22 percent of total union membership.

No easy generalizations can be ventured about how these new members viewed their union status or how the many hundreds of locals to which they belonged responded to them. Many men at first looked askance at the invasion by women of their working domain because they feared that it might jeopardize hard-won gains. They were concerned with protecting their seniority, which was made uncertain by changes in war production and large-scale calls for military service. Organized labor had long fought against employers who brought in women to cut wage standards. The initial attitude of many male workers, unorganized as well as organized, was suspicion, if not outright hostility. This was not surprising in the light of the unemployment of the preceding decade and the fact that the availability of women workers made it more likely that men would be called from their jobs into military service.

As the war progressed, it became increasingly clear that women workers were doing a good job and that their employment was not leading to a breakdown of union standards, at least in so far as the men were concerned. In many cases, newly hired women could acquire only limited seniority rights, or even no seniority whatever because of union opposition. In other cases, union leaders rather quickly reached the conclusion that the best way to protect standards was to insist that employers not differentiate between women and men, and they strongly supported the principles of equal seniority and equal pay. In any case, men usually got the better jobs because they had longer service and greater experience. When the rank and file men union members recognized that they were given preference for upgrading and promotion and that their security was being protected, they felt much less defensive about the large-scale invasion by women. Moreover, they had hopes that women would remain "for the duration only."

By controlling only wages and the employer's freedom to hire, the Federal government accepted the principle that the labor market would be altered only as employers and employees responded to new conditions. It has been seen that most employers gave little thought to hiring women early in the war, for they could not conceive how the still large numbers of unemployed men were likely to be absorbed, even with the demands of the war effort.

Some efforts to expand and improve the use of women workers by industry were bound to fail. Leadership and trained personnel were lacking for badly needed plant and community programs dealing with health, morale, and recreational needs of millions of new women workers.

It is difficult to determine to what extent the problems encountered by employers when they finally started to hire women in large numbers were the direct result of a lack of planning. The rate of accessions was so great that employers would have faced major problems even if all the new employees had been men. Nevertheless, faulty hiring and placement practices were very costly. Many employers failed to make a modest, but essential, investment in the initial industrial orientation of their new women workers. This would have helped the women to familiarize themselves with basic tools and machines, to establish new relationships, and to overcome their feelings of insecurity about undertaking new tasks. Many employers were slow to understand the importance of their foremen's attitudes and behavior. Usually responsible for the initial orientation of new workers, foremen not only influenced the way in which women would respond to their jobs, but also helped to condition the attitudes of male workers whose behavior could facilitate or retard the adjustment of women workers.

Management attitudes and policies determined not only when

women were hired, but also in what departments they would be employed. This latter decision was frequently made in response to a crisis situation, as when foremen or higher supervisors recognized that production schedules could not be met unless additional workers were taken on immediately. In many cases, women, the only source of additional labor, were not equipped to fill the jobs that were open. In other instances, foremen did not assign women to jobs they could have performed because there still were adequate numbers of male employees.

HOURS AND CONDITIONS OF WORK

Employers were advised by the Federal government that the continuing productivity of their women employees would depend upon the establishment of reasonable hours and working conditions. However, many employers were hard-pressed to meet their production schedules and felt they were unnecessarily hampered by state laws governing hours of work, shifts, rest periods, and other working conditions of women. They successfully sought the relaxation of much of this legislation, and many women were employed during the war under conditions formerly prohibited by law. This was usually made possible by granting exemptions from particular provisions of the law to individual employers or industries. Nevertheless, state regulatory agencies sought to preserve the basic intent of legislation designed to protect women workers.

The War Production Board noted in the summer of 1943 that production was slowing down. The War Manpower Commission concluded on the basis of a field investigation that the increasing absenteeism resulting from fatigue could be checked by setting a working schedule for women of approximately eight hours a day and forty hours a week, with a few extra hours allowed for emergency overtime. Many employers ran their plants on a fifty-four to sixty hour schedule, but the majority of women made their own rules. Few would work more than forty-eight or, at the most, fifty hours a week on a continuing basis, and there was good rea-

son to believe that very limited gains in production could result
from extending the working day of women. Many new women
workers had responsibilities at home as well as on the job; household help was almost impossible to secure; marketing became a
major challenge in most war production centers; and transportation was frequently time-consuming.

Some employers helped to meet the special needs of their
women workers by arranging opportunities for them to do their
shopping, attend to their personal needs, and engage in selected
recreational activities at, or very close to, their place of work.
Others facilitated their transportation to and from work. But such
measures were usually feasible only for the larger enterprises.
Only a few communities made the effort required to help meet
the special needs of women workers. The majority, in fact, were
unable to solve the host of problems precipitated by the entrance
of so many housewives into paid employment. The surprising
fact is not that some women who took jobs gave them up after
a trial period because they found themselves overwhelmed by
their double responsibilities, nor that many others took an occasional day off to catch up on sleep and to attend to long-neglected
household duties, but rather that such a large number stayed with
their jobs day in and day out to the end of the war.

THE SCALE OF CHANGES IN WOMEN'S EMPLOYMENT

Strenuous efforts were made to recruit large numbers of additional women workers from the middle of 1943 until nearly the end
of the war. Between April, 1943, and April, 1945, the female labor
force grew by 1.5 million. Compared to the early years of the war,
this was a modest increase, but most single women were already
at work by 1943. The remaining significant source of supply con-
sisted in married women, the overwhelming majority of whom
had household responsibilities. The difficulties of developing effective methods for helping women to discharge these responsibilities go far to explain why the recruiting efforts were much

less successful than anticipated. There were other obstacles to recruiting married women. There were many reports that women already at work were being poorly utilized, and some housewives questioned whether they were needed in war production. In certain communities there were deeply ingrained traditions against the hiring of white married women, especially in the South. And there was continued resistance to hiring Negro women, particularly in the South, even though they were sometimes hired before Negro men.

However reluctant they may have been to hire women, most employers eventually made a number of adjustments in selection, indoctrination, training, assignment, and promotion, in order to improve their utilization of women. By May, 1943, there were approximately 19 million women in the labor force, 3 million over the number for the previous May, or an increase of about 20 percent. With recruitment of aditional full time workers becoming increasingly difficult, employers began to experiment with a "victory shift" in order to utilize women on a part-time basis. The hope was that, with women working fewer hours daily, on alternate days, or only on weekends, absenteeism resulting from fatigue would be avoided and the total work force augmented. A daily four-hour shift, between two ten-hour shifts, however, made additional demands on an already overextended supervisory staff. It was found that many women who accepted weekend jobs also held down a full-time job, and their absentee and turnover rates were high. Moreover, the alternate-day cycle did not meet the needs of women with younger children.

As is true of other aspects of the employment of women during World War II, no simple comment can be made about the effectiveness of part-time work. Considering the fact that many women had never before worked and that others were employed in work that was new to them, it is not surprising that part-time work often proved a failure in war production industries. It was far more successful in the many supporting services and trades that had long made use of part-time help. In fact, their wartime needs for personnel could not have been met had they not been able to rely heavily upon women who could work only part of the day or week.

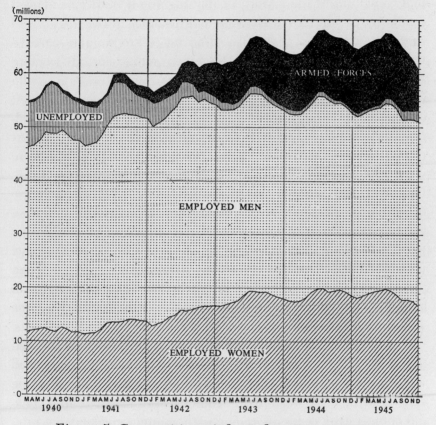

Figure 5. Composition of the Labor Force, 1940-45
Based on data from the U. S. Bureau of the Census.

Between 1940, the onset of the mobilization effort, and 1945, when the wartime labor force was at its peak, the number of women in the labor force expanded from less than 14 million to slightly over 20 million. Since there were about 2 million unemployed women in the labor force in 1940, but as few as one quarter of a million in 1945, employment increased by more than 7 million, as Figure 5 shows. In 1940, slightly more than 27 percent of all women aged 14 and over were in the labor force; at the peak in 1945, the percentage was 38. Women accounted for 25 percent of all workers at the beginning of the war, but in 1945 they represented 36 percent of the total civilian working population.

Certain important movements took place within these totals that warrant comment. Approximately one out of every six women in the labor force in 1941 had left by 1944—over 2 million in all. All but 7 percent of those who withdrew were occupied as housewives in 1944. On the other hand, the 1944 labor force contained 6.7 million women who had not been employed in 1941. Of these, 3.7 million had been keeping house full time, 3.3 million had been in school, and 0.7 million had not been employed in 1941 for a number of other reasons. Of the women who left housekeeping to go to work, two out of five became operatives, laborers, craftsmen, or foremen; one out of five went into clerical work; and one out of five into domestic or other service work. In the case of those who had been in school, more than two out of five went into clerical pursuits, about one out of four into skilled, semi-skilled and unskilled jobs, and only one out of eight into domestic or service employment.

Most of the 10 million women who had been employed in 1941 and were still at work in 1944 were in the same occupational fields, but 1.5 million of them had shifted to other types of work in the interim. There were three major types of shifts: from service and clerical work to production work in manufacturing; from production work and selling into clerical positions; and from agriculture into domestic service. These shifts contributed to major alterations in the structure of the female labor force during the war. Between 1940 and 1944, female employment was estimated to have increased about 51 percent. During this period women classified as craftsmen, foremen, operatives, and nonfarm laborers (mostly manufacturing) increased 119 percent and clerical workers increased 85 percent. Those employed in agriculture increased by 20 percent, but the number of women employed in domestic work actually declined by 20 percent.

In March, 1944, slightly more than two out of every five women workers were single. Approximately one third of the women who were working had husbands living at home with them. However, one eighth of all the women working were married women whose husbands were away, primarily in the services. More than half of the married women whose husbands were away worked, compared to one fifth of those with husbands at home.

EXPANDING OPPORTUNITIES FOR WOMEN WORKERS

World War II opened up new opportunities to women, primarily in industry. In many cases the work that women performed during the war had no relation to their pattern of prewar employment. For instance, in the latter part of the war there were large numbers of women employed in the shipyards, even on repair work, where earlier no women were found. Much the same order of transformation took place in the aircraft industry. Before the war there were only a few women employed in a limited number of positions, but at the peak of the war production effort they were to be found in practically every job in the aircraft industry.

Many employers learned at first hand during the war that women worked very effectively at the assembly of small articles and at inspection functions. They apparently did not respond as negatively as men did to repetitive operations. A 1942 study by the Women's Bureau—of 125 war plants engaged in the manufacture of electrical instruments, aircraft engines, machine and metal parts, and ammunition—found women concentrated in the following operations: assembling, machine operating, testing and inspecting, and packing and wrapping. Women also did well at riveting, welding, and blueprint reading. During the war, women replaced many men on drill presses, milling machines, lathes, punch and forming presses, and other machine tools. During the fall of 1942 and the following winter, women represented from one third to one half of the trainees entering pre-employment machine shop courses. During the latter half of 1943, women accounted for about the same proportions of employees entering more advanced classes in machine shop work.

Many foremen were impressed by how well women did on light machine work, and also by their ability to maintain work discipline. This does not mean that difficulties resulting from mixed work forces were unknown, but only that they were exceptional. Employers quickly recognized that new women workers caused fewer difficulties than they had anticipated.

At the same time, management never gave up its conviction that it was easier for a man than for a woman to supervise women, and that women themselves preferred to take orders from a man. Some women, presumably competent to assume supervisory functions, were apparently unwilling to do so, especially when they carried heavy responsibilities at home. A large number of women became supervisors in the textile, electronics, ammunition, and a few other industries, and their performance was generally reported as satisfactory. In the face of mangement's hesitancy, however, the advancement of women workers was very slow.

Some women succeeded in gaining access to better jobs by taking advantage of the scientific, engineering, and management courses that were sponsored by the government. Those with a talent for mathematics and the sciences had a chance to prepare themselves for work at the semiprofessional level. Striking increases took place in the employment of women by the Federal government, from about 250,000 at the time of Pearl Harbor to over a million in 1945. Because the number of men employed increased much less, women were two fifths of all government employees in 1945, compared to only one fifth in 1940. This provided opportunities for many women to rise to supervisory and specialized positions, primarily in the fields of clerical and office work.

POSTWAR EXPECTATIONS OF WOMEN WORKERS

During the war, many polls were taken to determine how many of the women who had entered the labor force intended to continue in employment once peace returned. This was a matter of public concern for a variety of reasons. There were significant groups of both men and women who continued to hold that the place of a married woman was in the home. Many male workers, organized and unorganized alike, had vivid memories of the high unemployment of the 1930's. They were afraid that jobs would be scarce when defense production came to an end and that, if many women remained in the labor force, the competition for jobs would be proportionately sharper. They were also concerned with the effects upon seniority and related job rights and benefits of the return of veterans to civilian employment and of the drastic changes involved in the shift to peacetime production. Many employers and government economists believed that the immediate postwar reconversion would result in a depression and that unemployment might reach 8 or 10 million. Many employers, consequently, had little interest in retaining their wartime women workers, even when they recognized their capabilities.

A survey by the Women's Bureau of 13,000 women in all occupations except domestic service employed in ten war production areas in 1944 and early 1945 revealed some startling findings. An average of three out of every four of these women indicated their intention to remain employed after the war ended. Among those who had not been either employed or looking for work at the time of Pearl Harbor—chiefly the younger girls who had still been in school and the older women who had been housewives—three quarters of the younger group and over half of the older group expected to keep on working. The survey also showed that 87 percent of the single and 94 percent of the widowed and divorced women planned to continue working. Even among married women, 57 percent indicated that they intended to remain in paid employment. What, in fact, did happen as the war came to an end? Between June and September, 1945, one out of every four women employed in factories had been dropped or quit work, and by the end of the year nonagricultural employment for women showed a decline of 2 million over the June peak. Most of these women left the labor market, and the number of unemployed did not increase significantly.

From June, 1945, to February, 1947, the female labor force dropped from 20.3 million to 15.9 million. Instead of 38 percent of all women aged 14 and over in the labor force, the ratio had shrunk to 29 percent. But—and this is of major significance—the decline was then reversed. Except for a very slight drop in women's employment at the end of the Korean hostilities, the trend has been steadily upward since 1947.

THE WAR'S INFLUENCE ON WOMEN IN THE LABOR MARKET

Many women who worked during the war remained at work afterwards as they said they would. But the war had an impact that went further and deeper. It helped to alter the traditional approach of women, particularly married women, toward paid employment. The war proved to many women that it was feasible for them to discharge their responsibilities at home and at the same time hold down a full-time job. If they could do so during the hectic war years, when hours of work were long and housekeeping particularly difficult, they could certainly do so under peacetime conditions. Many were now reassured about their ability to handle a job, although they may have had serious doubts about their adaptability to factory or office work when they were first employed. Not to be underestimated was the satisfaction that many found in bringing home a sizable pay check every week. Finally, many found their jobs interesting. For one or more of these reasons, women continued to work.

The war also left its mark on employers. They found that many of their beliefs about the difficulties that women would create turned out to have no foundation in fact. They had discovered that introducing women in considerable numbers did not set the stage for a war between the sexes nor was it a prelude to a breakdown in either factory discipline or sexual morality. Employers also discovered that for certain types of work women were more productive than men. Finally, they learned that for certain jobs their preference for younger women was not always justified by the facts, for absentee rates were frequently lower and over-all work adjustment better among older women.

Trade union leaders also learned several lessons as a result of the war experience. One of the most important was that the utilization of women workers by employers did not necessarily result in cuts in prevailing wage scales. The replacement of men by women might have taken place on rare occasions, but the men were usually able to secure better jobs. Moreover, they learned that the competition for jobs between men and women which they expected when the labor market weakened did not develop, for many women voluntarily withdrew from the labor force. Although many women without prior work experience had little knowledge of unions and played only a passive role after joining, a number did become interested and devoted union members, from whose ranks it was frequently possible to develop additional local union leadership.

The unions also found that it was to their advantage, as part of their broader goals, to be able to put forward demands that had specific meaning for their women members, for instance, more frequent rest periods, cleaner restaurants, or more liberal sickness leaves. Pressing for these gains did not detract from the objectives sought by their male membership, but served to broaden the range of bargaining items. When the feared postwar depression failed to materialize, unions generally recognized that no special risks were involved in the continued large-scale employment of women. Each of these developments helped to break down powerful traditions concerning the employment of women.

PROBLEMS OF MOBILIZATION AND IMPROVED UTILIZATION

The World War II experience has a bearing upon the nation's planning with respect to any future large-scale mobilization and upon the improved utilization of womanpower in a full-employment economy. At present, there is no clear agreement among those responsible for national defense policy about the assumptions that should govern planning for a future emergency. Some are convinced that if there is another war it will begin with full use of nuclear weapons and that it will be of very short duration. At the opposite extreme are those who hold that the use of nuclear weapons will be outlawed and that, if war comes, it will be fought with more conventional weapons and will probably be prolonged. In spite of the uncertainty about the probable nature and duration of a future war, certain observations may still be ventured on the basis of lessons learned during World War II.

One concerns the supply of potential women workers. There is now a much higher proportion of women in the labor force than there was in 1940. In terms of planning for mobilization within the next decade, it may be assumed that about 40 percent of the women over 14 years of age will be in the labor force. This is higher than the peak for World War II and suggests, first, that the expanded utilization of women for war work would depend more on converting them from other kinds of employment than was the case during World War II. Further, it indicates that a high proportion of the additional women workers who could be added from outside the labor force would be younger girls still in school, or wives with heavy homemaking responsibilities. World War II highlighted the fact that the rate at which women with extensive household duties can be drawn into the labor market depends heavily on the availability of others in the household or in the community to provide assistance in performing these duties. In terms of these considerations, therefore, it would seem that the higher the proportion of women at work at the beginning of hostilities, the more difficult it will be to draw additional women into employment. On the other hand, the existence of more favorable attitudes toward the employment of women would presumably facilitate expansion of the female labor force.

On the demand side, it is reasonable to anticipate that employers will be much more willing to accept women workers from the onset of hostilities, that they will be better prepared to absorb them, and that they will be more ready to use them at their highest level of skill. These assumptions are suggested by the experience of employers during and since World War II, a period which has seen ever-increasing numbers of women in new types of work.

In World War II the registration of women, even those with high skills, was not undertaken, and national service legislation never gained more than a few supporters. Current mobilization planning also favors a voluntary approach to the recruitment of women not only for the armed forces, but also for the civilian labor market. Whether this approach will be adequate in the event that full mobilization requires the use of the nation's total manpower reserves—of which women continue to form the largest portion—is open to question, especially if the speedy relocation of part of the working force is also necessary.

One of the major lessons of World War II, having applicability to almost any type of future emergency, is the need for advance planning and, to some degree, prior training, if women are to be utilized at their maximum potential skills. One of the problems that such planning will have to deal with, as World War II clearly indicated, is the mutual relationship between the household responsibilities of women and their employment outside the home. Because civil defense functions will be of critical importance in any future mobilization, there is additional reason to plan ahead for the utilization of women.

Far less speculative than the implications of World War II experiences for any future mobilization is the application of certain wartime lessons to the utilization of womanpower in a full-employment economy. World War II revealed that the occupational concentration of women was largely the outgrowth of tradition. When opportunities were provided for them in new fields of work, women responded eagerly and performed well. How well they performed depended on many factors, among them the extent to which they had a chance to participate in training programs. At first, they were excluded from many training programs and as a result were not in a position to fill essential jobs. As the war proceeded and they were able to secure the training required, both before employment and when they were at work, they did well—in some cases better than men.

It became apparent to employers during World War II that they could gain flexibility in meeting their labor-supply problems by drawing on reserves of womanpower, particularly married women. Moreover, the radical reconversion that took place immediately after the war helped to assure employers, as well as labor and the country at large, that when work was no longer available many women returned to their homes and did not compete with men for scarce jobs.

World War II helped accelerate long-run changes in the role of women workers in the American economy. It raised fundamental doubts concerning conventional notions about women and their suitability for work. It proved that there were relatively few jobs which they could not perform because of limitations of strength or unyielding social attitudes. It demonstrated that with proper training they could readily reach acceptable and in many cases superior levels of performance. It provided a small number of women with opportunities to rise to positions of authority in which they were effective. Most important, perhaps, World War II made it possible for a large number of women to combine marriage and work, and many found that they preferred this pattern of life.

VI. THE SECONDARY EDUCATION OF GIRLS

FROM THE BEGINNINGS of American secondary education in the nineteenth century, high schools have enrolled and graduated more girls than boys. The principle of equality of opportunity in education for all was established in secondary education long before many barriers to the employment of women were surmounted or contemporary patterns of work outside the home began to emerge. Consequently, developments in the high school education of girls during the present century seem modest when they are measured against the more spectacular changes in the paid employment of women.

The value of having girls and boys share essentially the same educational experiences during their high school years has long been taken for granted in the United States. The differences in the behavior of boys and girls in high school with respect to attendance and graduation, curriculum and subject-matter choices, and grades are equally taken for granted—judging by the lack of interest in studying their significance. These differences are intimately bound up with dominant views concerning the distinctive interests and abilities of girls and boys, and with the characteristic responsibilities and activities which they are expected to assume in adult life.

GROWTH OF A COEDUCATIONAL SYSTEM

The rule of having separate schools for boys and girls, derived from the practice of the early academies, was followed when the first public high schools were established. As the number of public secondary schools grew, essentially as an extension of elementary education, coeducational schools became increasingly common. Before the end of the nineteenth century, coeducation was a distinguishing feature of American secondary education. By 1900, only 2 percent of the nation's 6,000 public high schools were separate schools for boys and girls. Twenty years later, less than one half of 1 percent of the more than 14,000 public high schools in the United States were not coeducational. Between 1900 and 1956, the number of students enrolled in public high schools increased from a little more than half a million to almost 6 million. During this period, the number of graduates from public high schools rose even more strikingly—from 61,000 to over 1.3 million annually. Before the opening of the present century, girls accounted for almost two thirds of all public high school graduates; now they constitute slightly more than half. As Table 13 shows, both the number and proportion of boys completing high school have increased significantly during this period. Nevertheless, more girls still graduate from high school. Thus, in 1956, the number of boy high school graduates represented 57 percent of the seventeen-year-old boys in the population; the number of girl high school graduates, however, was 63 percent of the seventeen-year-old girls in the population.

When the issue of a coeducational system was debated in the nineteenth century, the primary argument against it held that girls and boys differed so greatly in nature, interest, and ability, as well as in the functions they would perform when they grew up, that coeducation could not adequately serve the needs of either. Their close association during adolescence, it was maintained, was improper, if not injurious. To some who opposed a coeducational system, it was clear that the boys would constitute

Table 13. *Secondary School Graduates from Public and Nonpublic Schools, by Sex, and as a Proportion of the 17-Year-Old Population, 1890-1956*

	Boys			Girls			Girl Graduates as Percent of All Public and Nonpublic Graduates	Girl Graduates as Percent of All Public Graduates
Year	Total Public and Nonpublic Graduates	Graduates as Percent of All Boys Aged 17 Years	Public Graduates as Percent of Total Graduates	Total Public and Nonpublic Graduates	Graduates as Percent of All Girls Aged 17 Years	Public Graduates as Percent of Total Graduates		
1956 [a]	634,300	57	n.a.	684,400	63	n.a.	52	n.a.
1954	612,500	56	89	663,600	62	88	52	52
1952	569,200	53	88	627,300	60	88	52	52
1950	570,700	54	89	629,000	61	89	52	53
1940	578,718	48	93	642,757	54	94	53	56
1930	300,376	26	89	366,528	32	89	55	55
1920	123,684	13	73	187,582	20	75	60	61
1910	63,676	7	69	92,753	10	73	59	61
1900	38,075	5	59	56,808	8	69	60	63
1890	18,549	3	41	25,182	4	56	58	65

n.a.=not available

[a] Preliminary figures

Source: U.S. Office of Education

a "vicious" influence upon the girls. Others were troubled by the possibility that corporal punishment—viewed as an indispensable instrument for educating boys—would not be inflicted in the presence of girls. The difficulty of administering large coeducational schools effectively and the lack of adequate facilities for girl students in existing school buildings—particularly in the Eastern cities—were additional reasons set forth for maintaining a system of separate instruction.

Coeducation, however, had the tremendous advantage of being less costly than a dual school system. Moreover, it was more convenient for families to send their daughters and sons to the same school. The proponents of coeducation firmly believed that it was "natural" and, consequently, more beneficial for girls and boys to associate with each other during their school years. The "refinement" of the boys, it appeared to others, would be an inevitable consequence of the presence of girls in common classes.

The victory of coeducation was won relatively quickly, but there have been few searching inquiries to appraise its consequences. One study of separate education, undertaken in 1906 in Englewood High School near Chicago, seemed to demonstrate that when the boys were in separate classes, their scholarship improved and their tendency to "show off" was lessened. The study also indicated that the boys could be more severely disciplined when they were in separate classes; that they performed better with male teachers in early adolescence; and that more of them were motivated to continue their schooling. Finally, the study appeared to support the conclusion that, when boys and girls were taught in separate classes, the school work could be better adapted to the needs, interests, and the character traits of each. These findings did little to prompt further investigation of the advantages and disadvantages of a system of separate instruction. Compelling considerations of economy and the strong belief of educators that students should not be segregated on the basis of sex assured the continued growth of a coeducational public high school system. Coeducational instruction has been growing among the nonpublic secondary schools of the country, but separate schools for boys and girls still remain a distinguishing feature of the private high schools. Only a little more than one fifth of the independent day and boarding schools are coeducational, and they account for less than 30 percent of all students enrolled in such schools. Of the Catholic high schools—which enroll over 85 percent of all nonpublic secondary school students—about half are coeducational.

CHANGING PURPOSES OF SECONDARY EDUCATION

Up to the middle of the nineteenth century, private academies and seminaries provided a secondary education for girls which was essentially "practical" and terminal. These schools emphasized reading, writing, and arithmetic, and sought to train girls in the social graces considered appropriate for women and to prepare them for homemaking duties. Girls were sometimes accepted by private schools offering courses designed to equip young men for the fields of commerce and industry. In addition, some of the private academies offering a choice of either a classical course, which was college preparatory, or one known as the "English" curriculum, which was considered more "practical," also accepted girls.

Public demand for schools that would provide "practical" education of a terminal nature, and the growing demand for more equal educational opportunities prepared the ground for the appearance of publicly supported secondary schools. By the middle of the nineteenth century, the principle of public education had won wide acceptance. By this time, too, the value of providing some form of "practical" schooling for girls was also generally recognized, and the movement for women's rights, as has been seen, had been launched. In the free public high schools which subsequently developed, girls were included almost as a matter of course. Indeed, in 1890, the public schools accounted for almost 60 percent of all girl high school graduates, in comparison with about 40 percent among the boys.

Although the public high school developed in part to provide a terminal education, its curriculum was for many years essentially academic and college preparatory. The majority of boys who graduated from high school did in fact go on to college at the close of the last century. Girls accounted for well over half of the public high school graduates, but only a small number of them attended college.

Around the turn of the century, the college preparatory character of the high school curriculum began to be modified as a result of the introduction of such subjects as industrial arts, home economics, physical training, and commercial education. During the first decade of the century, the growing strength of the movement for a distinctly "practical" secondary education was manifested in the founding of the National Society for the Promotion of Industrial Education in 1906. In the same year, the National Education Association called for publicly supported trade and industrial schools. By the close of the second decade of the century, the content of the high school curriculum was no longer so clearly determined by college entrance requirements. Under the pressure of expanding enrollments, the high schools were compelled to respond to the needs of the overwhelming majority of their students who would not be going on to college or professional schools. This development was epitomized by the influential report, *Seven Cardinal Principles of Secondary Education*, issued in 1918 by the Commission on Reorganization of Secondary Education. It stated the aims of secondary education as "health, command of fundamental processes, worthy home membership, vocational efficiency, civic participation, worthy use of leisure time, and ethical character."

The passage of the Smith-Hughes Act in 1917, by which Federal funds were made available for programs of vocational education, was another clear indication that the high schools were expected to help prepare their students, particularly the boys, for immediate entrance into gainful employment. In the eyes of the Congress, as well as of the public at large, vocational education for girls was viewed essentially as training in homemaking skills. The Act, consequently, made Federal funds available to encourage and develop home economics programs. In addition, the Act provided for reimbursement to the states for the training of girls in wage-earning occupations in trade, technical, and industrial pursuits under the trade and industrial programs.

The establishment of Federal support of vocational education at the secondary school level helped encourage the introduction of business education courses into the public high schools. The first comprehensive report on enrollments in these courses showed that in 1922 bookkeeping and typing courses each enrolled 13 percent and shorthand 9 percent of all students. Although the ratio of girls to boys among the students in these fields is not known, girls were probably in the vast majority.

During the 1930's, the objectives of the public high school, and, therefore, the scope of its curriculum, underwent further redefinition. Course offerings were added which were not required—and, indeed, often not accepted—for admission to college, and which had no direct relevance for preparing students for work. This is seen in the rapid growth of courses in social living, group guidance, personal problems, human relations, social adjustment, consumer buying, safety education, driver education, home management, and still other subjects. This development reflected the growing conviction that the secondary school had some responsibility for preparing students for life, as well as work, by contributing to their capacities for individual and social adjustment and for effective citizenship.

A report by the United States Office of Education shows that, between 1934 and 1949, enrollments rose in introductory survey courses in science and mathematics, but declined in specialized and advanced courses in these fields. The largest increases in enrollments occurred in courses in physical education and United States history (which increasingly became "required" courses), and in typing and general mathematics. The largest decreases took place in Latin and French courses. There were also substantial rises in enrollments in home economics and industrial arts courses. These changes were accompanied by modifications in teaching methods and practices and by the influence of what is known as the core curriculum approach, which emphasizes the relationships among different subjects and their common application to particular problem areas.

CURRICULUM AND SUBJECT-MATTER CHOICES OF GIRLS

The explosive growth of enrollments over the past half century has been accompanied by a transformation in the purposes of secondary education, as the high schools have sought to fulfill the needs and respond to the problems of all youth. This effort has led, in turn, to a preoccupation with those problems and needs common to all young people. A quite unintended byproduct of this development has been the paucity of statistical data about differences between girls and boys in curricula and subject-matter choices and in other aspects of their school behavior.

Significant new information has become available, however, as a result of a recent study of the educational and occupational plans of secondary school students. Undertaken early in 1955 by the Educational Testing Service for the National Science Foundation, this study, the first of its kind based on a large national sample, provides comparative data about public high school senior students in 1954-55. Further knowledge about differences between boys and girls as high school students has also been provided by the replies to a questionnaire circulated by the National Manpower Council in 1955 and 1956. Twenty-nine school systems, located in cities or counties in different parts of the country and of varying size, and five State Departments of Education generously supplied comparative information on curriculum and subject-matter choices, motivation, grades, graduation, guidance, and extracurricular activities.

The ETS study, as Table 14 shows, found that 35 percent of the girls were pursuing a commercial program, and another 6 percent were enrolled in what is described as a vocational curriculum. Not all of the girls in the last group, however, were actually receiving training for employment. Yet, it is safe to assert, about two out of five girls in the senior year of high school, in contrast to approximately one out of four boys, were enrolled in 1954 in courses of study where the primary emphasis was upon the development of skills qualifying them for employment immediately upon graduation. Among boys, 14 percent were enrolled in a curriculum identified as vocational in the ETS study, and 9 percent were in a curriculum identified as commercial. Among girls who do not go on to college, it appears that nearly one half are enrolled in a commercial curriculum, nearly one tenth in a vocational curriculum, and one third in academic and general curricula. Of the boys who graduate from high school but do not go on to college, nearly one fifth follow a commercial curriculum, over one fourth a vocational curriculum, and over one third an academic or general curriculum.

Comprehensive and statistically reliable information about the subject-matter choices of girls enrolled in the vocational and commercial curricula is, unfortunately, lacking. Data are available for students in the Federal-aided vocational education programs. These programs currently involve more than 1.6 million full-time day students, but they represent only part of what the schools are doing by way of vocational preparation. Girls constitute 58 percent of these full-time day students. Almost all of them, however, are enrolled in the home economics program, which is designed to provide training for homemaking rather than for paid employment. Of the total number of full-time day students enrolled in trade and industry courses, the girls constitute only about 16 percent. Only 40,000 girls are full-time students in

Table 14. Percentage Distribution of Girls and Boys in the Senior Class in Public High Schools, by Type of Curriculum, Region, and Ability Level, 1954

Type of Curriculum	United States		Northeast		N. Central		South		West		Students with Ability to Do College Work[a]	
	Girls	Boys	Girls	Boys	Girls	Boys	Girls	Boys	Girls	Boys	Girls	Boys
Total	100	100	100	100	100	100	100	100	100	100	100	100
Academic	29	38	36	45	26	34	23	29	36	45	54	66
General	19	28	12	22	23	33	24	29	16	24	13	18
Commercial	35	9	38	11	38	7	33	12	29	7		
Vocational	6	14	5	12	5	14	8	16	6	13	33	16
Other	7	7	7	7	6	8	7	7	9	7		
No response	4	4	3	3	3	4	5	7	5	4		

[a] Includes the top 30 percent of all senior students, as measured by a special intelligence test administered by the Educational Testing Service.

Source: Educational Testing Service study

Federal-aided vocational trade and industry courses, and most of these are studying practical nursing, cosmetology, dressmaking, the operation of sewing machines, and food preparation or handling. These subjects are obviously related to occupational fields in which women workers predominate.

The Federal-aided vocational education program also enrolls more than one and three quarter million evening and part-time students. Among these about two out of five are girls or women, most of whom are in homemaking classes. Less than 10 percent of the part-time and evening girl and women students are in the trade and industry programs, and about 15 percent are in the distributive education program, which provides part-time and evening training for selling and marketing jobs for persons employed in the field. Girls represent slightly more than half of all students in distributive education.

Replies to the National Manpower Council's questionnaire indicate that girls and boys in the commercial curriculum differ in their subject-matter choices. The girls show a distinct preference for typing, shorthand, and general business courses. Boys following a commercial curriculum, on the other hand, display a preference for courses in bookkeeping, commercial law, and selling.

The preference among high school girls for courses of study which promise to equip them for jobs immediately after graduation is also indicated by the fact that relatively few of them enroll in an academic curriculum. However, some educators report that a number of girls decide against a college preparatory program simply because the subject matter of many courses in other curricula is easier to master, and not because of occupational considerations. In any case, as Table 14 shows, about three out of ten senior year girls, compared to almost four out of ten boys, were enrolled in an academic, or college preparatory, curriculum in 1954. Among the senior year students who ranked in the top 30 percent on a special intelligence test, and were, therefore, presumed to possess the ability to do college level work successfully, a significantly smaller proportion of the girls than of the boys were pursuing an academic program. A larger proportion of boys than of girls with the ability to do college work were enrolled in the "general" curriculum, which may also serve to prepare students for college entrance. Relatively few students who pursue the other curricula go on to college.

The ETS study also shows that boys and girls are not equally prepared for college entrance with respect to science and mathematics courses. Thus, of senior year students, almost half of the boys, but less than a tenth of the girls, would have had more than six semesters of mathematics by the time they graduated. Almost a tenth of the girls would have had no mathematics at all, and as many as a fourth would have had only one or two semesters by graduation. In science, the difference between boys and girls, while not so great, was still substantial. Three fourths of the boys and half of the girls would have completed three or more semesters of work in science before graduation. Interest in additional courses in both science and mathematics was more pronounced among boys than girls, but almost 40 percent of the girls indicated that they wished they had taken more courses in both these fields.

A recent study by the U.S. Office of Education substantiates the finding that boys receive far more preparation than girls in mathematics and science. In 1954, almost as many girls as boys were enrolled in elementary mathematics courses in high schools. Boys made up about 60 percent of enrollments in plane geometry and intermediate algebra, however, and about 80 percent of enrollments in trigonometry and solid geometry. Girls outnumbered boys in biology courses by a narrow margin. But in chemistry classes three fifths, and in physics classes four fifths, of the students were boys.

The National Manpower Council's questionnaire returns also showed that, among the students in the college preparatory curriculum, a greater proportion of boys than of girls are interested in advanced courses in mathematics and physics. Judging from enrollments, there is a marked preference among girls for advanced courses in foreign languages. A number of school systems reported high interest among girls in courses in biology, chemistry, world problems, economics, social studies, history, English, and literature. All these subjects, however, turned up among the fields in which boys in other school systems showed interest.

Curricula and subject-matter choices in high school are related in part to what students expect, or consciously plan, to do after graduation. The ETS study shows that anticipation of college attendance is far stronger among boys than among girls. Of those students in 1954-55 high school graduating classes with the ability to do college work, 62 percent of the girls, in contrast to 78 percent of the boys, planned to enter college in the fall of 1955 or at some later date. Table 15 also shows that more girls than boys were not interested in going to college, or, even when interested, had made no plans to do so. Even among the students of marked

Table 15. Estimated Percentage Distribution of Senior Students in Public High Schools by College-Going Plans and Aptitude Test Scores, 1954-55 Graduating Classes

College-Going Plans	High Scorers[a]		Very High Scorers[b]	
	Girls	Boys	Girls	Boys
Total	100	100	100	100
With college plans	62	78	75	88
Going now[c]	42	47	58	59
Going later	20	31	22	29
Interest, but no plans	8	4	6	2
No interest, no plans	17	10	10	5
Miscellaneous	13	8	9	5

[a] The top 30 percent of all senior students in public schools, as measured by the mental ability test administered by the Educational Testing Service.

[b] The top 10 percent of all senior students, as measured by the Educational Testing Service.

[c] In the fall of 1955.

Source: Educational Testing Service study

ability—the top 10 percent—a significantly smaller proportion of girls than of boys planned to attend. In this group, one out of ten girls, but only one of twenty boys, had neither interest in nor plans to go to college.

The gross differences beween girls and boys in high school curricula and subject-matter preferences are the products of several factors related to fundamental differences in the lives they expect—and are expected—to lead as adults. The proportions of girls following an academic program in high school, and for whom college attendance is a goal, are strongly affected by family influences and by their expectations of marriage. The ETS study revealed, for example, that among the girls for whom college attendance was not a goal, half specifically indicated that it was not a goal because they would "rather get married."

For many girls still in high school the anticipation of becoming wives, mothers, and homemakers appears to be strong enough to turn them away from investing in more education. Marriage expectations or plans were apparently not part of the conscious thinking of the boys for whom going to college was not a goal. The major reasons they offered were that their occupational objectives were not yet defined, or that a college education is not required to fulfill their job aspirations. Economic considerations, as will be seen, also play a role in the decision not to go to college, as do certain social characteristics of the family.

The wives and the mothers who work outside the home are now familiar and accepted figures. Yet, most teen-age girls appear to take it for granted that their future lives will be centered chiefly, if not exclusively, around homemaking responsibilities. Although this expectation fits more closely the life of an earlier generation than the actual behavior of many women during the last decade and a half, it exercises a strong influence on the educational objectives of many girls in high school and encourages them to prepare for jobs which will be open to them immediately after graduation. Such jobs are overwhelmingly in fields already employing many women, and the curriculum and subject-matter choices of high school girls thus tend to respond to existing patterns of women's employment. It is not surprising, therefore, that more than one third of the girls in high school are enrolled in a commercial curriculum.

According to the ETS study, more than one fourth of all girl seniors named office or clerical work as the kind they would be most interested in having after graduation. Even among students of high ability, almost half of the girls who expressed a preference for jobs in office or clerical work indicated that they had no interest in further education and training at the college level. Only one fourth of the boys of high ability who preferred clerical work were not interested in pursuing a college course.

The ETS study sought to discover the fields of college study and subsequent employment which interested high school seniors with the ability to do college work. Among boys, the strongest preferences among fields of study were, in order of descending popularity, engineering, physical science, business, liberal arts, and the health professions. Among girls, the health professions ranked first and were followed by education, business, liberal arts, and fine arts. Among those who wanted to study one of the health professions, the boys were primarily interested in medicine and the girls in nursing and technicians' occupations. When asked to name in what occupation they wanted to be engaged fifteen years hence, on the assumption that with hard work they could be successful, about half the girls chose education, office or clerical jobs, nursing, or medical technicians' work. About half of the boys, on the other hand, chose engineering, business, science and mathematics, or medicine.

The findings on field of study and occupational preference once again suggest that marriage is a central concern among high school girls and that their occupational leanings reflect the existing distribution of women in the labor market. Their occupational preferences seem to be reinforced rather than altered by the vocational guidance and counseling available at the high school level. The replies to the National Manpower Council's questionnaire indicated that the opportunities for guidance and counseling are approximately the same for boys and girls. At the same time, most of the school systems indicated that their students were counseled in terms of the existing differences between boys and girls in education, work interests, and employment opportunities.

There is evidence that boys as well as girls are likely to express educational and occupational preferences which reflect more their acceptance of adult judgments, voiced both at home and at school, than their own positive interests. In some cases, the adult judgment provides an educational or career objective when youngsters lack positive interests. The ETS study showed that a fifth of the girls named education as their probable field of study, but it also revealed that only a tenth indicated that this was their field of greatest interest. Similarly, although two fifths of the boys listed engineering as their probable field of study, only a fourth indicated that it was the field in which they were most interested.

Most girls in high school assume that they will have some experience working outside the home after they complete their formal education. But they also take it for granted that paid employment will not constitute the central focus of their lives. Moreover, they see their future job opportunities largely in terms of a relatively restricted range of occupations growing out of existing patterns of women's employment. These are overwhelmingly in clerical and sales work, and in fields associated with the traditional functions of women—the care of the sick, the training of children, the handling or preparation of food, the manufacture of clothing. Even among girls in high school who have an interest in and plans for going to college, educational and occupational aspirations tend to be concentrated in traditional women's occupations or in new fields in which women predominate.

SCHOOL PERFORMANCE

It is not clear why girls achieve, on the average, better grades in high school than boys. But, on the basis of the measures used, there is no question that they do. Up to college, as Table 16 shows, girls outdistance boys in the number of years of schooling achieved. Those who replied to the National Manpower Council's questionnaire also reported that girls earn better grades than boys; that a smaller proportion fail; that they constitute a majority of the honor roll and scholarship society students; and that their grades, in relation to their intellectual ability, are higher than is the case with boys. About two thirds of the school systems reporting indicated that girls remain in high school on a full-time basis longer than boys, regardless of the curriculum they are studying.

The recently developed National Merit Scholarship testing program also indicates that girls, on the average, do better than boys in high school. The first step in the program involved the screen-

Table 16. Estimated Percentages of Young Men and Women Completing Specified Amounts of Education, 1950[a]

Educational Attainment	Young Men	Young Women
Less than high school	26	20
Some high school	19	20
High school graduation	29	46
Some college[b]	11	6
College graduation	11	6
Some graduate work	1	
Master's degree	2	2
Doctorate	1	
	100	100

[a] These estimates are designed to indicate the educational attainments of young men and women at the time their formal schooling terminates.

[b] The majority of this group pursue a baccalaureate college program, but an unknown number enroll in technical institutes, vocationally oriented junior college programs, and other post-high school educational or training programs.

Source: Based on data from U.S. Bureau of the Census and The Commission on Human Resources and Advanced Training.

ing of students in all the high schools of the nation in order to select those qualified to compete for a National Merit Scholarship. On the basis of the standards used—grades and class standing—girls made up 55 percent of the total selected to compete. Boys, however, accounted for 69 percent of all of the scholarships awarded on the basis of a special test. The results of the College Entrance Board Examinations tell a similar story: boys make up a larger proportion of the students who qualify for college entrance or scholarship aid on the basis of tests measuring ability to do college work.

It is generally agreed that the reasons for the superior performance of girls in high school, or for the better record achieved by boys in college entrance examinations and scholarship competitions, do not lie in differences in native ability between the sexes. The results of tests of intelligence show that highly developed ability is more or less equally distributed between boys and girls. The distribution of intelligence test scores among the senior high school students covered in the ETS study, however, reveals slight, but still significant, differences. The scores in this test ranged from zero to twenty, and a score of eleven or less designated an intelligence level below the ability to perform college work. The median score for boys was 8.2, compared with 7.9 for girls. The same proportions of boys and girls—just about one third—scored below 6. One half of the girls, in contrast to 45 percent of the boys, scored between 7 and 13. More important is the fact that 20 percent of the boys, but only 16 percent of the girls, scored between 14 and 20. Other studies point up the fact that boys do somewhat better than girls with respect to intelligence test scores toward the close of their high school experience, even though girls achieve, on the average, a superior grade record.

THE PROBLEM OF MOTIVATION

Several explanations have been offered of the differences between boys and girls in high school performance and college entrance and scholarship examination results. In one way or another these explanations point to differences in the motivations of boys and girls during their high school years. Some educators hold that the better grades which girls achieve reflect in part the less demanding commercial and vocational courses many of them select. The evidence supporting this contention has been very much disputed. Although many girls do distinguish themselves intellectually in high school, it is also asserted that a majority are reluctant to appear outstanding for fear that they will be less sought after by boys. The report of the Commission on the Education of Women, *How Fare American Women?* cites recent investigations which indicate "that the intelligence quotients and grades of girls in high school become lower when they consider that successful academic work militates against their popularity or feminity."

The point has been made that the tests used in selecting candidates for admission to college and for scholarship aid merely reveal the poorer preparation of girls in mathematics and the sciences, a reflection of their curriculum choices. Most tests involve both verbal and mathematical components, and girls score less well than boys primarily because of their weakness in the latter. This may indicate that boys are better prepared in mathematics, but it may also suggest differences in mathematical aptitude. It is commonly assumed that boys are better endowed than girls, on the average, in mathematical aptitude. However, the ways in which this aptitude has been measured have been questioned, and doubts, consequently, have been raised about the asserted superiority of boys. It has been argued that an adjustment in the relative weights of the verbal and mathematical test components, in favor of the first, would result in better average scores for girls, who presumably excel in verbal aptitude.

Replies to the National Manpower Council's questionnaire frequently asserted that, although girls, on the average, are better students in high school than boys, the range from low to high in the performance of boys is greater than among girls. One school system in a large city presented data showing that "while more boys than girls earn very low or failing grades, more boys than girls are likely to rank within the top 5 percent of their graduating class." Educators and school administrators report that girls are, by and large, better motivated than boys with respect to learning, and suggest that this accounts for their superior record of performance in high school. Many respondents to the Council's questionnaire described the girls as being more curious about the subject matter of their courses, more conscientious in applying themselves to their work, and more concerned with high marks and academic achievement. They were said to take more pride in high grades. However, many also asserted that girls are much more likely than boys to conform to the requirements of the school situation and to measure up to the standards set by those in authority.

Just why this pattern of conforming behavior should be characteristic of girls is far from clear. It has been suggested that one reason is to be found in the influences which shape the personality of girls during their formative years. These, it is claimed, condition them to place a higher value than boys do upon conforming to the norms of social behavior. Meeting the standards of approved student conduct is, according to this contention, merely one expression of a basic orientation toward all social behavior. The point has also been made that the high school experience is much more likely to be regarded by girls than by boys as an end in itself. Boys, as they approach maturity, tend to view and evaluate their schooling as a means for realizing other objectives, such as further education or long range vocational goals. Girls, on the other hand, are more inclined to respond to the educational situation on its own terms and, consequently, to conduct themselves in ways which win approval by school standards, one of which is "good" marks. The predominance of women teachers, particularly in the lower grades, is another reason offered to explain why girls apparently display a marked impulse to measure up to the idea of being "good" students in high school. Differences in school performance are also traced to the fact that girls mature earlier than boys, and this is alleged to result in a more adult attitude toward grades and in a more realistic sense of the consequences of indifferent or poor school performance.

Such explanations, it may be remarked, themselves raise many questions, and some of them merely restate the assertion that girls generally exhibit conforming behavior. Moreover, it is important to bear in mind that little is known about the interplay of factors affecting motivation. All large-scale generalizations about differences in motivation are subject to almost endless qualification, and any representation of such differences in black and white is bound to be misleading. There is considerable evidence that differences among students enrolled in various high school curricula are greater than differences between girls and boys pursuing the same program of study. Students in the college preparatory program, for example, are said to be generally "better motivated" than those in the commercial or general curricula. While credited, on the average, with being better motivated in school, girls are more heavily represented than boys in the latter curricula. Within the academic curriculum, educators assert that boys whose educational or occupational goals are fairly well defined are certainly no less interested in learning than are girls.

Experienced teachers and school administrators remain convinced, however, that girls as a group are more responsive than boys to social pressures to do well in school, and are more disposed to measure up to the standards of conduct which the school sets. These characteristics, they believe, help to explain the differences between girls and boys in high school performance. Boys are reported to be more responsive to social pressure to excel in sports, while girls, according to some educators, are more likely to strive for academic achievement and recognition.

One respondent wrote in answer to the National Manpower Council's questionnaire that "The attitude of boys changes from one of calloused indifference to real concern about grades between the first and last years of their high school experience, whereas the attitude of girls remains about the same throughout, namely one of sensitivity and concern with the matter of grades." Although such a change in attitude can be related to the emergence and clarification of vocational or career objectives among the boys, it still remains true that the pattern of curriculum and subject-choices among girls points to a relatively high concern with short-run employment considerations. This is particularly noticeable, as a number of respondents pointed out, among students in the commercial curricula, who are aware that employment opportunities often depend heavily upon the record of their performance in high school.

If the vocational goals of girls tend to be secondary to the expectation of marriage and to be defined in terms of the jobs they are likely to hold immediately after completing high school, it is understandable why most of them do not view their educational experience as a means of preparing themselves for a lifetime of activity in paid employment. Replies to the National Manpower Council's questionnaire strongly suggest that the occupational and career objectives of boys, particularly in the later years of high school, are likely to be more sharply delineated than among girls, to be long run rather than short run in outlook, and to be more ambitious than those of girls.

PLANS FOR GOING TO COLLEGE

While in high school, girls and boys look with different eyes upon continuing their education in college. Just as there are gross differences between boys and girls with respect to curricula, subject-matter choices, and performance, so there are significant variations between their plans to attend college. Ability, vocational objectives, and level of high school performance all affect these plans. At the same time, it is clear that family circumstances can be particularly influential in the decisions of boys and girls alike to go or not to go to college.

Thus, wanting to go to college is closely related to the educational and occupational level attained by the student's father. The positive leaning toward college attendance is markedly stronger among boys than among girls. But the ETS study shows that it is true of girls, as well as of boys, that the higher the educational attainment of the father, the more likely it is that his children will want to attend college. If the father's education was the equivalent of high school or less, the proportion of girls planning to go to college was substantially below that of boys. However, where the father's education reached graduate or professional school level, about the same proportion of girls as of boys planned to attend college.

Roughly the same situation is found when the father's occupation is correlated with children's plans for going to college. According to the ETS study, the higher the father stood on the occupational ladder, the more the girls' pattern approximated that of the boys. Among the sons of businessmen, 85 to 91 percent planned to go to college, depending upon the specific occupational status of the father. Among the daughters of businessmen, somewhat smaller proportions—70 to 74 percent—planned to go to college. From 90 to 95 percent of the sons of professional men were planning to go to college, and the proportions of college-oriented daughters of professional men ranged from 79 percent, for those whose fathers were in scientific occupations, to 94 percent, for those whose fathers were physicians. At the lower end of the parental occupational scale, the proportions of boys planning to go to college were considerably larger than among girls.

Levels of education and occupation are associated with income, and these findings point to the significance of the economic resources of the family as a determinant of college attendance. Among the high school seniors in the ETS study who did not plan to go to college, half of both the boys and the girls stated that the cost involved was one of the important reasons. Further evidence of the influence exercised by economic resources appears in the ETS finding that the chances of college attendance are reduced for both the able boys and girls as the number of children in the family rises. The proportion planning to go to college sometime in the future, rather than immediately after graduation, was also higher in larger than in smaller families.

The ETS study throws no direct light on whether parents are more inclined to make the effort to send sons rather than daughters to college, when expenses are a major consideration. The study did find, however, that a much higher proportion of boys than girls in wage-earning families plan to go to college. It is, therefore, reasonable to assume that among lower-income families parents are more likely to make sacrifices to send sons, rather than daughters, to college simply because the latter are expected to be supported by the men they will eventually marry.

Different career and economic objectives also help to explain why more boys than girls go on to college. Thus, the ETS study revealed that among senior high school students who planned to attend college, 59 percent of the boys, compared with 47 percent of the girls, planned to go to college because a degree was required for the work they wanted to do, or because of the higher earnings which would result from a college education.

The differences between boys and girls in high school are reflected in how they respond to the opportunities which the educational system offers them. These responses, in turn, help to determine whether or not they go on to college. It will be seen that the difference in the behavior of boys and girls in college has significance not only in its own terms, but also because of its effect on their later lives, particularly their different patterns of work.

VII. POST-HIGH SCHOOL EDUCATION AND TRAINING

Every attempt to define the purposes of American higher education and to state the most effective means for realizing them is an invitation to disagreement. This is understandable, for its functions and forms, shaped by changing historical circumstances, reflect the needs of a large and heterogeneous student population and the influence of conflicting educational philosophies. Every attempt to specify the purposes of higher education for women in particular encounters additional difficulties.

To inquire how women should be educated, or whether they should be educated in the same way as men, or differently, does not merely raise queries concerning the structure of educational institutions and methods of instruction. It also asks how young men and women are to be prepared to assume those adult responsibilities which society views as distinctive of each sex. Consequently, almost every utterance on the education of women is likely to express a judgment—at least by implication—on the degree to which women resemble or differ from men in general intelligence, abilities, and aptitudes, in "nature" or "psychology," or in functions.

It should not be surprising, therefore, that there has been a continuing debate over whether higher education should serve primarily the needs and interests of women as homemakers, as workers, or as citizens. Enormous changes have occurred in the course of the past century in the status of women in American society, in the ways they conduct their lives, and in the extent and content of their education. These changes have profoundly altered the terms and manner of that debate. They have not, however, resolved the underlying question: Should the primary emphasis in the college education of women be given to preparing them for adult responsibilities and functions which essentially differ from or resemble those of men?

This question is obviously related to the concern which has frequently been expressed that only a small proportion of the girls who graduate from high school go on to college. Even more prominent than those which appear earlier are the differences in the educational behavior and experience of young men and women after high school. As has been seen, fewer young women than young men enter and graduate from college. Women are heavily outnumbered by men in graduate study. In many respects, of course, their college or university education is identical, but, both as undergraduate and graduate students, young men and women differ significantly with respect to the fields in which they specialize. Furthermore, men and women do not make the same use of noncollegiate educational and training facilities.

Yet, there has been less dissimilarity in college attendance and graduation between the sexes in the United States than in most other western societies. Even where, as in France, Italy, and England, the ratio of women to men students is roughly similar to that in the United States, a much smaller proportion of the total population is enrolled in colleges and universities. From a comparative point of view, the extent to which American women are educated beyond the secondary school level is quite remarkable. Since 1949, more than 100,000 bachelor's and first professional degrees have been awarded annually to women—a number which is substantially larger than the total college and university enrollments of Great Britain. From 1946 to 1955, a total of almost one million women earned bachelor's and first professional degrees in the United States. In recent years, about one third of all such degrees have gone to women. In 1950, 2.25 million—or about 43 percent—of the 5.25 million college graduates aged 25 years and over were women.

GROWTH OF COLLEGIATE EDUCATION FOR WOMEN

College education for women, comparable in quality to that available for men, began in the United States in 1837, when Oberlin College opened its doors to four young women. The first women's college, Vassar, was founded twenty-eight years later. By the close of the nineteenth century, women comprised one third of the nation's college and university students. At first, higher education for women, whether provided by establishing separate women's colleges or by admitting women to men's institutions, was staunchly resisted. The early arguments in opposition took for granted the innate inferiority of the female sex and represented college education for women as a device for undermining the superior status of the male. It was maintained that women possessed neither the physical strength nor the mental ability to do college work; that a college education was incompatible with their functions and status; that it would decrease their chances for marriage—for men were repelled by "learned" or "intellectual" women—and destroy their distinctive feminine qualities; and that it would have no utility after marriage.

These and other objections were more than counterbalanced by forces which produced an increasingly vigorous and gradually successful movement for women's rights. This had its educational as well as its legal, social, economic, and political aspects. Much later, however, when the right of women to a college education had clearly been established, the lower marriage and birth rates of women college graduates provided fresh ammunition for those who resisted the break with tradition. They ascribed these developments to college attendance alone and cited them as proof of the undesirable consequences of higher education for women. The proposal that men's institutions be opened up to women was countered on additional grounds. It was contended that this step would "feminize" the institutions, for new courses designed to meet women's needs would be introduced, or men would be discouraged from attending existing courses likely to attract many women, particularly in the liberal arts. Some opponents of educational equality believed that the coeducational system would encourage immorality, or promote early marriages, or weaken the family by leading women to question the superior status of the husband. Such convictions and the weight of tradition contributed to the establishment of the "coordinate college" for women, associated with, but still separate from, the men's institution.

How much had been won in the struggle to provide opportunities for higher education for women, even before the close of the nineteenth century, appears in the fact that women then accounted for more than one third of the still small number of college and university students. Since that time, women have represented from 30 to 50 percent of the enrollments in institutions of higher education.

The growth in college attendance during the present century, which rests upon the foundation provided by the tremendous expansion in high school attendance and graduation, is one aspect of a continuing trend toward more years of schooling for young people. It is a measure of the value which Americans attach not so much to intellectual attainment as to formal education. A growing national income, a substantial rise in family income, and expenditures of public funds for higher education have been crucial in the increase in college attendance. So have the needs

of a complex, technological society for highly trained and specialized personnel. These needs are reflected in the extent to which
college training is held to be desirable for employment, and in the
professionalization of a number of occupations by establishing
a college or professional school degree as a minimum requirement.

Young women and men go to college for much the same basic
reasons: because they have compelling intellectual interests;
because they regard college as essential preparation for a fruitful
adult life; because they want to enter one of the professions or
prepare for a career in business; because they view college attendance as a means for attaining higher social status; and even
because going to college is an acceptable substitute for going to
work for those young people who are under no pressure to earn an
income. Each of these reasons, as well as others that might be
specified, rarely operate alone. The decision to go to college is
shaped by social and economic circumstances, a variety of personal considerations, and the influences exerted by parents, relatives, teachers, and others.

It has been seen that the expectation of marriage and of an
adult life defined primarily in terms of functions centered in the
home goes far to explain why a smaller proportion of girl than of
boy high school graduates go on to college. The available evidence
indicates that vocational interests and aspirations are important
reasons for college attendance among the young women who do
go. These reasons, however, are on the whole still more significant
with men. For example, a recent study, "Occupational Planning
by Undergraduates of the State College of Washington," found
that "women as well as men appeared to be impressed by the
vocational importance of college training, although a higher proportion of the men (92 percent) than of the women (77 percent)
stated that occupational preparation was the most important
reason for coming to college."

TRENDS IN COLLEGE GRADUATION

From 1900 to 1955, there was an elevenfold increase in the number of bachelor's and first professional degrees conferred. Since the number of women graduating from college was twenty times greater in 1955 than in 1900, the proportion of these degrees awarded to women did not quite double between these two points in time. Early in this century, women constituted a much larger proportion of college students than they did of graduates. They accounted for about one third of the students—almost as high a proportion as today—but, as Table 17 shows, for only about one fifth of all recipients of bachelor's and first professional degrees. A partial explanation of this situation is that many young women who intended to teach attended college or normal school for only one or two years, which were then sufficient to meet the requirements for certification. The significant increases in the numbers of women college graduates occurred after 1920, and since that date the ratio of women to men has been about the same for degree recipients as for college students.

Since 1920, moreover, there has been no consistent growth in the ratio of women to men among college graduates. In 1920, women constituted one third of all the bachelor's and first professional degree recipients. In 1930 and 1940, they received two fifths of all of the degrees awarded. During World War II, which temporarily checked the long-run growth in college enrollments and graduations, women constituted a substantial majority of all college graduates for the first time. Even though the actual numbers of women graduating from college rose after the war, they accounted for much smaller proportions of the total recipients of degrees because of the influx of male veterans into the colleges and universities. In 1950, only one out of every four degrees was awarded to a woman. Since then, as Table 17 indicates, there has been a steady growth in the proportion of women among college graduates, but this is unlikely to continue in the future.

Table 17. Bachelor's and First Professional Degrees Awarded to Men and Women, 1900-55

| Year | First Degrees Awarded | | | | Men Receiving First Degrees as Percent of All Men Aged 22 Years | Women Receiving First Degrees as Percent of All Women Aged 22 Years |
	Total	Men	Women	Percent Women of Total		
1900	27,410	22,173	5,237	19.1	3.0	0.7
1910	37,199	28,762	8,437	22.7	3.1	0.9
1920	48,622	31,980	16,642	34.2	3.5	1.7
1930	122,484	73,615	48,869	39.9	6.8	4.3
1940	186,500	109,546	76,954	41.3	9.7	6.6
1942	185,346	103,889	81,457	43.9	8.8	6.5
1944	125,863	55,865	69,998	55.6	4.5	5.4
1946	136,174	58,664	77,510	56.9	4.9	6.2
1947	272,144	175,987	96,157	35.3	14.5	7.7
1948	271,019	175,456	95,563	35.3	14.9	8.0
1949	366,634	264,168	102,466	27.9	22.5	8.6
1950	433,734	329,819	103,915	24.0	29.6	8.9
1951	384,352	279,343	105,009	27.3	25.0	9.1
1952	331,924	227,029	104,895	31.6	21.6	9.2
1953	304,857	200,820	104,037	34.1	19.1	9.4
1954	292,880	187,500	105,380	36.0	17.3	9.6
1955	287,401	183,602	103,799	36.1	17.4	10.0

Source: U.S. Office of Education and U.S. Bureau of the Census

The rapid increase in college graduations may also be shown by comparison with the growth in the numbers of young men and women in the population. Around the turn of the century, the number of women graduating from college annually was equivalent to less than 1 percent of the total number of women 22 years of age. The ratio of men graduating annually to the male population aged 22, however, was 3 percent. By 1955, as Table 17 shows, the ratio for women came to 10 percent, and for men to 17 percent.

Many persons graduate from college when they are in their later twenties or early thirties. For example, 19 percent of the women who received bachelor's degrees in June, 1955, are reported to have been 23 to 29 years old, and another 8 percent were 30 or over. It is, therefore, somewhat misleading to compare the number of college graduates in any one year with the number of high school graduates four years earlier. Nevertheless, such a comparison does help illuminate differences between the sexes with respect to high school completion and college graduation. The number of girls graduating from high schools was equivalent to three fifths of all the 17-year-old girls in the population in 1950. Male high school graduates came to more than half of the 17-year-old male population. The number of women graduating from college or professional school in 1954 was equal to 17 percent of the number of girl high school graduates four years earlier. The number of boys completing college in 1954 was 33 percent of the number graduating from high school in 1950. Over the last two decades, the proportions of boys and girls graduating both from high school and college have increased substantially. There have been only moderate gains, however, in the proportions of high school graduates who have gone on to complete college. In each case, the increases for boys have been somewhat greater than those for girls.

All estimates point to a striking growth in the future size of the college-educated population. Such forecasts are based on rapid

increases in the college-age population and on the assumption
that the underlying social and economic causes for the past
growth of higher education will continue to operate in the
future. The proportion of young people who complete college
may grow at an even faster rate than in the past, particularly if
the high level of demand for college-trained men and women
continues, as it gives every promise of doing. Projections prepared
by the U. S. Office of Education, indicating that women will
make up about a third of all college graduates, show 145,000
women recipients of bachelor's and first professional degrees in
1959-60, and 246,000 ten years later, compared to slightly over
100,000 in recent years. These projections also assume, of course,
that teaching personnel and physical facilities required for the
expansion in enrollments will be available.

UNDERGRADUATE EDUCATIONAL PATTERNS

Variations in educational patterns appear not only in college
enrollment and completion, but also in the types of institutions
men and women attend. Three types of institutions award the
overwhelming majority of bachelor's and first professional degrees—universities, liberal arts colleges, and teachers' colleges.
As Table 18 shows, a much higher proportion of the women graduates come from teachers' colleges than is the case among men.
A significantly smaller proportion of women than of men graduates
earned their degrees in universities in 1953-54, while the reverse
was the case in the liberal arts colleges. Women are most poorly
represented among the graduates of technological schools.

Coeducation is not nearly as prevalent in American higher education as it is at the secondary level, but it is still characteristic
of the college and university scene. In 1953-54, only three institutions classified as "men's universities" did not grant bachelor's
degrees to women. Coeducational colleges conferred about three
fourths of all of the degrees granted by liberal arts institutions.
There are more than twice as many separate women's colleges as

Table 18. Bachelor's and First Professional Degrees Awarded to Men and Women, by Type of Institution, 1953-54

Type of Institution	Total		Men		Women		Women as Percent of Total Receiving Degrees
	Number	*Percent*	*Number*	*Percent*	*Number*	*Percent*	
Total	292,880	100	187,500	100	105,380	100	36
Universities	141,819	48	102,472	55	39,347	37	28
Coeducational	138,989	47	99,642	53	39,347	37	28
Non-coeducational	2,830	1	2,830	2	--	--	--
Liberal arts colleges	88,384	30	47,136	25	41,248	39	47
Coeducational	67,245	23	39,015	21	28,230	27	42
Non-coeducational	21,139	7	8,121	4	13,018	12	62
Teachers' colleges	34,938	12	13,311	7	21,627	21	62
Technological schools	14,316	5	12,942	7	1,374	1	10
Other	13,423	5	11,639	6	1,784	2	13

Source: U. S. Office of Education, and Richard H. Ostheimer, *A Statistical Analysis of the Organization of Higher Education in the U. S., 1948-1949*, New York, 1951.

men's, and about one third of the degrees earned by women in liberal arts institutions were granted by women's colleges. Only one sixth of the degrees granted to men by liberal arts colleges were awarded by separate men's schools.

In presenting data on women in the labor force, earlier chapters stressed the fact that they are concentrated in relatively few fields of employment even though they are found in virtually all occupations. This is also true for the fields of undergraduate study pursued by young women. Thus, almost two out of every five women who graduated in 1954-55 majored in the field of education, and an additional one out of seven prepared for teaching, even though she specialized in some other field. Almost as striking is the contrast between men and women college graduates with respect to specialization in the basic and applied natural sciences. One third of the men graduating in 1954-55 majored in these fields, as Table 19 shows, in contrast to one eighth of the women. Engineering, for men the most important single field of concentration among the natural and physical sciences, claimed less than 1 percent of the women, but in several scientific fields, such as botany, bacteriology, physiology, and mathematics, there were roughly similar proportions of men and women graduates.

The several social sciences accounted for a substantially larger proportion of the men (about one third) than of the women graduates (about one fifth). Within the social sciences, men and women tend to specialize in different disciplines. For example, economics attracted very few women compared to the number of men among graduates in 1954-55, while a much larger proportion of women than of men had majored in sociology. In liberal arts fields of study, in which about one out of every five women and one out of every seven men college graduates specialized, there were large differences in the proportions of men and women majoring in English, the fine arts, foreign languages, and religion and philosophy.

Four areas of specialization in which the great majority of

Table 19.   Bachelor's and First Professional Degrees Awarded to Men and Women, by Field of Study, 1954-55

Field of Study	Percent Distribution		Women as Percent of Total Receiving Degrees
	Men	Women	
Total	100	100	36
Natural sciences, basic and applied	32	13	18
Biological	3	2	28
Physical	5	1	13
Healing arts and medical sciences	9	7	31
Engineering	12	1	--
Mathematics	1	1	33
Science without major	2	1	16
Social sciences	35	19	25
Basic [a]	11	8	29
Applied [b]	20	7	17
Psychology	2	2	46
Other	2	2	41
Liberal art subjects	15	22	45
English	3	8	61
Fine arts	4	8	53
Foreign languages	1	2	60
Religion and philosophy	4	2	17
Arts without major	3	2	27
Agriculture	4	--	2
Education [c]	8	37	72
Home economics	--	7	99
Journalism	1	1	36
Law	4	--	4
Library science	--	1	75
Military science	1	--	--

-- = less than 0.5 percent.
[a] Includes anthropology, economics, geography, history, international relations, political science, and sociology.
[b] Includes business and commerce, social work, and public administration. Master's degrees in social work, where they are the first professional degree granted by a school, are also included.
[c] Most students who prepared for high school teaching are included in other fields of specialization and not in the education category.
Source: U.S. Office of Education

graduates were women—education, nursing, library science, and home economics—accounted for exactly half of the bachelor's and first professional degrees earned by women in 1954-55. Two thirds of the degrees granted to women were in these four fields and in English and fine arts, where women also outnumbered men. Women were also granted a majority of the degrees in foreign languages, sociology, and social work.

The fields of study which attract women most strongly are those which prepare them for employment in professional occupations long viewed as peculiarly suited to women and in which they are already heavily represented. Teaching, nursing, library work, and the occupations based on home economics study currently account for almost 70 percent of all women employed in professional occupations. The opening up of employment opportunities in science and technology since 1950 has not yet significantly influenced the choices which young women make with respect to fields of college study.

Employment opportunities alone could not determine choices among fields of study, for many young women do not view college in purely vocational terms. There are those who hope that their college years will help them, not so much in paid employment, as in their activities as wives, mothers, and citizens. For some young women, as for some young men, interest in a field of study overrides considerations of employment opportunities. Others might have majored in one of the natural sciences, for example, rather than in one of the "women's" fields, if their high school studies had prepared them for such specialization. Some are greatly influenced in their choices by the strength of a department or even of a single teacher. With others, specialization in college may be affected by the knowledge that their chances of continuing with graduate study are slight. Even if it were possible, it would not be very useful to assign precise weights to these diverse reasons for the relatively heavy concentration of women college students in a few fields of study. For the important points are that a combination of factors results in distinctive and persisting patterns of choice among fields of study and that traditional modes of behavior are not readily altered.

GRADUATE STUDY

At the level of graduate study, women and men behave similarly in one major respect. Just about the same proportions of women as of men college graduates obtain master's degrees. This is not a recent development, for in 1900, when women earned about one fifth of all of the bachelor's and first professional degrees, they also received about the same proportion of master's degrees. In the mid-1950's, about one third of all first degree and of all master's degree recipients were women. In recent decades, the number of master's degrees awarded has increased considerably, in good part because so large a proportion of those entering the teaching profession have gone on to advanced study.

In graduate, as in undergraduate, study women enter almost all fields, but most are found in a handful of specialties. Of the almost 19,500 master's degrees awarded women in 1954-55, about 12,500, or just under two thirds, were earned in the field of education. Two fifths of all the men receiving master's degrees that year earned them in education. Five fields of study—education, English, home economics, nursing, and fine arts—accounted for about four fifths of all of the master's degrees conferred on women.

In only three fields—nursing, home economics, and library science—were the overwhelming majority of the master's degrees granted to women in 1954-55. Even in education, more men than women were granted master's degrees. In social work and some foreign languages (French, Spanish, and Russian) there were more women recipients than men, and in English the master's degrees were equally divided between the sexes. Women who go on to earn a master's degree generally represent a smaller proportion of the total than do those who majored in the same field as undergraduates. Thus, in English and in foreign languages, fields in which women earned about three fifths of the bachelor's degrees, they accounted for about half of the master's degrees granted. In fine arts and psychology, women received about half of the bachelor's degrees, but a third of the master's.

Relatively few women continue with graduate study to the Ph.D. level. The proportion of all doctoral degrees earned by women has fluctuated greatly since the close of the nineteenth century. Women constituted about 6 percent of all doctoral degree recipients in 1890 and 1900, but for 12 to 16 percent in the three decades after 1910. At the close of World War II, they earned about one fifth of all the doctoral degrees conferred. Since then, the number of doctorates granted to women has more than doubled, but the increase in the number granted to men has been even greater. Consequently, the proportion of all doctoral degrees earned by women has declined, and since 1949, about one tenth of those granted have gone to women.

As at the bachelor's and master's level, the majority of doctoral degrees earned by women are in education, and this one field accounted for 30 percent of the 826 doctoral degrees conferred on women in 1954-55. Another one third of all of the Ph.D.'s awarded to women were in six other fields—psychology, English, home economics, fine arts, chemistry, and history. At the Ph.D. level, women accounted for most of the few degrees in home economics, Russian language studies, social work, and nursing. On the other hand, they represented a small fraction of the Ph.D.'s granted in mathematics and the physical sciences, and about 10 percent in the social and biological sciences and psychology.

The vast majority of college men and women do not contemplate further study. In the case of the women, pursuit of an advanced degree is more or less foreclosed by marriage either before or shortly after graduation from college. How significant a role marriage plays can be seen in the findings of a study undertaken jointly by the Women's Bureau and the National Vocational Guidance Association of the women college graduates of the class of June, 1955. Six months later, 12 percent of the single women from this class were enrolled in school full time, most of them in graduate courses. Of the married women, only 4 percent were attending school, and of those with children, 2 percent were in school full time. Of all women graduates of the class of June, 1955, enrolled as full-time students six months later, however, 15 percent were married.

The married woman graduate student was exceptional years ago. It has been estimated that today almost one third of the women working toward an advanced degree are married. Marriage is only one factor affecting graduate study by women. Some young women who do not engage in graduate study would do so if they had the economic means. It has been asserted that some able women do not make the investment of time, effort, and money in a master's or doctor's degree because men are preferred for top positions, even in occupations in which women predominate, such as library service and teaching. There is also reason to believe that most women who look forward to combining paid employment with homemaking do not aspire to top level jobs for which graduate study would be a prerequisite. Most women who enter employment after graduation and who continue to work after marriage see no need to acquire a graduate degree for a successful career, particularly if they find themselves in business or industry. Moreover, there are few professional fields in which substantial numbers of women are found where the opportunities for either employment or advancement depend heavily upon advanced study.

POTENTIAL ABILITY FOR HIGHER EDUCATION

The growing demand for college and university trained personnel in recent years has focused attention upon the nation's resources of individuals with the ability to pursue formal education beyond the high school level. All the available studies demonstrate that there is a substantial reservoir of young men and women intellectually capable of doing successful college and graduate work whose education stops with high school graduation, if not before.

There is certainly little reason to maintain categorically that everyone with the intellectual ability to graduate from college should go to college. Able individuals are needed for a wide range of occupations and functions for which college education and training are neither required nor essential. There is ground for contending that much of the value assigned to college study is a recognition of its worth for attaining social status rather than for developing potential ability. College study, moreover, is only one of several ways in which talents and abilities may be realized. Nevertheless, formal education is the major instrument through which potential ability is developed, and from this point of view the undereducation of those capable of advanced schooling is a measure of wasted ability and talent.

Various investigations have estimated the extent to which potential ability fails to be developed by formal schooling at the high school as well as at the college level. In *Who Should Go to College?* Byron S. Hollinshead estimates that of the boys and girls who score in the top 25 percent in intelligence, almost one fifth do not graduate from high school; two fifths graduate from high school but do not go to college; and only two fifths enter college. Of the young people who attain an Army General Classification Test score of 120, which is equivalent to the intelligence score of the average college graduate, more than 60 percent now do not complete college. Almost all the young people who score in the top 5 percent in intelligence—and are, therefore, considered capable of earning a Ph.D. degree—complete high school, but only about half of them, according to Dael Wolfle, graduate from college. Less than 2 percent of them secure a doctoral degree.

Most investigators agree that about the same proportions of individuals of high ability are found among the members of each sex. Variations between the sexes in intelligence or aptitude test scores are ascribed, as has been seen, not to innate differences but to cultural and motivational factors. A slightly larger proportion of girls than boys capable of doing college work—those with an AGCT score of 120 or over—graduate from high school; of this group, half of the boys, but only one fourth of the girls, enter and graduate from college. Among those with the intellectual ability to earn a doctoral degree, 37 percent of the girls, in contrast to 55 percent of the boys, graduate from college. In this high ability group, one out of 30 men and one out of 300 women actually earn a Ph.D. degree. Among college graduates who are capable of earning a doctoral degree, about 6 percent of the men but only 1 percent of the women do so. Young women probably account for about three out of five of those who have the ability to graduate from college but do not, and for slightly over half of those who could obtain a doctoral degree but do not.

Much attention has understandably been directed to economic reasons in explaining why so many individuals with high ability fail to continue their education beyond the high school level. The evidence is clear that in the absence of economic barriers many more able young people would continue with their formal education. An increase in scholarships providing substantial financial assistance would no doubt enable a significant number of capable young men and women to attend college who today cannot afford to do so. The *Fifth Annual Report of the National Science Foundation* observes that "a total of from 60,000 to 100,000 seniors have the ability and the desire to go to college, but will not do so. Presumably, if financial support were available, many of this group could be salvaged for higher education."

The Educational Testing Service study cited in Chapter VI indicated that scholarship aid can be effective not only in encouraging able students to go to college, but also in inducing them to study in a particular field. It is interesting to note, however, that scholarship aid contingent on a willingness to study in one of the physical or natural sciences seems to be less of an inducement to girls than boys. Financial assistance appears to be more influential with girls when the fields in which they would have to major, in order to secure scholarship aid, are those in which college women normally concentrate—that is, the liberal arts, the fine arts, and education.

There is reason to believe that even if generous scholarship aid were offered to all able young people who do not go to college, a substantial proportion of them would not be induced to do so. For a variety of individual and social reasons, the motivation to do well in high school or to go on to college is lacking in many potentially able young people. Girls are better motivated to achieve good grades in high school than boys, as has been seen, and boys and girls in families at the top of the educational and occupational scale behave very much alike with respect to college attendance. In families at the lower end of the educational and occupational scale, however, able girls are even less interested than boys in going to college.

OTHER FORMS OF POST-HIGH SCHOOL EDUCATION

Full-time regular college and university enrollments represent only part of the entire post-high school student population of the United States. There are, to begin with, summer session students, many, but far from all, of whom are full-time students during the academic year. In addition, there are the part-time, extension, and correspondence students enrolled in college and university programs. Their number has come to about one million in recent years. Another large and rapidly growing group of post-high school students attend junior and community colleges. The American Association of Junior Colleges reported full-time enrollments of 276,000 in 1955. Junior and community colleges also have "adult," "special," correspondence, and other groups of part-time students, many of whom are not high school graduates, and their total student population was estimated at nearly 700,000 in 1955. Technical institutes of various kinds frequently resemble junior and community colleges. In 1955-56, there were over 31,000 full-time and an additional 36,000 part-time students enrolled in the technical institutes covered in the annual survey conducted by Dean Leo Smith of the Rochester Institute of Technology. There are also a number of schools maintained by trade groups, such as the American Banking Association, which provide specialized occupational training. However, no over-all data are available on them. Correspondence schools may be regarded as still another form of post-high school education, even though it is not known how many of their students are high school graduates and to what extent the students take courses above the secondary school level. The number of correspondence school students may be estimated at over one million, with almost one fifth being enrolled in courses conducted by universities.

Information about the many opportunities and facilities for post-high school education and training which are not strictly "collegiate" in character is either fragmentary, outdated, or unreliable. Consequently, it is almost impossible to specify their significance for the education of women or to delineate precisely the ways in which men and women make use of them. There are, however, many indications of differences between the sexes in this large and as yet unmapped area of post-high school education.

The junior and community colleges offer young men and women an opportunity to continue their education beyond high school at a much lower total cost than is involved in attending an out-of-town, traditional four-year college. They also represent an attempt to build a new kind of two-year terminal education, and an expansion of the facilities of publicly-supported education. Most of these institutions, particularly the newer community colleges, are decisively oriented toward the occupational interests and needs of both their student bodies and local industries. The public junior college has flourished particularly in California, but many other states, Texas and New York among them, have allocated a significant share of their educational expenditures to them. New, ambitious programs for public, junior, and community colleges are under way in Florida, Mississippi, Iowa, Ohio, North Carolina, and other states.

Young women account for approximately the same proportion of total enrollments in junior and community colleges as in four-year colleges. There are about seventy separate women's junior colleges, mainly in the northeastern and southern states, but almost all of the publicly controlled and the majority of the private institutions are coeducational.

While there are no data on the distribution of students among fields of study by sex, it appears that the curricula of many schools are specially geared to the vocational needs of young women. Training for semiprofessional and office, clerical, and technicians' occupations, in which women are heavily represented, is provided by many junior and community colleges. In California, for example, where special programs are offered in secretarial work and practical nursing, a majority of students in some junior colleges are women. The extent to which these institutions serve adults is indicated by their many part-time students. It is also suggested by the fact that the average age of the student body of one junior college in California is almost 30. In that state in 1952, according to a National Education Association survey, there were about a quarter of a million students participating in junior college adult education programs, half of whom were women. Among the women, 15 percent were housewives.

The student body of technical institutes is overwhelmingly male. In 1953-54, the last year for which data are available, women made up only 13 percent of all full-time students in the 60 institutes included in the annual survey. Eighty percent of the women were enrolled in the state and municipal institutes in New York, while the Rochester Institute of Technology accounted for another 10 percent. Most women pursue courses in fashion design, beauty culture, dental hygiene, and office occupations, and relatively few women follow programs of study in industrial or technological fields.

A variety of schools which do not grant degrees also train both younger and older students for "women's" occupations in the health and other fields. Most student nurses, for example, are trained in hospital and other non-degree granting schools. Practical nurse training has in recent years been offered in almost 300 programs approved by state agencies or the National Association of Practical Nurse Education and conducted by public schools and other institutions. Several programs also specialize in training medical technicians. Note should be taken of the many private secretarial and business schools—about 1500—which offer post-high school instruction, and of the other kinds of proprietary vocational schools in which an unknown number of women are enrolled.

The fragmentary data available on correspondence schooling indicate that women constitute an important segment of the total student body. Housewives preparing to return to work are apparently well represented among women students. In one school with an enrollment of 120,000 in 1956, more than half the students were women, of whom nearly 75 percent were under 25, 35 percent were employed, and 65 percent were housewives. In this school, the "high school" program was most popular with women students, and those enrolled in it showed a particular interest in homemaking, commercial, and retail merchandising courses. Other courses for which women showed a preference provide training for office and clerical jobs.

The return to employment of married women with professional training, for teaching and nursing in particular, has been facilitated by special training and refresher courses. In the case of nonprofessional occupations, this is a responsibility carried by a vast array of vocational training facilities. Adult vocational training, conducted under both public and private auspices in classrooms and on the job, is of special moment to the many women who want to return to work in later life but who lack specialized skills. How many women are participating in such training, to what extent it serves their needs, what role it plays in lifting the skill level of the society, and what bearing it has upon the existing structure of women's employment are all questions which invite study.

THE CONTINUING DEBATE

The women's colleges were founded as part of the larger movement for equal rights for women and out of a need for education and training which was not centered on homemaking functions. There were, however, early critics who took them to task for modeling themselves after the men's colleges in purpose and curriculum and, therefore, for educating women as if they were men. Since then, the purposes and the content of women's college education have been subjects of controversy. The search for an "ideal" college education for women will, of course, continue, but it will not be made easier by the likelihood that more women, as the Commission on the Education of Women has observed, will lead more "complex lives" in the future, "encompassing homemaking, gainful employment, and community service."

In recent years, the proponents of a broad liberal arts education have maintained that it provides the best foundation for individual self-development and, therefore, for meeting the challenges of homemaking, paid employment, and citizenship. Neither the training designed to serve vocational goals alone, nor that shaped to prepare women for their unique functions as wives and mothers, it has been argued, adequately recognizes the extent to which adult women participate in different, if not competing, spheres of activity. A special claim is made for the women's liberal arts colleges on the ground that their students do not compete with men for leadership positions in the college community, and therefore, have richer opportunities to prepare for responsible leadership in adult life.

The liberal arts program of education, however, has been charged with several weaknesses. Some of its critics have asserted that, in seeking to prepare young women for all patterns of adult life by stressing their individual self-development, it establishes a goal which cannot be realized. There is, of course, considerable evidence that some liberal arts graduates have found their education severely inadequate in the light of subsequent experiences both in marriage and in paid employment. Whether or not such evidence should be taken as compelling proof that a liberal arts education cannot possibly serve the needs of most women who continue their education beyond secondary school is, of course, another matter.

Other critics have found a liberal arts program lacking because it does not develop in young women a positive motivation toward paid employment, even though it may provide them with some of the knowledge and skills essential for an occupation. The extent to which women are found in college programs which are primarily, if not exclusively, vocationally oriented demonstrates that the liberal arts colleges do not provide the occupational training—whether for short-run employment or a continuing career—which increasing numbers of young women have come to desire.

In spite of modifications in their content, which represent an adjustment to demands for more directly "practical" courses, liberal arts programs still express a belief in the value of an educational experience built upon the needs, capacities, and values which are common to men and women alike. From this point of view, the severest critics of the liberal arts philosophy have been those whom Mirra Komarovsky has identified as "neo-anti-feminists." While rejecting any imputation of inferiority to women, this group insists upon the importance of the differences between them and men, and, therefore, would construct a college education for women based upon distinctively feminine abilities, interests, and functions. One forceful exponent of these views, Lynn White, has called for a curriculum which emphasizes courses of study "dealing with the institution of the family and all that contributes to its well-being through food, beauty and warmth, shelter and security." Some of those who have urged the value of a distinctively "feminine higher education" have maintained that to educate women through a program of study designed for the needs of men is to lay the basis for frustrations in adult life.

The advocates of an educational philosophy which emphasizes homemaking functions are in turn criticized by those who would encourage more professional training among women. The need for this development, they contend, is demonstrated, on the one hand, by the new place of work in women's lives, and on the other, by the society's needs for more highly trained workers. In addition, the economic role of women both within and outside the home has stimulated proposals for changes in the collegiate education of women which call for still a different emphasis. It has been argued by Louis William Norris, for example, that their education should have the effect of encouraging women who want to enter paid employment "to choose work as a means of self-expression and personal enrichment" for themselves and their families, rather than for material gains alone, and to consider what their unique contributions as workers might be. He would also have their education encourage women to make decisions as consumers and investors more effectively and with greater recognition of the consequences, both for their families and the economy, which flow from these responsibilities.

These and still other approaches taken toward the higher education of women in recent years testify to the variety of needs which formal education is called upon to fulfill. They suggest, moreover, that the search for a single educational format which will serve equally well to prepare women for three spheres of activity —the home, paid employment, and the community—may well be self-defeating. A single or dominant mode of education was to be expected when college study was, for practical purposes, the privilege of only a small and more or less homogeneous group of young women. Today, the group which continues formal education beyond high school, while still a minority, is much larger and more diverse in composition. The patterns of women's lives have changed, as have the reasons why young women attend college. These and other developments have been reflected in the growing variety of institutions, programs of study, and purposes which mark the higher education of women. This diversity underscores the plenitude of the facilities and the opportunities for higher education, but obviously makes it difficult to characterize women's college education in simple and precise terms, and it means that the college diploma symbolizes a variety of accomplishments.

CURRENT PROBLEM AREAS

The continuing problem of where the emphasis in women's post-high school education should fall has been both transformed and complicated by the emergence of new issues. How much of the responsibility for the vocational training of women now carried by four-year colleges may be assumed in the future by junior and community colleges is one which has been raised but not yet thoroughly investigated. The rapid growth of these institutions may be viewed as a response to the need for some form of intermediate education between high school and college, which could serve as a bridge to the latter for some, but could also provide highly practical, terminal education for others. For many occupations in which women are well represented, one or two years of post-high school study is adequate preparation, and such training is emphasized in the curricula of junior and community colleges. These institutions have also developed new curricula which have helped to give semiprofessional status to certain occupations. There is good reason to expect a more rapid expansion of junior and community colleges in the future, but it is hard to predict what consequence this will have for four-year college attendance and graduation among young women.

Another new problem area has emerged in connection with the possibilities for undertaking college education later in life. For some time, college attendance has not been narrowly confined to the 18 to 22 year age span. The educational benefits extended to veterans meant a departure from convention at the upper end of this age range, and there is now a conscious effort being made to regularize the admission of able young people to college at 16. The growth of college and university programs of study specially geared to the interests and time schedules of adults has made college attendance and graduation in the later twenties and thirties a commonplace occurrence. How much more can be done to facilitate college attendance by more mature men and women remains to be seen. Meanwhile, some institutions, among them Columbia University's School of General Studies, have already begun to explore what might be done by taking into account the experiences which adult students have had outside the classroom as a basis for experimenting with greater flexibility in programs of study and years of attendance required.

Manpower objectives and changing employment opportunities have given fresh emphasis to two areas of concern. One involves the encouragement of a larger proportion of able young women to undertake undergraduate and graduate study. The second turns on the possibility of reducing, at least to some degree, the tendency of women to concentrate in a few traditional fields of study. The high demand for scientific and professional workers in particular has prompted suggestions for encouraging more young women to specialize in physical science fields in which they are now poorly represented. The point has already been made that altering traditional patterns of choice among fields of study depends upon far more than the existence of new job opportunities. It involves changes in dominant ideas about suitable work for women, in employment practices, and in the way in which young women are guided while in high school and college in planning for the future, and in making decisions about courses of study.

The expansion in the employment of married women whose children are of school age, and the consequent combining of work with homemaking functions, have obviously raised new guidance and counseling problems. Many women would benefit if they could plan their education with an eye not only to marriage and employment early in life, but also to possible reentry into the labor market later on. Conceivably, such planning might also make it easier to tap the reservoir of ability among married women whose family circumstances permit them to return to work.

The point is made in Chapter XI that it is difficult to do much more at the high school and college level than to establish an awareness and an understanding of the varied kinds of adult lives which women now lead and will be likely to lead in the future. Whether much more than this can be done through early guidance and counseling to help those women who, after a dozen or more years of preoccupation with home and family, may desire to go to work, is an open question. It may not be feasible to attempt to provide ways of helping such women with their educational and occupational problems until they reach the point in their lives when they are interested in and able to work outside the home.

In any case, it may be assumed that greater anticipation of a return to employment will to some degree influence decisions about courses of study and college attendance and completion. Because more and more married women are returning to work in their thirties, and the range of jobs open to them is constantly being broadened, young women in high school and college will be less likely to think about paid employment solely as a short interlude between the completion of schooling and the arrival of the first child. Teachers and guidance counselors can, of course, help create greater awareness of recent trends in women's employment and of their implications for educational decisions. An understanding of the educational experience in relation to an adult life which encompasses both the home and paid employment could have various consequences. It might lead some young women to decide to enter college; to complete their studies rather than drop out along the way; to be more deliberate about the subjects in which they major; to take their studies more seriously; or, finally, to make the added investment of going on to graduate school.

VIII. THE LABOR MARKET BEHAVIOR OF WOMEN

MEN AND WOMEN have very different employment experiences with respect to the amount and character of their work while they are still in school; the jobs they first enter after they leave school; their work experiences later in life; their earnings; and their advancement into higher-level jobs. Analysis of these differences illuminates such distinguishing features of women's employment as discontinuity in work, occupational concentration, and the return to the labor force of significant numbers of older married women.

Many of the differences between men and women in paid employment are well known, but the reasons for them continue to be debated. In part, the lack of agreement is the product of attempts to generalize about the behavior of all working women on the basis of what is known about specific groups. In part, it reflects the conflict between older assumptions about the abilities or characteristics peculiar to women and more recent views that challenge these assumptions. In spite of the intensive and valuable research of recent years, key aspects of the labor market behavior of both men and women are not yet adequately understood.

INITIAL WORK EXPERIENCE OF MEN AND WOMEN

The part-time and temporary employment of boys and girls while they are still in school offers a preview of many features of their later behavior in the labor force. Like their elders, high school boys are far more likely to be employed than high school girls. Thus, in October, 1955, among 16- and 17-year-old students, one fifth of the girls and nearly two fifths of the boys were in the labor force. These boys worked much longer hours than the girls. Among older students, young men were also about twice as likely to work as women, and they, too, tended to work longer hours. There is, consequently, some correspondence with the adult pattern, for most men are full-time workers, and part-time work is common among the minority of women who are in the labor force.

The occupations of girl students mirror to some extent the distinctive activities of women in the home and in the labor market. Among high school student workers, about half the girls, compared to only 12 percent of the boys, held domestic or other service jobs, including baby-sitting. About one tenth of the girls, but hardly any boys, were in clerical jobs. On the other hand, over one fourth of the boys, but very few girls, were laborers, operatives, and craftsmen. Among older students, over 40 percent of the women students, but only 16 percent of the men, held clerical jobs; hardly any women, but nearly 40 percent of the men, were operatives, laborers, or craftsmen.

Concentration in relatively few fields is characteristic of the initial employment of women, just as it is of their fields of study in high school and college. Currently, about 45 precent of all girls, compared to about 30 percent of all boys, terminate their formal education with high school graduation. Over two fifths of these girls have followed clerical or commercial curricula and about three fifths of those who enter employment secure clerical jobs. Even among girls who do not graduate from high school—who currently account for about 40 percent of all girls—over one fourth of those who enter employment find clerical jobs. Jobs in this field are held by about one half of the girls who have some post-high school education, but do not graduate from college, and by about 15 percent of the college graduates. The types of jobs held by girls who enter clerical work vary significantly with their education. Thus, about 25 percent of those with less than a high school education, 40 percent of the high school graduates, and over 60 percent of the college graduates are employed as secretaries, stenographers, and typists.

Only 10 percent of all women complete college, and another 6 percent secure some education beyond high school. Among those who seek employment, the large majority of the first group and a large minority of the second enter professional and related occupations, especially teaching. A recent survey of employed women college graduates some six months after graduation revealed that more than 60 percent of them were teaching, although less than 40 percent held degrees in education. Many women with degrees in other fields qualified themselves for teaching by including education courses in their programs. Another 20 percent entered other professional and related occupations as nurses, recreation and social workers, biological technicians, home economists, copywriters and reporters, etc. Of the women who enter employment with some post-high school education, but without a college degree, about 30 percent enter professional or related occupations, most of them as teachers, nurses, and medical technicians. Less than 10 percent of girl high school graduates enter these occupations, most of them as student nurses.

Among the young women who graduate from high school, who have some education beyond high school, or who graduate from college, no less than 70 percent and as many as 95 percent are found in clerical, professional, and semiprofessional occupations. On the other hand, these occupational fields account for only 30 percent of the girls who do not graduate from high school. Of the non-high school graduates, about one fourth work on farms, and successively smaller proportions become operatives, especially in light manufacturing; service workers, especially waitresses and counter girls; private household servants; and sales workers. Except for farming, a similar range of jobs attracts those high school graduates who do not become clerical, professional, or similar workers. Almost all the young women who have some college education and who do not enter clerical, professional or semi-professional work, are found in service and sales jobs.

At each educational level, the types of jobs secured by young men and women differ, and, except for those who do not finish high school, men are found in a wider range of occupations than women. Among college graduates, for instance, 60 percent of the men, compared to 80 percent of the women, enter the professions. The largest single group of men enter engineering, but they represent less than 25 percent of the graduates. Moreover, the degree of specialization by men within engineering and most of the other professions is considerable. Most of the remaining men become clerical workers, salesmen, or proprietors and managers. Few women college graduates, on the other hand, become managers or enter sales occupations.

Among the men who have some post-high school education but do not complete college, nearly 20 percent enter clerical work, and smaller but still significant proportions become sales workers, semiprofessional workers, operatives, and craftsmen and foremen. Among boys who go to work after high school, those who become semiskilled operatives comprise the largest single group, but they account for only one fourth of the total. The rest find employment as clerical, farm, skilled, unskilled, and sales workers, in that order. Only among those who do not graduate from high school is a greater degree of concentration found among boys than girls, for one third of these boys are in farm work, one fourth become operatives, and one fifth become unskilled laborers.

THE EARNINGS OF MEN AND WOMEN WORKERS

Women workers are concentrated at the lower end of the income scale. In recent years, their median annual income from wages and salaries has been well under half that of men. There is a widespread conviction that women are generally paid less than men for similar work. An important reason for the lower median income of employed women, however, is that a far greater proportion of them than of men works part time or part of the year. For instance, the median wage and salary income of women who were employees sometime in the course of 1955 came to only 38 percent of that of men. However, among full-time workers—those employed no less than 50 weeks during the year and working 35 or more hours in most of these weeks—the median wage and salary income of women was almost two thirds that of men. The Bureau of Labor Statistics reports that the hourly earnings of women production workers in manufacturing average about 70 percent of the earnings of men production workers.

Most of the remaining differential can be attributed to the fact that men and women are employed in different kinds of jobs, and that wages are generally higher in the jobs that men hold. It has been maintained that the pay differential between "men's" and "women's" jobs is the result of the lower level of skill and responsibility required in most women's jobs. So many factors affect wage rates, however, that it would be almost impossible to prove or disprove this assertion. It is true, of course, that women tend to be employed in such low paying jobs as assembler, machine operator, and clerical worker, while men tend to be employed as mechanics, craftsmen, and supervisors.

In the past, it was clear that men received much higher wages than women for comparable work. One study before World War I found that women with apparently the same skill and experience worked for half the wages of men, although even then it was almost impossible to find men and women in closely comparable jobs. Such wage differentials were largely taken for granted on the ground that most women worked only temporarily for "pin money" or, at most, to support themselves, while men worked to support their families. The wage differential was apparently great enough to encourage employers to substitute women for men in many cases, especially in manufacturing, if women could do the work adequately.

Because they are rarely utilized interchangeably, it is almost impossible to determine statistically whether men and women now receive the same pay when they are doing comparable work. A recent study by the Bureau of Labor Statistics of earnings in the machinery industry found few cases where men and women held the same job title in the same plant. Matching workers as closely as possible, the study found that women's earnings averaged from 95 to 99 percent of men's earnings on jobs paid on an hourly basis. On incentive or piece rates, women's earnings averaged from 88 to 99 percent of men's. It was believed that even these differences were due in part to actual differences in the jobs performed by men and women, even though their job titles were identical.

There is evidence that women are sometimes paid less for essentially the same work. It is common, although far from universal, for men to receive higher wages than women in entry jobs in manufacturing. Sometimes this difference reflects the higher physical strength requirements of the men's jobs. However, since entry jobs usually involve no special skills, men may, in some instances, be receiving a higher wage solely by virtue of their sex.

Occasionally, explicit differentials for similar work are maintained at higher-level jobs as well. Overt differentials, however, are becoming increasingly rare. Most unions oppose separate pay schedules on principle, even though they are occasionally provided for in union-management contracts. The growth of job evaluation systems, which stress the function performed rather than the worker, has reduced the use of separate pay scales. It is charged, however, that some systems give undue importance to manual effort in setting the wage rate, thereby favoring men over women.

Women are more likely to receive lower pay than men in very

small establishments, or where salaries are set informally, than where pay scales are determined by union-management contract, civil service regulation, or other formal procedures. Separate pay scales for men and women teachers have disappeared in most places, although teachers in some communities receive higher pay if they have dependents, and this practice tends to favor men over women. The Federal civil service has followed the principle of equal pay for equal work since 1923. Sixteen states and Alaska have adopted laws prohibiting discrimination in pay on the basis of sex, but, as Chapter XII indicates, the practical effects of such legislation are not clear.

Frequently, a woman performing the same job functions as a man is given neither the same job title nor the same wage. It has been asserted that women are sometimes used exclusively in certain occupations and men in others in order to maintain differences in pay levels. Occasionally, women are substituted for men at the same pay, on the grounds that women as a group are better qualified. If women obtained at the same rates as men are actually better workers, there is in effect a wage differential.

ABILITIES AND TRAITS OF MEN AND WOMEN WORKERS

It has been noted in earlier chapters that women are hired for some jobs but not for others because both employers and employees hold certain views about where women should and should not work. These views are generally supported by assertions that men and women differ in ways which affect their job performance. It is frequently stated, for instance, that women do not have as much mechanical ability as men, but that they have greater manual dexterity; that they are more emotional and unstable, but that they are admirably adapted to routine or detailed work. Many of these judgments are based on opinion rather than careful investigation, but their wide acceptance strongly influences the occupational distribution of women.

In the leading study of physical differences between men and women relevant to their suitability for work,[1] Professor Anna Baetjer concluded, on the basis of data from World War II and earlier, that:

Women are on the average only 85 percent as heavy as men and have only about 60 percent as much physical strength. Therefore, they cannot lift or hold as heavy weights, they cannot direct as much weight or strength to the pushing or pulling of loads and their grip is not as strong.

Women are built on a smaller anatomical scale than men, their standing and sitting height, arm length and size of hands and feet all being smaller. Because of this, machines built to the scale of men often require excessive reaching or stretching on the part of women and the height of the work bench is often unsuitable.

Such differences are clearly relevant in some industrial or manual jobs, but strength is seldom necessary in many industrial, service, and other occupations. Size and physical strength are steadily becoming less important as an advancing technology provides substitutes for human muscle and as the proportion of the labor force employed at unskilled labor declines. Dr. Baetjer also observes that:

The fact that women are less strong than men does not necessarily imply that they will fatigue more easily except on jobs requiring heavy physical labor. In most occupations today, the type of fatigue which is associated with a decrease in production ability is due chiefly to changes in the nervous system or to psychological states rather than to chemical changes in the muscles or blood. Women may fatigue more rapidly than men but this is probably due partly to a lack of background training in industrial work and, chiefly, to the fact that they usually have household duties and responsibilities which require many hours of work in addition to those spent in industry.

Employers frequently declare that men, or women, as the case may be, have greater aptitudes for specific kinds of work, but it is not clear whether they have firm evidence to support such

[1] Anna M. Baetjer, *Women in Industry: Their Health and Efficiency*, Philadelphia, 1946.

contentions. A recent review of industrial studies of aptitude test results, prepared for the U.S. Bureau of Naval Personnel, concluded that "in normal times most civilian jobs are held predominantly by members of one sex or the other, and hence the practical problem of the influence of sex differences on predictive measures of aptitudes has not been investigated to any extent by those who are conducting personnel research in industry."

Ability to perform is closely related to general intelligence, and decades of investigation by psychologists have made it clear that there is little, if any, difference between men and women in general intelligence. Girls and women usually score somewhat higher than boys and men on tests of verbal and clerical aptitudes, but do less well on tests of mechanical and computational aptitudes. These differences do not seem to be sex-linked, but are apparently the product of differences in background, interest, and experience. There is some scattered evidence, moreover, that women studying mechanical and technical subjects receive better grades than men who score equally well on aptitude tests. This has been the experience of the U.S. Air Force and the British armed forces.

Whether women also do better on the job than men with equal aptitude test scores is not clear. One study of women in the British armed services indicated that they do. A study of the performance of inexperienced men and women as lathe operators during World War II, reported by the Women's Bureau of the U.S. Department of Labor, found little difference between them. Aside from certain physical limitations of women workers, the sole difference appeared to be that "training time, including time for general orientation to the machines and shop environment, may be a little longer for women than for men. However, this difference relates primarily to acquired characteristics and not to a basic difference in learning capacity between men and women. It arises out of such considerations as acquaintance with industrial surroundings, and knowledge of machines, mechanical processes and tools, and the technical vocabulary of the machine shop."

Such demonstrated average differences as exist between the physical attributes, intelligence, and aptitudes of men and women have limited relevance, since men and women are not generally assigned to the same work. The point need hardly be made that some women are larger and stronger than some men, and that many women have greater mechanical and computational skills than most men. Variations in average ability and aptitude might help to explain why differing proportions of men and women are employed in various occupations, but not why so many jobs are filled almost entirely by persons of one sex.

Nevertheless, employers report greater aptitude on the part of men or women for certain jobs. In particular situations and at specified wage rates, employers may be able to hire women who have greater aptitude for a job than can be found among men seeking work. But this reflects the different interests and employment opportunities of men and women rather than their aptitudes.

It is often said that women have difficulty making decisions; that they are conscientious about details; or that they perform well in routine, repetitive jobs. These and other alleged personality traits are frequently cited by employers to explain why they use women in some jobs and men in others. Such differences between the sexes are often considered to be innate, but, to the extent that they exist, it seems more accurate to regard them as motivational differences arising from different influences and experiences throughout their lives.

Very little is known about such motivational differences, and only tangential evidence is available. Women show a greater tendency to be absent from work than men. This higher rate of absenteeism has been assumed to reflect a higher incidence of illness, but more careful analysis suggests that it is due to differ-

ent attitudes toward illness and toward performing one's accustomed functions.

Dr. Anna Baetjer, in her exhaustive study, concludes that:

There can be no doubt that women have a much higher sickness
rate than men and lose more time from work as a result of this. . . .
The greater incidence of illness among women as compared with men
occurs at all ages from fifteen to sixty-four years, among those not
employed as well as those who are employed and among women and
men in various occupations. The sickness rate of women is greater for
the majority of the diseases common to both sexes (with a few notable
exceptions), for both acute and chronic diseases and for illnesses caus-
ing disabilities of all durations from 1 day to 1 year. This excess illness
has been observed during years of war and depression as well as during more stable years, and in Great Britain as well as in this country.

Although women report themselves as ill more frequently than
men, there is no reason to believe that they are more susceptible
to disease. The mortality rate for males exceeds that for females
at all ages. The wartime hospitalization rate for WACS was about
the same as for male personnel. Dr. Baetjer indicates that the
higher rate of absences among women

may be due merely to the fact that women take their minor illnesses
more seriously than men. This is supported by the fact that the average
duration of sick-absences is shorter for women than men. Many persons
believe that the excess sick-absenteeism among industrial women is due
to the fact that they frequently attempt to do two jobs at once, their
work in industry plus their duties at home, which may demand heavy
labor, worry and interference with proper rest. Part of the excess absenteeism among women may be due to a less serious attitude toward
their work, so that they take time off for minor ailments or report un-
justified absences as due to sickness more frequently than men.

Fragmentary reports indicate that there may be significant differences in absentee rates due to menstruation and illness among
women in white collar and manual work, older and younger wom-
en, and women from different racial and ethnic groups. This suggests that there are also important differences among women in
their response to physical discomfort or ill-health.

THE PROBLEM OF COMPARATIVE LABOR COSTS

It is frequently asserted that female labor is cheaper than male labor, and employers have often been accused of substituting women for men in order to cut costs. Employers generally deny this charge, and, moreover, frequently maintain that they cannot afford to use women in particular positions. At times, the employment of women does entail added costs. When women are hired for the first time, it may be necessary to provide separate rest room and other facilities, to provide cleaner, more agreeable working conditions, or to employ a few extra men to handle occasional heavy tasks. Such additional costs to the employer, however, are minor in the few cases where they occur.

Many employers state that they do not want to employ women for some jobs because they are likely to quit after an investment has been made in their training. It is significant that in two of the most important occupations for women—clerical work and teaching—new workers must have acquired their basic skills before starting to work and employers provide little additional training. On the other hand, male high school graduates are commonly hired on the basis of their general qualifications and trained on the job. Many men college graduates are hired on a similar basis, and even those with professional training, such as engineers, are frequently not considered fully qualified until they receive additional training after they are employed. Since training is closely associated with opportunities to advance, the question of whether or not an investment in the training of women is likely to be wasted will be discussed later in connection with the problem of their opportunities to advance.

On the basis of the existing evidence, it cannot be asserted that women generally constitute a cheap source of labor as compared with men. As far as can be seen, employers do not hire women for particular jobs because of differences in wage costs alone. The employment of women, as of men, always depends upon many other factors. Thus, the relative productivity of men and women in particular jobs has a bearing on the decision to hire one or the other whether or not their wages are the same. Women may not have the skills, interest, and other qualities necessary to perform at a high level of effectiveness in some jobs, even though they might be willing to work at them, and the same may be true for men in other jobs. For both men and women, possession of the required skills, interest, and other qualities is frequently directly related to the value they place upon particular jobs and working conditions, as well as upon work in general.

In some cases, relative wage rates appear to have a direct influence on the hiring of men or women. Because employers are often reluctant to hire women for many positions, a woman may be forced to accept a lower wage if she is to obtain the job she wants. Several studies indicate that the female labor force in small communities may increase rapidly when new enterprises move in. This suggests that the presence of a potential supply of women willing to work when the opportunity appears may have a depressing effect upon women's wage rates. This may help to explain why many manufacturing plants operating on narrow profit margins are set up in rural areas or small towns.

CULTURAL DETERMINANTS OF "MEN'S" AND "WOMEN'S" JOBS

More often than not, conventional notions of what activities or tasks may be appropriately performed by each sex explain why some jobs are "men's" and others are "women's." The assignment of sex labels to jobs is part of a universal tendency to give sex labels to a wide range of activities and objects, such as games, social events, clothing, and machinery, as well as institutions, mental and emotional traits, physical characteristics, and the like. Comparisons between different cultures, between groups within a particular culture, or between different periods in the history of a single culture reveal that items having a masculine or feminine or neuter designation in one instance, are often differently labeled in others. Thus, there are societies where singing and dancing are masculine, and work, in the economic sense, is feminine, and others in which the reverse is true.

The concentration of women within a much narrower range of jobs and the division of jobs into "men's" and "women's" have been repeatedly emphasized as outstanding characteristics of the labor market for women. Indeed, the extent to which many jobs are differentiated according to the sex of the employee tends to be obscured by the available statistical data. Sex labels are applied to most jobs in every occupational group, but they are not always consistently applied. The same job may be considered male in one region, city, company, plant, or department, and female in another. Although the label tends to be viewed as permanent, women are sometimes substituted for men without apparent difficulty. When this happens, the new sex label tends to be as firmly attached to the job as the old one. In some work situations, men and women employees are segregated, and departments as well as jobs carry sex labels. In others, men and women work side by side, but at different jobs. Even when men and women fill apparently similar jobs, the situation in which they find themselves may not be the same. A man may work at a clerical job in order to gain a minimum of experience for promotion, but the woman who holds such a job is likely to stay in it. In some occupations and places of employment, of course, sex labels are not applied, and even where sex distinctions are maintained, they are occasionally ignored.

Sex labeling has a major influence on the distribution of jobs between men and women. Employers hire persons of the sex supposedly possessing the characteristics considered necessary for effective job performance. Once a job is performed by members of one sex, for this or other reasons, its sex label tends to persist. It has been maintained that men are frequently hostile to the introduction of women into "men's" jobs because they feel that if women can do the work, its value will be diminished. Both as employers and workers, men are in a position to act upon such feelings to exclude women from certain jobs. Another reason for the persistence of sex labels is that a job may develop in such a way that its assignment to members of one sex becomes particularly appropriate. For example, because men perform a particular job, new machines may be designed so that it requires considerable manual effort and so-called "dirty" work, thus insuring that the job will continue to be done by men.

Open positions tend to be filled by replacements not only of the same sex as the existing work force, but also of the same color, nationality, social origin, and approximate age. Since the most usual method of locating a job is through information from friends who work where the vacancy exists, workers tend to "reproduce" themselves. Employers are not likely to introduce new workers who might not be acceptable to the old work force. So long as the flow of replacements is adequate and the basic characteristics of a job remain stable, new workers are not likely to differ in any major respect from those already employed.

Growth in the employment of women appears to have been accomplished more through increased employment in occupations held by women and by the emergence of new "women's" occupations than through the entrance of women into occupations formerly considered exclusively male. Nevertheless, women have entered some traditionally male fields, and the sex labels of jobs do change in response to manpower shortages, technological alterations, or for other reasons. The shift from men to women workers requires a certain willingness to accept the new workers on the part of all concerned—the existing work force, employers, and customers. The extent to which the members of different socioeconomic or occupational groups are willing to accept women in new jobs varies enormously. Employers have encountered both surprising acceptance and unexpected resistance when they have attempted to introduce women into "men's" jobs. The resistances appear to be strongest in occupations where job status is significant, as well as where new women workers are thought to represent a direct threat to the job security of men.

The willingness of employers to make the change is crucial, for, even when faced with manpower shortages, they almost always have alternatives to hiring women, which include modifying hiring standards or changing production methods, products, or materials. During the Korean conflict, for instance, when the supply of male workers in a suburban area was exhausted, rather than employ women, one manufacturer went to great lengths to get permission from the government to increase his wage rates and to offer extensive overtime work in order to attract men from other parts of the metropolitan area.

When an industrial plant has difficulty meeting its manpower requirements, adjustments involving the subdivision of functions frequently take place. Either men or women may be hired for the new jobs, depending on the nature of the work and labor market conditions. If there is a significant reorganization in work patterns because more women are employed, it may also be necessary to increase the number of supervisory personnel. In responding to manpower shortages, new machinery and equipment may be developed, possibly less versatile, but more automatic, and the presence of women in the work force may, of course, influence the nature of changes in technology.

In young, rapidly expanding firms in new industries, where manpower shortages are most likely to occur, conditions may change so rapidly that a division of jobs according to sex does not become firmly fixed. Even in old industries, the sex designations of jobs may be changed rather easily when plants are established in new localities. New plants also afford an opportunity to introduce changes in working methods or machinery that would not be profitable or would meet with strong resistance in older ones. Among the many factors which influence the location of new plants—such as the costs of materials, labor, transportation, and taxes—the possibility of tapping a potential supply of women workers may be an important or a trivial consideration. Industries or firms in which the work force is contracting, or even growing slowly, frequently offer relatively low salaries and provide limited advancement opportunities. They may, as a result, also face difficulties in recruiting employees, and, therefore, turn to women workers. The recent opening of opportunities for women in many banks and insurance companies may in part be traced to such conditions.

Managements may shift to the employment of women as a matter of preference even when they are not pressed by shortages of male personnel. Innovations in technology which reduce the skill or strength requirements of a job, for example, may facilitate, if not prompt, the employment of women. Changes in the nature of the consumer market may have similar consequences. The recognition of women's importance as purchasers has had a direct effect upon the employment of women in sales, demonstration, and advertising. Women are now commonly employed to sell men's shirts and other men's furnishings in department stores because it was found that women constituted a majority of the buyers of these items. Changes in the jobs open to women have also been influenced by the increasing acceptance of the principle of equality as the basis for hiring and promotion policies, not only in public employment but also in private enterprise.

OPPORTUNITIES FOR ADVANCEMENT

A distinctive aspect of women's employment, as has been noted, is the limited extent to which they are found in higher-level jobs. Until recently, employers gave little attention to promotion policies in their personnel planning. Even less thought was given to the problems involved in, or the gains realized from, the advancement of their women workers. Broadly speaking, employers' decisions about utilizing women workers for higher-level jobs have been shaped by conventional attitudes, which generally lead to decisions to promote men. Even in fields of employment where women predominate, as in teaching, the top positions tend to go to men.

It is commonly believed that women do not make good supervisors. Most men and many women probably prefer a man to a woman as a supervisor, for they are more accustomed to finding men in positions of authority over adults. It may be that because women exercise supervisory functions infrequently many of them are poorly prepared for and reluctant to assume them. Many companies, of course, successfully employ women as supervisors over other women. To a much smaller extent, women are given supervisory and executive responsibilities over men. Where they have been so utilized in private enterprises, government employment, and the armed services, and where there has been careful selection, adequate training, and support by their own superiors, women have demonstrated that they can supervise men or women effectively.

It would be a serious error, however, to explain the low occupational status of most women exclusively in terms of the reluctance of male employers to promote them. No person achieves a high position without wanting and preparing and working for it, and the evidence is strong that women are, on the whole, less desirous of and less well prepared for promotion than men. This situation results, in part, from the fact that most women workers divide their energy and interests between home and family on the one hand and work on the other. In part, it is to be traced to the fact that most women do not acquire as much seniority, experience, and skill as men because they do not have continuous work careers. Employers are reluctant to invest in their training, fearing that it may be wasted, although the grounds for this belief are frequently weak. Moreover, women appear to share with men most conventional notions about their own abilities and the kinds of positions they should fill.

Another factor which strongly affects the promotion of women to higher-level jobs is that, by and large, they tend to enter occupations which offer restricted opportunities for advancement. Women are not likely to be employed in those entry jobs which constitute the first step on a more or less well-defined route of promotion leading all the way to the top. Most college trained women, for instance, work as teachers, nurses, social workers, librarians, etc., for public or other nonprofit agencies, where promotion and income possibilities are limited for both men and women. Strict training and licensing regulations in the medical field set limits to the extent to which the range of a nurse's medical functions may be enlarged, no matter how much competence and skill she acquires through advanced study or experience. Supervision over practical nurses, nurses' aides, orderlies, and other registered nurses is the principal means for gaining promotion. In other professions, women may secure advancement into administrative jobs, but these opportunities are more likely to go to men.

The factory and service occupations which most women enter offer even less opportunity for advancement. In many manufacturing industries which employ large numbers of women production workers, jobs tend to be quite narrow in scope and workers have little opportunity to acquire the experience necessary to advance to a highly skilled job. In these and other industries women are not likely to be hired for jobs that equip a worker for promotion. In household-service occupations opportunities for advancement are, of course, negligible. The nonhousehold-service fields, on the other hand, are characterized by many small establishments in which there are few higher-level jobs.

There is a close connection between the concentration of women workers in jobs where promotion opportunities are rare, and the attitudes and behavior of both employers and women with respect to promotion. Many women do not expect to reach higher-level positions, either because they believe that opportunities are not available or because they do not wish to advance, and therefore do not prepare themselves for promotion. They appear to be more willing than men to accept jobs with limited opportunities for advancement. Employers who believe that women do not want to qualify for advancement, on the other hand, neither create promotion routes for women nor assign them to jobs which serve as training grounds for promotion.

Many women workers who remain employed for a considerable time, however, may advance some distance beyond their first job, and some of them go quite far. Generally, they follow a promotion system which is specific for women, and do not compete with men. In the largest single area of employment for young women, the clerical field, a girl who begins as a typist may advance to stenographer, become secretary to a group of junior executives, and finally, secretary to an executive. From this point on, her progress is likely to depend on that of her boss. If he moves up to a top position, she may become his executive secretary with a staff of her own and the power to make decisions, but usually in his name rather than her own. In some fields, such as publishing and advertising, an ambitious secretary with a good education has a chance to become an executive in her own right.

Opportunities for promotion are greater in some places, industries, firms, and occupational areas than in others. Federal and many state and local civil service regulations prescribe equal opportunity for advancement without regard to sex. Although such regulations may be evaded to some extent, and are partially vitiated by veterans' preference or other civil service provisions, the opportunities for advancement available to women are greater in public than in private employment. In part this is due to the fact that the latter generally offers better opportunities and higher salaries to men, thus reducing the number of able men available for government employment.

Women are likely to find the opportunities for promotion better where large numbers of women are employed. Employers may open up promotion opportunities to forestall discontent, to provide an incentive for improved performance, to induce women to undertake training, and to facilitate the recruitment of more able workers. Where the great majority of workers in a field are women, opportunities for promotion arise because there are few, if any, men qualified for higher-level jobs. Thus, almost all executive secretaries and head nurses are women because few men work as stenographers or floor nurses. With increasing numbers of women acting as first-line clerical supervisors, there are growing opportunities for them in higher supervisory posts. In almost every organization, however, a point is reached where further promotion would involve supervision of men. At this point, and sometimes even before, women are likely to be passed over in favor of men. The same consideration usually limits the promotion of women to top staff positions in personnel, training, and similar departments.

Sometimes the opportunities for advancement in a traditional woman's field expand, but men, rather than women, may benefit. In the social work and library fields, for instance, the number of workers is growing, greater emphasis is being placed on professional standards and university training, the number of administrative posts is increasing, and salaries are rising. These developments attract men, who tend to be hired for the better administrative positions. Indeed, it has been suggested that the best way for a man to insure his advancement is to prepare for a field of work in which most employees are women.

Sometimes, the special suitability of women for a particular position is unquestionable. There are far more women than men qualified by interest and training as food or women's fashion editors. In other cases, however, the association of women with a particular kind of top-level position seems to be another instance of conventional sex-labeling. Women have gained considerable acceptance in personnel work, although many are restricted to dealing with the women employees of their firms. Women are apparently gaining increasing acceptance in research in chemistry and biology. Some employers maintain that they are especially effective in consumer relations work, but others assert that they can use women in advanced positions only where they do not come into direct contact with customers. Women have a much better chance of gaining responsible staff than executive or supervisory positions, partly because of the widespread belief that they are conscientious and careful with detail and so make good assistants or researchers.

Department stores offer perhaps the most striking opportunities for women to advance to top positions, although the total number of women in such positions is not large. Women can and do move from selling to merchandising and buying, and even to the highest administrative positions. Even here, however, jobs tend to receive sex labels, and a woman is more likely to deal with women's and children's clothing than with furniture and appliances.

In the fields where small business enterprises predominate or independent practice is possible, a few women create their own opportunities. Some women own and operate public stenographic offices, real estate and insurance businesses, small retail stores and service establishments such as beauty parlors and restaurants, or private employment agencies. Sometimes, a woman who has acquired considerable experience enters business in partnership with a man. Many women help to manage their husbands' businesses, and some women become proprietors and managers when their husbands die or are incapacitated.

TURNOVER

The widespread belief that women workers are likely to quit their jobs at any moment constitutes a serious limitation on their opportunities for promotion, as well as on the range of jobs for which they are hired. There is no question that women are much more likely than men to leave the labor force during any given period of time. Each month a great many people, most of them women, enter and leave the labor force, some temporarily and others more or less permanently. In 1952, an average of about 5 percent of all persons who were in the labor force during any one month were not in it during the previous month, and a nearly equivalent group not in the labor force were in it the previous month. Thus, the gross labor force turnover rate was 10 percent per month. Gross turnover is very high among both men and women under 20 and over 60, but higher for women than for men in the last age group. The monthly turnover rate averaged 17 percent or more for women throughout the age range 20 to 60, but it was less than 7 percent for men in this age range and less than 2 percent among men aged 25 to 44 years.

From the point of view of a return on an investment in training, the important consideration is whether the worker will leave the employer—whether or not he or she also leaves the labor force. When a man quits a job, he rarely leaves the labor force; that is, he almost always takes another job. When a woman quits a job, she often leaves the labor force as well, but the available evidence indicates that on the average women are no more likely than men to quit their jobs. A recent survey, under the auspices of the Social Science Research Council, of the work experience of the labor force in six cities found that men held an average of 2.7 jobs and women an average of 2.5 jobs between 1940 and 1949. Younger workers held more jobs than older workers, but in each age group, women held fewer jobs than men, largely because they spent fewer years in the labor force. The available data probably obscure differences in turnover rates between men and women in particular occupations or from particular social backgrounds. Still, they show that among groups of men and women who were comparable in terms of age, marital status, length of time in the labor force, and migration patterns, women held about the same number of jobs as men.

The fact is that American workers, both men and women, are very mobile, particularly during periods of high employment. In 1951, over one third of all employed women and one fourth of all employed men had held their current jobs for one year or less. Forty percent of the men and nearly 60 percent of the women had been on their jobs for three years or less. At that time, the proportion of workers with short service was increased somewhat by job shifting during the Korean mobilization.

Among employees of manufacturing concerns, women show a greater tendency to quit jobs than men. During the period 1950-55, an average of 24 out of each thousand women in manufacturing quit their jobs each month, compared to 18 per thousand men. Part of this difference reflects the fact that the women are younger than the men. Most of the difference is due to the fact that men and women do not respond in the same way to unfavorable employment prospects. When employment is expanding and there are many alternative job opportunities, both men and women tend to quit their jobs more readily. Under this condition, the quit rate for women is usually only slightly higher than for men. When employment is falling, quit rates decrease considerably, but more for men than for women. The quit rate among women remains relatively high under adverse economic conditions probably because they are far more likely than men to stop working for personal and family reasons and because many of them are not compelled, to the same extent as men, to work because of economic necessity.

The quit rates for both men and women vary a great deal in different areas of employment, as well as from time to time. In October, 1952, although the quit rate for women was at its highest since 1950, a larger proportion of men than of women quit in the following industries: ordnance, lumber and wood products, furniture and fixtures, and stone, clay, and glass products. In other industries, the rates were higher for women, and in still others, they were about the same. Usually, the quit rates for women exceed those for men by a larger margin in nondurable than in durable goods manufacturing, perhaps because the lower wages prevailing in nondurable industries present to women a less attractive alternative to keeping house.

There are indications that much of the job-leaving by both men and women is concentrated among particular groups and that a fairly large group of women remain employed more or less continuously. The Social Science Research Council study of six cities found, for instance, that among the women who were working in both 1940 and 1950, one third had had only one employer during the decade. Among these, half had worked continuously and half had withdrawn from the labor force and returned to the same employer in the course of the decade. Thus, an employer's investment in the training of his women workers is not necessarily wasted if they leave, because a significant proportion return later on.

Employers can gain as well as lose from high turnover. For some firms, women provide a seasonal labor supply. For others, where the wage rate automatically advances with length of service, high turnover helps to hold down wage costs. An employer may also avoid the necessity of having to create opportunities for promotion, and further, can avoid high pension costs.

These limited data on turnover suggest that the widespread belief that women are more likely than men to quit their jobs is, in large part, a vestige from the past, when the female labor force was made up mainly of very young women. During the last decade, the differences in turnover rates between men and women workers in manufacturing have declined. As more and more older women return to and remain in the labor force, the differences which still exist are likely to diminish even further. Labor force turnover among women—as distinct from job turnover—is also likely to decline in the future. It will, however, remain much greater than among men, and, therefore, will continue to limit the work experience, seniority, and promotion of women.

PART-TIME AND TEMPORARY WORK

After their initial introduction to work, most women do not remain in paid employment continuously, but many work part-time, temporarily, or intermittently. For instance, nearly one tenth of all women over 25 years of age reported that because of household and family responsibilities, they either worked for less than half of the year during 1955, or for less than 35 hours a week, which the Census defines as part-time work. An equal number reported a similar amount of work experience, but offered as explanations lay-offs, unemployment, illness, and similar reasons. These two groups made up about 40 percent of all women over 25 years of age who worked at any time during 1955.

Family farms and domestic service are by far the most important areas for part-time, seasonal, and temporary work. Of the approximately 8 million women who worked part time during 1955, nearly 25 percent worked in agriculture and over 20 percent as private household workers. Many full- and part-time farm and domestic-service workers are employed the year round; but many others work only part of the year. Large numbers of women help out on farms in the spring or early summer and again in the fall of each year.

Employers generally will not make special efforts to hire a person for a part-time job, except as a means of solving a specific problem. Some firms may be characterized by seasonal or irregular business, busy periods or peak loads, or a short work week or day. Others may have hours or days of work somewhat longer than usual, but not long enough to warrant hiring more full-time workers. Some employers make special arrangements to retain experienced employees who no longer want to work full time. In an emergency, other employers may adopt part-time schedules to secure persons with scarce skills, such as nurses or secretaries. Generally, employers hesitate to undertake the training of part-time workers. They may, however, seek to hire trained and unusually competent personnel for part-time work.

After farm and domestic-service work, retail selling is the major field of part-time and seasonal employment for women, accounting for about one eighth of the part-time women workers. The seasonal pattern in retailing is roughly the reverse of that in agriculture, with employment diminishing in the summer and expanding during the fall, winter, and preholiday seasons.

Many seasonal jobs for manufacturing operatives reflect the seasonal patterns in agriculture and retailing. This is true in such industries as food processing and clothing manufacture. Relatively little part-time work is regularly scheduled in such industries, but women may be temporarily laid off or asked to work only a few days a week in slack periods. It should be noted that short periods of unemployment are welcomed by some women, for they can rest or attend to their homes and families. Some part-time and temporary work is available in clerical and various nonhousehold-service occupations. A substantial number of cashiers, bookkeepers, and various other clerical workers, but relatively few typists and secretaries, hold part-time jobs. Many women hold part-time, irregular, and seasonal jobs as beauticians, waitresses, cooks, charwomen, janitresses, and practical nurses.

In the professions, part-time and temporary work is far less common, even though some part-time salaried teaching positions are available, and a number of women teach foreign languages, music, or dancing in their own homes or studios on a part-time basis. Small libraries offer considerable part-time employment to librarians. Part-time work is common in journalistic occupations and has recently been increasing among nurses and medical technicians.

THE RETURN TO WORK AMONG OLDER WOMEN

The return to work among older women as their children grow up and their homemaking responsibilities lessen is a recent development, and the information available about it is not commensurate with its growing importance. Between 1940 and 1950, there was a net increase of 420,000 in employment in the group of women aged 25 to 34 years in 1940. During the same period, there was a growth of 530,000 in the number employed among women aged 35 to 44 years in 1940. Similarly, between 1950 and 1955, there was a net increase of 740,000 in employment among women aged 30 to 39 in 1950, and of 320,000 among women aged 40 to 49 in 1950, as those in both age groups grew five years older.

As Table 20 shows, these increases were distributed among almost all of the major occupational groups. The figures in this table, however, must be used with caution. They show net increases and do not include the reentry of women who had been employed in either 1940 or 1950, but left the labor force and returned in time to be counted as employed in 1950 or 1955, respectively. The figures also reflect changes in occupations by some women between 1940 and 1950, or 1950 and 1955, respectively. Studies of such occupational shifts suggest that, for the period 1940-1950, Table 20 tends to understate the return to service, sales, and professional work, and overstate the return to managerial, operative, clerical, and craftsman and foreman occupations.

It appears that more than one fourth of the women returning to work between 1940 and 1950 went into service occupations and another one fourth entered sales occupations. Probably less than 20 percent became operatives, and about 10 percent, most of them 35 years of age or over in 1940, reentered the professions and related work. Many of those who returned held proprietary and managerial positions in 1950, but some of them may have first held other jobs from which they subsequently secured advancement. Many women aged 35 to 44 in 1940 returned to clerical work, but there was no apparent return to clerical work among those ten years younger. The numbers returning to other occupations were not significant.

About one third of the net increase in service workers took place among cooks in places other than private homes, and another one third was divided equally among charwoman and janitresses, practical nurses, and waitresses and counter workers. The largest increases in employment among operatives took place in the clothing and food processing industries. In the professions the largest absolute increases took place among teachers and nurses,

Table 20. Net Increases in Employment in Major Occupational Groups among Women in Selected Age Groups, between 1940 and 1950 and between 1950 and 1955

Occupational Group	Net Increase 1940 to 1950 (in thousands)		Net Increase 1950 to 1955 (in thousands)	
	Among Women Aged 25 to 34 in 1940	Among Women Aged 35 to 44 in 1940	Among Women Aged 30 to 39 in 1950	Among Women Aged 40 to 49 in 1950
Operatives and kindred workers	140	110	120	--
Service workers, except private household	130	110	170	80
Sales workers	100	100	40	60
Managers, officials, and proprietors, except farm	120	70	40	-60
Clerical and kindred workers	-10	100	190	130
Farm laborers and foremen	30	30	80	10
Craftsmen, foremen, and kindred workers	40	20	30	10
Professional, technical, and kindred workers	-10	70	100	30
Farmers and farm managers	10	--	-10	--
Laborers, except farm and mine	--	--	10	10
Private household workers	-160	-110	-30	50
Occupation not reported	30	30	--	--
Total net change	420	530	740	320

-- = less than 5000.
Source: Based on data published by the U.S. Bureau of the Census and unpublished data prepared for the National Manpower Council by the Bureau of the Census.

with the first accounting for nearly one third and the second for one tenth of the increase. Larger relative increases, however, occurred among librarians, musicians and music teachers, social workers, and other professional groups.

Since 1950, there has been considerable change in the occupations entered by older women returning to work. Relatively few entered clerical employment prior to 1950, but this field has since become the most important, accounting for 30 percent of the increase in employment between 1950 and 1955 among women aged 30 to 49 in 1950. Women returning to clerical occupations are apparently younger than formerly, as Table 20 indicates. Those who returned to this field between 1940 and 1950 were largely in the age group 35 to 44 in 1940, while those who returned between 1950 and 1955 were largely in the age group 30 to 39 in 1950. Those who reentered the professions after 1950 also tended to be younger than formerly. The proportions of returning women who secured professional positions were about the same in both periods.

Reemployment in the service occupations, other than as domestics, continues to be important, accounting for one fourth of the net gain among these women between 1950 and 1955. In contrast to the previous trends, there was also a small increase in the number of domestic servants among women aged 40 to 49 in 1950. The return to semiskilled and sales work has apparently become considerably less important than formerly. While there was a sizable increase between 1940 and 1950 in the number of older women in managerial and proprietary occupations, there was an actual decline after 1950.

Older women now returning to work undoubtedly face several disadvantages. Traditionally, employers have often favored young workers, and the bias against older women appears to be even stronger than against older men. Unfortunately, studies of older women workers have not differentiated between those who have worked continuously and those who have not, or between those who work because of some family dislocation and the growing number who have a choice between working and not working. Women in the latter group may be less burdened by household responsibilities, and also have quite positive attitudes toward paid employment. This is especially true for those who return and stay at work, signifying that their choice has been satisfactory. Some employers have actively begun to seek such older women because, among other reasons, they are often more stable and responsible workers than young girls.

Discontinuity in work creates problems for the older woman who returns to employment. In many cases, a worker's position is closely governed by formal or informal systems of seniority, and a new employee starts out in one of the lowest-ranking jobs. Advancement comes when the worker is able and willing to take advantage of such opportunities for promotion as appear. Frequently, if a woman wants to return to work, she can do so only if she is willing to accept a low-ranking job. Maternity leave provisions sometimes protect a woman's position, but rarely for more than two years. Consequently, many older women who return to work may not achieve status and pay corresponding to their skills.

Because workers may lose skill and competence while not working or fail to keep abreast of new developments in their fields, it has been urged that arrangements be made to maintain skills through part-time or intermittent work. In the professional, managerial, and skilled occupations, the maintenance of skills is most important but it is also most difficult. Employers usually do not think it feasible to use part-time or temporary workers in these occupations. A few employers are willing to hold on to employees on a part-time basis, especially if they encounter difficulty in replacing them. Most employers, however, have been unwilling to provide part-time work in order to enable women to maintain their skills. On the other hand, the demand for many kinds of women workers has been so great, especially in the professions, that many women have been able to return to work, assisted in some cases, as in teaching and nursing, by special training courses which provide needed skills.

IMPLICATIONS FOR EMPLOYER ACTION

The main findings of this chapter challenge widely held convictions about the characteristics of women in relationship to their employment. It is quite clear that the labor market behavior of women differs in many ways from that of men. The precise nature and the reasons for the differences, however, remain in doubt because of the paucity of reliable data and because so much of the available data relate to labor-market conditions of an earlier day. For example, it appears that women workers, particularly married women, show different geographical mobility patterns from men, but this specific question has not yet been investigated thoroughly. Available studies of occupational advancement do not distinguish between women who work continuously and those who do not. It is known that many men advance by obtaining a series of better jobs in different organizations, but it is uncertain whether this is also a significant route to higher-level jobs for women. There has been much discussion of the question of equal pay, but only one thorough investigation of the pay received by men and women in comparable jobs has been published, and it is of limited scope.

Although the evidence is overwhelming that differences between men and women in work performance are largely culturally determined, very little reliable information exists about the attitudes and motivations of men and women toward their work, and about personal relationships between men and women in the work situation. Even though employers have had considerable experience in attempting to alter the attitudes and behavior of both men and women workers, much remains obscure about how such changes can be brought about.

Some employers have, of course, been quite willing to introduce new policies and practices in order to utilize the capacities and skills of their women employees more effectively. Many employers have successfully challenged assumptions that one job or another belongs to a particular sex. There seems to be increasing willingness to abandon traditional sex labels of jobs. However, it cannot yet be asserted that employers as a group have critically examined the effect which the existing distribution of jobs by sex has upon the supply of labor available to them and its utilization. As a result of current practices, employers often deny themselves capable employees, and the abilities of many women are underutilized and, therefore, in good part wasted. Certainly there is good reason for more employers to challenge the assumption that jobs must be assigned to one sex or another. If employees were assigned on the basis of individual ability, skill, and motivation, employers would have greater flexibility in adjusting to alterations in the supply of male and female workers induced by changes in economic activity. It would also enable them to adjust more easily to other factors affecting the supply of labor, such as changes in military manpower policies, in marriage and birth rates, in attitudes toward work on the part of married women, and in educational and occupational choices of men and women.

It also seems clear that the more effective utilization of womanpower will require employers to reexamine their policies involving the training and promotion of women workers. High levels of employment, employer concern with turnover problems, and the changing age characteristics of women workers—quite apart from other considerations—warrant such an undertaking. The mere fact that an increasingly larger number of women are spending a greater proportion of their lives in paid employment can lead to important changes in their attitudes toward work and occupational advancement. As work becomes more significant to more women, and as they manifest a greater desire and willingness to move up the occupational ladder, the practice of maintaining separate systems of training and promotion for men and women workers becomes increasingly open to question.

Many women apparently want to be engaged in both work and homemaking functions but do not want to be totally absorbed in either. Conceivably, new kinds of part-day, part-week, or part-year arrangements could be developed that would be attractive to potential women workers and enable employers to secure more competent personnel than they could otherwise attract. By being absent or quitting their jobs from time to time, many women are in fact working out their own solutions to the problem of combining work and home activities, but frequently at a relatively heavy cost to themselves and their employers. Some firms, of course, do have a policy of granting leaves of absence to women workers which safeguard their status and facilitate their return to work. How much could be done to invent new patterns of part-time employment which would tend to reduce absenteeism and turnover invites consideration.

Discontinuity in employment poses the problem of skill maintenance for those women who temporarily leave the labor market and of skill development when they return. There is already a concern with refresher courses for older women workers and also with training programs designed to develop their potential skills. Just how much more can be done to maintain and improve the skills of married women who are partially relieved of household duties but not yet available for full-time employment still remains to be explored.

IX. SHORTAGES OF HIGHLY TRAINED PERSONNEL

THE RAPID development of manpower studies in recent years has been strongly encouraged by a widespread concern with persistent shortages of scientists, professional workers, and other highly trained personnel. Among the fields where shortages have prompted determined efforts to expand the supply of personnel are several in which women predominate—health, education, and social work. In others, including engineering and the physical sciences, men constitute the overwhelming majority of workers.

Proposals for expanding the supply of workers for occupations where shortages exist have generally assumed that there will be no change in the sex characteristics of occupational fields; that is, that shortages of nurses and of engineers, for example, will be alleviated primarily by encouraging more young women, in the first instance, and more young men, in the second, to train for these professions. Since all professional occupations—including nursing —are open to men and women, some attention has also been paid to the possibility of relieving shortages by attracting more workers of whichever sex is in the minority. Because there are important differences between the ways in which men and women prepare for work and behave in the labor market, shortage situations in "men's" and "women's" professional occupations, as will be seen, pose different problems.

MANPOWER SHORTAGES

The term "manpower shortages" refers to imbalances between the demand for and the supply of particular kinds of workers. The significant manpower shortages of recent years can be traced, either directly or indirectly, to change and growth in the economy, resulting in rapid increases in the demand for certain kinds of workers which cannot be met from personnel currently available. The international tensions of the postwar period, which led to efforts to enhance the economic and military strength of the United States, have been a special factor in stimulating the demand for highly trained personnel. The high level of expenditures for research and development during this period, financed in large part by Federal appropriations, has been an important influence on the heavy demand for scientific and professional workers. A rising national income and a growing population have, moreover, contributed to the demand for expanded and improved health and educational services, and, therefore, to the need for highly trained personnel. From one point of view, manpower shortages may be regarded as evidences of a dynamic economy and of striking advances in science and technology. From another, they may be conceived of as reflections of higher aspirations for educational, health and other services, or as consequences of responses to threats to the nation's security. From still a third point of view, manpower shortages may be thought of as barriers to the attainment of national security or economic or social objectives.

Manpower shortages are always felt as inadequacies in the supply of particular kinds of personnel to fill specific kinds of jobs. It is quite clear, however, that each of the shortages of highly trained manpower that has won attention in recent years is not an isolated phenomenon which can be relieved without reference to larger considerations of manpower demand and supply. Common factors are present in both the causes of shortages in different occupations and in the means for alleviating them. Steps taken to

cope with a shortage in one professional or scientific occupation
have a bearing upon demand and supply relationships in others.
Thus, a large increase in the number of young women preparing
to enter scientific employment might seriously reduce the relative
size of the supply available for teaching. Similarly, a rapid growth
in the number of young men studying engineering and the physical sciences might cut into the supply preparing to enter other
professional occupations, such as medicine. Thus, the price of
alleviating shortages in one field may be contractions in the
supply of personnel available for others. Moreover, the utilization
of personnel in one occupational field is affected by its dependence upon related, supporting occupations. The relief of shortages
in engineering, for instance, depends in large measure not only
upon ways in which professional engineers are now utilized, but
also upon the availability and use of such semiprofessional personnel as draftsmen and engineering aides. Shortages in professional nursing have to be seen within the context of a larger
complex of personnel — doctors, hospital administrators, practical
nurses, medical technicians, and other auxiliary medical personnel
—and are affected by the manner in which all these groups are
utilized.

Some of the aspects of supply-demand relationships significant
for the employment of women have received attention in the
preceding chapter. Shortages of highly trained personnel are an
important aspect of this larger subject because of the strategic
role such workers occupy with respect to the nation's present and
future well-being. In the case of occupations for which relatively
little skill is required, interoccupational shifts and brief periods
of on-the-job training can be relied upon to assure fairly
rapid expansions of the supply. A comparable capacity for
expansion, however, is not characteristic of the supply of personnel for professional and scientific occupations. The qualifications
for employment in these fields entail lengthy, expensive, and demanding programs of formal education and training. The total

supply available for college and graduate study is limited not only by the size and the age composition of the population, but also by the proportion with the ability and motivation to pursue formal schooling through college and beyond. Professional standards and codes and legal regulations often have the effect of controlling the size of the supply entering an occupation.

There is, however, always some elasticity in the supply of personnel for scientific and professional occupations. Professional workers trained for one field may be effectively employed in another. Such interoccupational mobility, while serving to satisfy high demands in some fields, may contribute to the emergence of shortages elsewhere. Thus, high school teachers of science have shifted to jobs in private industry, but there is reason to believe that better salaries could induce some to return to teaching. The annual loss in an occupation due to retirement may be reduced, when there is a shortage, by raising the retirement age.

More important is the fact that in recent years the substantial number of married women in their thirties and forties who are graduates of colleges or professional schools, and who are not currently in the labor force, has become a significant source for expanding the supply. By contrast, virtually all men in this age group are employed. This establishes a major difference in the elasticity of the supply between professions in which women predominate and those in which they are a small minority.

CRITERIA USED IN DETERMINING SHORTAGES

Every assertion that a manpower shortage exists rests upon the criteria employed to assess both the intensity of the demand for a particular category of workers and the characteristics of the available supply. Judgments about the scale and seriousness of a given manpower shortage, as well as about the steps necessary to correct it, frequently differ. Lack of agreement can be traced not only to incomplete or conflicting data, but also to the fact that different criteria are invoked in determining whether the relationship between demand and supply is such as to constitute a shortage situation.

In a free market economy, an unfulfilled demand for any resource is, in theory, both manifested in and remedied by an upward movement in price. Consequently, differential wage or salary increases for specific categories of highly trained workers are frequently used as criteria in deciding whether demand is running ahead of supply. Yet, in certain fields where inadequacies in the supply of personnel have aroused concern—as in teaching, for example—salaries have not risen more than in other occupations. The Fund for the Advancement of Education reports that between 1943 and 1947 teachers in the public schools suffered an actual decline in purchasing power. Since 1947, their salaries have increased, but at a rate no greater than that for industrial workers.

In recent years, no manpower shortage has received more public attention that that of engineers. For the past several years, the Engineering Manpower Commission has estimated that private and governmental employers would like to hire between 30,000 and 40,000 newly graduated engineers annually, a total well above the output of the nation's engineering schools. Beginning salaries for engineering school graduates have increased in recent years, but so have beginning salaries for other college graduates. Northwestern University reports that between 1950 and 1955 average starting salaries for all its new graduates employed by business enterprises increased by 39.2 percent, compared to 38.8 percent for engineering graduates alone. While the typical engineering graduate hired by industry in 1949 received a beginning salary 6 percent greater than that of other college graduates, after five years of employment the salary difference in favor of the engineer had all but vanished. Outstanding graduates in other fields were likely to surpass the outstanding engineers in earnings after five years on the job. The existence of a continuing shortage of engineering manpower is not clearly confirmed by upward salary movements. It is, however, easy enough to demonstrate high demand for newly graduated engineers, who make up only a small fraction of total personnel in the occupation.

Salary increases are commonly thought to be a first and basic step for relieving shortages of professional and scientific manpower. However, the identification of such shortages seldom rests solely on data showing comparative salary changes. What may be called noneconomic criteria, such as social need or aspiration, standards of professional service, or conceptions of national security, are also used to make judgments about manpower shortages. One reason for this is the extent to which professional manpower is engaged in providing basic social services, as in the fields of education and health. Moreover, a very large proportion of total professional personnel is employed by public or other nonprofit enterprises which respond more slowly and unevenly to changing labor-market conditions than do profit-seeking enterprises. Where salary schedules are set by law, for example, many difficulties stand in the way of changes which might attract additional personnel. Not the least is the reluctance or inability of communities to translate their expressed desire for adequate educational, health, and other social services into higher taxes and appropriations. Unless this occurs, the demand for personnel is not, in economic terms, an effective one.

Noneconomic criteria are implicit in judgments about manpower shortages made on the basis of inability to fill budgeted positions in public and nonprofit enterprises. This criterion is frequently employed to measure shortages of personnel in the health field, where large numbers of women are found. It was reported, for instance, that 23 percent of the budgeted positions for nurses and auxiliary personnel in hospitals in New York State were unfilled in 1954. The most severe shortage, 33 percent, was reported for general duty nurses, but shortages of between 4 and 12 percent were reported for head nurses, supervisory nurses, private duty nurses, practical nurses, and ward clerks. It was reported in 1952 that 18,000 budgeted positions for paramedical personnel in hospitals throughout the country, or 21 percent of all such positions, were unfilled. In the two largest occupations, laboratory and X-ray technicians, about 13 percent of the positions were not filled, as was the case with at least 27 percent of the positions for other paramedical personnel, including occupational therapists, dietitians, medical social workers, medical record librarians, and physical therapists. It has been reported on a similar basis that in 1955 there were at least 3,000 vacancies for professional social workers—whose salaries have long been held to be inadequate—in public assistance and child welfare programs.

The explicit use of criteria of social need or aspiration to measure shortages may be illustrated from the educational and health fields. Most educators hold that for effective teaching, a class should have no more than thirty pupils. In 1955, however, 27 percent of all elementary and secondary students were enrolled in classes of more than thirty-five, and still others were in classes which met for only half a day. The National Education Association has stated that a "reasonable effort to reduce class size and to eliminate double sessions would require at least 20,000 additional teachers." When the President's Commission on the Health Needs of the Nation reported in 1952-53 on the dimensions of the shortage of nurses, it used as a standard of minimum need for each state the ratio of 237 nurses per 100,000 population, the actual ratio found to obtain for the nation as a whole in 1951. On this basis, the Commission concluded that the expected supply of nurses in 1960 would fall more than 40,000 short of the number required, if every state was to meet even this minimum standard.

In establishing standards of education, training, competence, and conduct for their members, professional groups influence popular conceptions of what constitutes adequacy in the provision of essential services. Professional societies not only seek to maintain and elevate such standards, but also to insure in other ways the effective performance of functions for which their members are responsible. In achieving these purposes, however, professional groups must depend upon public acceptance and support in one form or another. Thus, the teachers in a community, reflecting the views of the profession as a whole, may protest that effective instruction is prevented because of class size. The local school board, however, may not feel that large classes are undesirable, while the taxpayers of the school district may be divided on both sides of the question. If the community at large fails to underwrite the judgment of the educators, action to change the situation will not be forthcoming.

Improvements in professional standards are usually sought once old standards have been met. This dynamic aspect of the criteria used to identify shortages in certain occupational fields appears in many judgments about inadequate supplies of personnel which are based upon qualitative considerations. Thus, most estimates of the dimensions of the current shortage of teachers make some allowance for replacing teachers who do not meet minimum certification requirements with better qualified personnel. It is even possible to "create" a persistent shortage, so to speak, by applying qualitative considerations far out of line with current practice. An example of this may be taken from the nursing field. According to the American Nurses Association, about 20 percent of the positions now held by registered nurses should be filled by nurses with master's degrees. For another 30 percent of the positions, it is maintained, bachelor's degree preparation would be desirable. At present, however, only 1 percent of the nurses hold master's degrees and 9 percent bachelor's degrees.

Qualitative considerations, moreover, transcend standards of formal education and training. Thus, for every group of highly trained workers, it may be said that there is always a shortage of individuals possessing unusual abilities. The need for broadly trained, imaginative leaders in all fields has long been stressed.

Increasing attention has been given to the problem of attracting and retaining a larger proportion of first-rate teachers in all fields, and special efforts are being made to secure more able and inspiring teachers of high school science and mathematics. In engineering and the sciences, the emphasis has been placed not only upon expanding the total supply of personnel, but also upon increasing the number of individuals with exceptional creative powers.

National security objectives, as has been observed, are also invoked in reaching judgments about shortage situations. Thus, difficulties encountered in fulfilling the requirements for certain types of highly trained manpower in the armed services are frequently cited as proof that the demand for such personnel is greater than the available supply. The same criterion is used in identifying shortages among scientific and professional workers required if research and development programs supported by Federal funds are to be successfully carried out. The degree to which such programs achieve their stipulated goals within a given time schedule also serves as a measure for determining whether the supply of needed personnel is adequate.

Still another commonly used yardstick is the number of students who complete their education and training for scientific and professional occupations in the Soviet Union. Some who employ this measure visualize the United States as losing out in a race for highly trained manpower because about twice as many new engineers are currently being graduated in Russia as in the United States. A doubling in the number of engineers graduated each year by American schools has even been urged in order to keep pace with the gains made by the Soviet Union. It is worth noting in this context that there are annually some 13,000 women graduating as engineers in the Soviet Union, compared to well under 100 in the United States. In the Soviet Union, moreover, women also make up a substantial majority of the new supply of physicians.

FACTORS AFFECTING THE SUPPLY OF PROFESSIONAL PERSONNEL

Developments affecting the supply of highly trained personnel are, obviously, no less significant for manpower imbalances than are changes in demand. Scientific and technological advances have established pressing demands for relatively new kinds of highly trained personnel, while the continuing rise in national income and the expansion in employment result in a steady rise in the demand for virtually all kinds of scientific and professional workers. On the other hand, the supply of workers for all these fields has been affected by such underlying factors as changes in the size and age composition of the population, in the proportion graduating from college, in educational and training qualifications for employment, and in the ways in which personnel are utilized. These basic demand and supply factors have not had the same impact upon all professional occupations in recent years, but they have led to situations which prompt questions about the adequacy of the present and future supply of new personnel for a number of fields.

In terms of education and training, the supply of most kinds of workers is drawn from a variety of sources. By contrast, professional and scientific occupations rely almost exclusively on college, professional school, and university graduates. Consequently, the supply of new personnel for these fields has been especially vulnerable in recent years to demographic developments which have reduced the size of the population of college age. The low birth rates of the 1930's have limited the growth in the number of college graduates. At the same time, as has been seen in Chapter VII, the proportions of young men and women of college age earning bachelor's and first professional degrees in the mid-1950's have been substantially greater than in the period before World War II. This has partly made up for the decline in the size of the college-age group. The fact that the number of bachelor's and first professional degrees awarded in the mid-

1950's has been smaller than it was in 1950 is due chiefly to heavy college enrollments of World War II veterans up to 1950.

Only relatively small changes have occurred in the numbers of young women awarded first degrees each year between 1949 and 1955, because higher proportions of smaller college-age groups were completing college. The fact that the number of women graduates remained relatively stable during this period has a two-fold significance. First, they are heavily concentrated in fields where the demand has been high, such as teaching, social work, nursing, and still other professional occupations in which women predominate. Second, in contrast to what happens among men, a sizable portion of the new supply in these occupations does not remain in employment. Each year, for instance, about 7 percent of all teachers leave the profession. Some are men who enter other occupations, but most of them are young women who stop working in order to care for their families and homes. The supply, therefore, must be large enough to meet the needs for replacements as well as to fill new positions.

What other effects recent demographic changes have upon the supply of women entering the professions is still uncertain. Thus far, the decline in the average age of marriage and the earlier onset of childbearing, for example, have not apparently cut down the number of young women completing college. Nor do these developments seem to have had any marked impact on the proportion of all young women in the labor force. Striking changes have occurred in the age of marriage and in childbearing patterns among women who are college graduates. Today, more of them marry, more of them have children, and, on the average, they are having larger families than before. As a result, relatively fewer women college graduates devote themselves exclusively either to careers or to home and family; more of them are combining professional employment with homemaking functions.

New additions constitute only one factor affecting the total number of workers available for employment in each occupation.

Also important is the extent to which individuals move out of a profession and into other fields, or withdraw from the labor force for shorter or longer periods of time. In the case of professional occupations where the vast majority of workers are men, continuity both in the labor force and in the profession is characteristic. It is true, of course, that in recent years compulsory military service has led to some reductions in the supply available for civilian employment. Moreover, in some of these occupations, as in engineering, a significant proportion of the supply ultimately finds employment outside the profession.

Marriage, childbearing, and childrearing account for significant losses from the current supply in professions in which women predominate, but many married women also return to employment, usually after their children have reached school age. This is the situation in teaching and nursing, where women can resume employment on the basis of their original preparation for the field, or after some additional training which may be necessitated by changes in knowledge and techniques or in legal requirements. In nursing, at any given time a sizable minority of the licenses or registrations—perhaps two fifths—are held by women who are not employed in the profession, most of whom are married and over thirty. In teaching, the return of married women to the profession is now a significant factor in expanding the total supply. Through refresher courses for those who once taught, and special educational programs for those who graduated from college but were not fully prepared to teach, additional personnel can be qualified for employment. In 1956, over 100 colleges and universities, located in twenty-seven states and the District of Columbia, were conducting special programs to prepare "mature college graduates" for teaching.

THE TEACHING PROFESSION

The high demand for teachers in recent years is largely the product of a rapid rise in the number of children of school age, and of continuing efforts to provide more years of schooling and better education for all children. The birth rate went up sharply during and again after World War II. This development, together with the long-run increase in the percentage of children of all ages attending school, has enormously expanded school enrollments. Thus, as the Fund for the Advancement of Education pointed out early in 1956 in its bulletin, *Teachers for Tomorrow:*

In 1950 elementary enrollments rose to 22 million after remaining fairly constant at about 20 million throughout the Forties. Each year since 1950 has brought a further increase. When school opened in September, the U. S. Office of Education estimated 1955-56 elementary enrollments at 29 million.

But further increases are yet to come. Most of the children born in the last five record-breaking years have not yet started to school. The more than four million babies born last year [1955] will not reach kindergarten age until the school year 1959-60, when the first group of postwar children will be moving on to the ninth grade. *By 1960, elementary enrollments will be 68 percent above 1946 and 28 percent above 1954.*

Secondary school enrollments, which have been rising gradually for 10 years, will increase considerably in each of the next five years, and by 1960 will begin to reflect the full impact of high postwar births. *By 1969, the children already born will push secondary school enrollments to more than 70 percent above the 1954 level.*

While the number of school children has been growing rapidly, efforts have been made to reduce the number of students per class. At the same time, the demand for teachers and other professional personnel has also been stimulated by the expansion of such educational services as special programs for both gifted and retarded children, remedial reading classes, health instruction, and guidance and counseling functions.

As in most other professional fields, the qualifications for employment in teaching have been steadily raised. Not only have more hours of work in specialized education courses been demanded of those preparing to teach in recent years, but a bachelor's degree is now almost universally required for high school teaching. In a few states, permanent high school teachers must have a master's degree, or its equivalent, to be licensed. The teaching profession has also been striving to have a bachelor's degree recognized as the minimum qualification for elementary school teaching, and in 1953 it was required for an elementary certificate in 31 states. In the past, completion of three years of work in a normal school, or even high school graduation, was regarded as adequate preparation for the teaching profession. Today's qualifications, consequently, have the effect of confining the potential supply from which new teachers can be drawn largely to college graduates. Higher qualifications also imply that older women who want to return to the profession and who were eligible to teach in the past may not meet current requirements. Longer preparation means later entrance into employment, and this, together with early departure from the profession on the part of many women, reduces the number of teachers available at any one time.

The future growth in the number of college graduates will be particularly important for teaching and other professions where annual replacement needs are high because women predominate. In 1955, over 287,000 persons received college and first professional degrees. The Fund for the Advancement of Education has estimated that, if past trends in college attendance continue, 355,000 persons will graduate by 1960, and over 500,000 by 1965. Some estimates by the U. S. Office of Education indicate that there may be even larger increases.

Between 1949 and 1955, the proportion of graduates qualifying for teaching rose from 21 to 30 percent. But this change is largely accounted for by the drop in the number of men graduating and by the high proportion of women majoring in education. Employment opportunities, better salaries, recruitment campaigns, and other inducements may now constitute greater incentives to enter the teaching profession than were present in the past. They do not appear, however, to have drastically altered the proportion of men or women entering teaching, and they have certainly not been as influential in redirecting the occupational objectives of college students as current incentives to prepare for engineering. Engineering students increased sharply from 11 percent to 16 percent of all male college freshmen between 1950 and 1952, and have remained at about 17 percent since 1953.

Table 21 indicates that there is good reason to expect steady future increases in the supply of new teachers graduating from college. This judgment rests, in the first instance, upon expected increases in the number of men and women completing college; and, second, upon the assumption that the proportion of graduates meeting the requirements for teaching certificates and entering the profession immediately after graduation will remain at 40 percent for women and increase to 12 percent for men. Some 8 to 11 percent of the men graduates have been going into teaching in recent years, but growing employment opportunities for high school teachers warrant the assumption that at least 12 percent will be doing so in the future.

Even if a larger proportion of the students in an expanding college population were to enter teaching upon graduation, this alone would not assure closing the gap between demand and supply. For the past several years, new college graduates who had specifically prepared for teaching have accounted for slightly less than half of the annual additions to the supply. The remainder of the additions have obtained teaching jobs on the basis of substandard licenses; or have met the qualifications in their states without being college graduates; or have fulfilled the requirements for certification sometime after graduation; or have been former teachers; or, without prior teaching experience, have been qualified on the basis of college graduation and certification sometime in the past. In the 1954-55 school year, for instance, 6 percent of the persons holding their first teaching jobs in urban school systems had not yet graduated from college at the start of the school

Table 21. Estimates of Teacher Supply and Demand, 1955-64
(thousands)

Supply of Qualified Persons Entering Teaching

School Year Starting Fall of	Estimate A		Estimate B		Demand for Teachers as Replacements and to Meet Increased Enrollments		Total Supply B Estimate B as Percent of Demand Estimate II
	From among College Graduates of Same Year[a]	Total from All Sources[b]	From among College Graduates of Same Year[c]	Total from All Sources[b]	Estimate I[d]	Estimate II[e]	
1955	6.30[f]	100.7	63.0[f]	100.7	145.2[g]	136.4[g]	74
1956	70.9	113.5	64.1	102.5	148.5	138.8	74
1957	75.8	121.3	68.6	109.7	152.5	142.1	72
1958	84.3	134.8	69.7	111.6	158.8	147.4	76
1959	89.4	143.1	70.7	113.2	160.0	148.0	77
1960	93.0	148.9	75.6	121.0	152.0	140.0	86
1961	96.0	153.6	78.9	126.2	152.9	139.5	90
1962	97.9	156.7	80.4	128.7	154.0	139.7	92
1963	102.2	163.5	86.1	137.8	152.0	137.6	100
1964	110.2	176.4	94.1	150.6	151.7	137.0	110

[a] Based on projection of annual number of male and female college graduates by U. S. Office of Education. Assumes 12 percent of male graduates and 40 percent of female graduates enter teaching immediately.

[b] Assumes that for every 5 persons who enter teaching immediately upon graduation, 3 other qualified persons coming from other sources enter the profession.

[c] Based on projections of total college graduations by Fund for the Advancement of Education. Assumes same ratio of men to women graduates, and same proportion of each sex enter teaching as in Estimate A.

[d] Teachers needed to replace annual loss from the profession to housekeeping, other occupations, etc., and to meet increased enrollments as projected by the U. S. Office of Education. Assumes annual loss of 7.5 percent, and one new teacher for every 25 additional secondary students or 30 additional elementary pupils.

[e] Same as Estimate I, except that it assumes 7 percent annual loss and one new teacher for every 30 additional secondary students or 33 additional elementary pupils.

[f] Actual number is estimated to be slightly more than 62,000 on the basis of National Education Association survey of college graduates meeting teacher certification requirements.

[g] Actual number hired has been estimated as 130,706 by the National Education Association.

Sources: Based on data from U. S. Office of Education, National Education Association, and Fund for the Advancement of Education.

year; 26 percent had graduated in 1953 or earlier; and 9 percent in 1950 or earlier. Those who delayed taking their first teaching jobs until some time after graduating from college had been engaged, during the interval, in further study, military service, work in other occupations, and homemaking and childrearing.

Adequate information is lacking on the sources of supply for teaching except for those who prepare for the profession and enter it immediately after college graduation. There are data, however, on the number of teachers holding emergency or substandard certificates. The U. S. Office of Education reported that almost 79,000 elementary and secondary school teachers held emergency licenses in 1955 because they did not meet the established minimum requirements for certification. From the data available, it would appear that from 20 to 25 percent of all additions to the teaching profession in recent years have held substandard certificates in their states. It is reported that while some of these leave teaching, about 20,000 in this group have been completing the requirements for standard certificates each year.

On the basis of the inadequate data available, annual new additions to the supply of teachers appear to be distributed roughly as follows: almost half are current college graduates with the required preparation for teaching; more than one fifth hold emergency licenses; and the remainder—about 30 percent—is made up of former teachers, college graduates of previous years, and nongraduates who meet the requirements of their states. These last three groups could account for more than 30 percent of new additions to the supply in the future, particularly if special educational and training programs designed to help qualify former and potential teachers were expanded.

Two sets of estimates of future supply are presented in Table 21. Both assume that the relationship between current college graduates entering teaching and the other sources of qualified new additions to the supply will remain at the present ratio of about five to three, and that teachers' earnings will remain as attractive as they now are relative to other occupations they might enter. One of these, Estimate B, rests upon more conservative projections of future college graduating classes. Table 21 also presents two estimates of future demand based on the need to replace those leaving the profession and to provide additional teachers for a growing school population. Demand Estimate I is based on replacement needs to meet a 7.5 percent annual loss from the profession, a rate suggested by the U. S. Office of Education, and on the provision of one new teacher for every additional 30 elementary or 25 high school students. Demand Estimate II, which shows smaller annual figures, assumes an annual turnover of 7 percent—the rate now employed by the National Education Association in estimating demand—and one new teacher for every additional 33 elementary or 30 high school students, which appears to be characteristic of current practice. Turnover, it should be noted, may be lower in the future, if more men enter the profession and if more older women return.

Depending on the combination of future estimates used, Table 21 indicates that demand, in purely quantitative terms, would no longer exceed supply possibly as early as 1960, and no later than 1964. An intensified effort to secure more qualified teachers from all of the sources of supply might relieve the shortage earlier, but even without new efforts the gap between demand and supply will be reduced steadily each year after 1957. After 1959, the number of additional teachers needed annually to meet increased enrollments will decline, and after 1962, the number of college graduates will rise dramatically. Under these circumstances, fewer and fewer new posts would have to be filled with emergency teachers, the gradual replacement of emergency teachers with better qualified personnel would become possible, and, subsequently, some reduction in average class size might be feasible. The anticipated growth in the demand for college and junior college instructors over the same period might have the effect of attracting some of the potential high school teachers into the field of college teaching. However, the greatest demands for post-high school teachers will come at about the same time that a rough balance is achieved between demand and supply in the case of high school teachers.

A numerical balance between the national demand for and the supply of teachers will not in itself assure that the schools in every community will be adequately staffed. In urban as well as rural areas where salaries and working conditions are relatively poor, shortages may persist. Nor would deficiencies in the supply of teachers of certain subjects necessarily be remedied. The secondary schools compete more directly with private industry for individuals who can teach science, mathematics, and a variety of vocational courses than for those prepared to teach in other subject areas. Abundant and attractive employment opportunities in industry for technical personnel will continue to make it difficult to relieve shortages of science and mathematics teachers. School systems have drawn upon skilled workers to increase the needed supply of trade and industrial teachers by modifying, or waiving entirely, requirements with respect to educational preparation. Such new personnel are usually given some training in educational methods after they are hired. It has been proposed that the supply of mathematics and science teachers could be expanded if similar steps were taken to qualify personnel recruited for teaching from private industry.

Between 1950 and 1955, the total number of college graduates prepared to teach in high school declined by 41 percent, compared to a more than 50 percent decline in the number prepared to teach mathematics and science. This development reflected not only the high industrial demand for technical personnel after the beginning of hostilities in Korea, but also the fact that the number of men graduates fell sharply. Women college graduates constitute a significant source of supply for high school teachers of science and mathematics, even though most of those now teaching in these fields are men. The high demand for technical personnel leads a substantial number of students who might under different circumstances seek a career in teaching to prepare themselves for a career in industry instead. Because there are more employment opportunities for men with scientific and mathematical skills, they are more likely than women to be diverted from the choice of teaching as a career.

As with other teachers, new additions to the supply of high school teachers of mathematics and science, do not come solely from current college graduates. A study by the National Education Association shows that of the 8,464 science teachers hired in September, 1955, in 32 states, less than 30 percent were newly qualified graduates. The remainder came from other sources, but, as Dr. Robert H. Carleton, Executive Secretary of the National Science Teachers Association, has observed, it is not known, "how many come from programs of graduate study, or from completion of their military duty, or from industry, or from other sources; we do not know how many were employed on temporary or emergency certificates."

In teaching, as in other professional occupations, minimum standards of formal education and training are established as a basic step toward securing competent personnel. Highly successful performance in a profession, however, is not assured solely because formal employment qualifications are met. The peculiar abilities of the individual, his working environment, including the stimulation and the opportunities it provides for skill acquisition, together with the whole of his educational experience, all enter into the development of the first-rate teacher, doctor, or engineer. Among those formally qualified to teach, there are some who discourage learning; a much larger number who, though competent, are still far from excellent teachers; and relatively few who are capable of inspiring their students. Increasing the proportion of first-rate teachers constitutes a significant problem whatever the demand-supply relationship may be. It is not a problem which is automatically solved by achieving a balance between supply and demand.

It has often been argued that teaching does not get a fair share of the high ability group because the inducements to enter other professional occupations are much stronger. There is evidence that many teacher training programs have attracted less able students, and that this has affected the quality of the curriculum and instruction in these programs. Qualitative deficiencies in the profession would not be corrected solely by expanding the total number entering training. It would also be necessary to attract more able men and women to teaching, improve the quality of formal preparation, and retain first-rate individuals within the profession, or, in the case of women who leave it, facilitate their return.

HEALTH SERVICE PERSONNEL

The increased demand for teachers is largely the result of a rapid rise in the number of children in the population. The steady growth in the demand for better medical care has resulted not only from advances in medicine, which have opened up new possibilities for improving the health of the population, but also from the greater ability of the society to pay for medical care. The demand for more educational service is expressed in demands for more teachers—mainly women—and more classrooms. Similarly, the demand for more health services has been expressed in a demand for more doctors, nurses, and hospital facilities. But it has also taken the form of new demands for other personnel, both professional and semiprofessional. Consequently, the health field has experienced major modifications in the ways in which its personnel are utilized, even though the functions performed by the several groups of professional and technical personnel and the requirements for employment are still sharply defined.

In spite of a significant rise in the demand for medical services, the number of physicians has grown relatively slowly. In 1950, the ratio of doctors to population was about what it was in 1920, but somewhat higher than in either 1930 or 1940. During these decades the number of registered nurses employed grew much more rapidly than the population, though at a steadily decreasing rate. The ratio of active graduate nurses to the population increased by 79 percent in the 1920's, by 23 percent in the next decade, and by 15 percent between 1940 and 1950. During this same period the number of nonprofessional personnel providing some form of nursing service grew rapidly, and several new professional and semiprofessional occupations appeared in the health field.

The expansion of employment in the health service occupations is directly related to major changes in the scope and methods of medical care in recent decades. The increase in hospital facilities, the growth of public and industrial health programs, the growth of medical insurance, and many other developments have enabled a larger proportion of the population to obtain more and better professional medical care. At the same time, the appearance of new diagnostic and therapeutic techniques has broadened the range and improved the results of medical treatment. The increased employment of nurses, technicians, and related groups is partly the result of these advances in techniques, many of which have facilitated the effective utilization of such personnel. The demand for these workers has also been heightened by the fact that they have taken over functions formerly performed by physicians—a tendency linked with the relatively slow growth in the number of physicians.

The demand for nurses has been further increased by a number of developments. Even though physicians keep their patients in hospitals for a much shorter period than formerly, so many more people enter hospitals for treatment that the number of patients in hospitals at any one time has increased considerably. Patients are now hospitalized for shorter periods because modern practice encourages convalescence at home. This means that a greater proportion of those in the hospitals are acutely ill or undergoing intensive diagnostic or therapeutic procedures, and therefore require more nursing care.

Another development increasing the demand for nurses has been a continuing reduction in their work week—from over fifty hours in 1930 to between 40 and 44 hours today. In addition, the number of student nurses in hospitals decreased markedly after World War II, as the special wartime training programs were discontinued and as smaller numbers of young women reached the age for entering training. Student nurses, moreover, spend less time in bedside care, not only because of the reduction in hours, but also because of the growing emphasis on classroom instruction.

The rising demand for nursing services could not be met by the growth in the number of diploma and degree nurses—who are commonly designated professional nurses—nor by the contribution made by student nurses. Consequently, hospitals came to rely increasingly upon nonprofessional personnel in providing nursing service. Since 1950, nearly half the nursing personnel in hospitals have been nonprofessional attendants, practical nurses, and nurses' aides. About 35 percent have been professional nurses and 15 percent student nurses.

The supervisory and administrative responsibilities of professional nurses have been increasingly stressed because of the greater use of nonprofessional personnel. Leaders of the profession, concerned also with raising its status, have maintained that more nurses should be prepared for supervisory and administrative functions by completing a four or five year college training program which leads to a bachelor's degree. The number of nurses completing degree programs is rising, but over 85 percent of new nurses are still graduates of diploma programs.

Some leaders in the nursing profession have argued that the three-year diploma training program is outmoded. They have proposed a division of nursing functions between college trained nurses, whose duties would be mainly supervisory, administrative, and instructional, and either diploma nurses trained in a new two-year program, or practical nurses with one year of training, who would provide bedside care. Hospitals have not generally responded to these suggestions with enthusiasm, in part because they carry most of the cost of nursing education. Two-year training programs would severely limit the amount of bedside care and other services provided by student nurses, through which hospitals are partially compensated for their training expenditures. There has, however, been a considerable expansion of practical nurse training, and some registered nurses have been trained in two-year diploma programs. The Health Amendments Act of 1956 reflected dominant views in the nursing profession by providing grants for the collegiate education of graduate nurses and practical nurse training in public vocational education programs.

Qualifications for employment in the nursing service field have changed in a number of ways, largely as a result of advancing medical techniques and the performance of more medical functions by nurses. Professional nurses tend to be somewhat more highly qualified than formerly, even in the face of severe shortages. Most practical nurses have acquired their skills through on-the-job experience, but more of them are now completing training programs of a more formal character. Although it still remains largely voluntary, there has been considerable growth in the licensing of practical nurses. Attendants and nurses' aides rarely complete formal training, but hospitals have increasingly stressed on-the-job training for them. Almost all technician and other paramedical occupations have organizations which maintain registers of qualified personnel. The standards for registration have risen over the years, and in some cases college graduation is necessary.

Considerations similar to those which encourage estimates of an expanding future supply in the teaching profession apply to the nursing field. Since the mid-1940's, the proportion of girl high school graduates entering the nursing field has remained relatively stable—about 6 or 7 percent. Even if this proportion does not rise, the increase in high school graduation among girls and the growth in the college-age population promise gains with respect to the size of the new supply in the future. More important, as

*Table 22. Nurses Graduating from Nursing Schools, Colleges,
and Universities: Number and as a Percent of Women
Aged 21 Years, 1940-54*

Year	Nurses Graduated	As Percent of Women Aged 21
1940	23,600	1.99
1941	24,899	1.97
1942	25,613	2.09
1943	26,816	2.07
1944	28,276	2.34
1945	31,721	2.55
1946	36,195	2.91
1947	40,744	3.40
1948	34,268	2.88
1949	21,379	1.81
1950	25,790	2.23
1951	28,794	2.53
1952	29,016[a]	2.63
1953	29,308[a]	2.66
1954	28,539[a]	2.75

[a] Includes Hawaii and Puerto Rico.

Source: American Nurses Association, *Facts about Nursing*, 1955-1956 edition, and U. S. Bureau of the Census

Table 22 indicates, the number of professional nurses graduated each year as a proportion of the female population aged 21 has been growing steadily in recent years. If this trend continues, it will result in more new graduates as the size of the age group increases. There are expected to be about 35,000 nursing graduates in 1960, or one third more than in 1950. Loss from the profession due to marriage and childbearing is high, as in the case of women teachers, but the total supply can be increased by the return of qualified personnel. Hospitals have encouraged this development, and have established retraining programs to facilitate the return of married women.

Married women with children of school age constitute a crucial source of supply of both practical nurses and nurses' aides. Since personnel for both of these groups require relatively little investment in training, their supply can be expanded quite rapidly. The growth of formal training programs conducted by hospitals, high school, and junior and community colleges for both younger and older women who wish to become practical nurses can also help enlarge the supply. Where women constitute a significant proportion in other nonprofessional health occupations, initial entry or re-entry of married women into employment, after their children reach school age, may also make for some elasticity in the total supply. In some of the newer technician occupations, however, the number of trained women who are not working is relatively small.

In the health professions dominated by men, those persons once trained who dropped out of employment are insufficient in number to afford significant new additions to the supply. Only about 6 percent of the total number of physicians and surgeons in 1950 were women. Moreover, losses as a result of marriage and childbearing are negligible, for almost all of the women who train for medicine stay in the profession. On the other hand, with high competition from engineering and science for potential male medical students, a significant rise in the proportion of women doctors could occur. Between 1930 and 1950, women made up a growing proportion of physicians, and their numbers rose from over 7,200 to almost 11,800.

IMPROVING UTILIZATION PRACTICES

The demand for and the supply and utilization of highly trained personnel are interrelated in complex and constantly changing patterns. Any change in utilization inevitably affects the character of the demand, which, in turn, influences the supply. In recent years, it has become increasingly clear that changes in utilization practices provide a major key to the alleviation of shortage situations involving highly trained personnel.[1] The effectiveness with which their capacities are used depends upon a variety of factors. An obvious step toward better utilization is to improve the equipment and facilities used by highly trained personnel. Outmoded, unreliable equipment, crowded working space, and similar conditions can be responsible for the waste of time and skills. This is an especially serious problem in such nonprofit establishments as schools and hospitals, where funds are often not available to introduce more efficient working conditions.

Another important approach to improved utilization is to insure that highly trained personnel are employed for functions for which they are especially qualified. Frequently, a highly competent professional worker can gain a substantial salary increase only by accepting promotion to an administrative position. This may result in the loss of valuable professional services without necessarily providing good administrative leadership. It is difficult to provide adequate rewards for superior professional performance in public and nonprofit institutions where most professional women are employed. In teaching and nursing, for instance, salaries are largely based on seniority and formal qualifications, rather than on a system of differential rewards for unusual competence.

Major improvements in utilization can frequently be secured by reallocating some of the functions of professionally trained personnel to less highly trained workers, as in the medical field, and, to a lesser degree, in engineering. Teaching, on the other hand, has perhaps made less use of auxiliary personnel than any other profession. A study in Bay City, Michigan, made possible by a grant from the Fund for the Advancement of Education, found that teachers spent from 21 to 69 percent of each working day on housekeeping, clerical, and other activities requiring little or no professional training, and more than four hours each week outside

[1] See, for example, National Manpower Council, *Proceedings of a Conference on the Utilization of Scientific and Professional Manpower*, New York, 1954.

school on records, report cards, and other clerical tasks. Experimental elementary classes were established with forty-five to fifty-two pupils in which the teacher was supported by an aide who performed some of these duties. The pupils in these classes, it appeared, achieved better grades than those in classes of thirty with an equally good teacher but no aide. Similar experiments elsewhere point to the possibility of developing a hierarchy of functions within the teaching profession which might permit more effective utilization and better compensation for highly competent teachers. This might attract more able persons to teaching and at the same time create opportunities for employing able women who are not college graduates as teachers' aides. It should be noted, however, that some leading educators question the findings of the Bay City experiment and the feasibility of drastically restructuring teaching functions.

Each professional group establishes policies which affect the utilization of its own members and of related personnel. The purposes of these policies are not only to clarify the changing functions of the group and to guarantee minimum standards of performance, but also to protect the status of the profession. In pursuing these aims, most groups tend to draw increasingly specific and rigid distinctions between their own functions and those of other groups, and to bar entrance to the profession except through a specific program of formal training. However, if full advantage is to be taken of the skills and abilities present in all kinds of workers employed in the same general field, some flexibility in the redesignation of responsibilities must be maintained.

SEX LABELS IN PROFESSIONAL OCCUPATIONS

In spite of the growth in the number of women workers in professional and semiprofessional occupations, they represent today a smaller proportion of these segments of the labor force than they did a quarter of a century ago. Women now constitute a smaller proportion of all professional and semiprofessional workers than formerly largely because of the rapid increase in the number of engineers, nearly all of whom are men. In 1930, 15 percent of all women workers were found in professional and semiprofessional occupations, and women constituted almost half of all workers in these occupational groups. In 1956, only 10 percent of the women workers were in professional and related jobs, and they represented only 35 percent of all workers in professional occupations.

Even though both men and women are employed in all professions, most professional occupations still represent, for practical purposes, "men's" or "women's" jobs. Thus, women account for 98 percent of the professional nurses and 94 percent of the dietitians and nutritionists, but for only 1 percent of the engineers and 3 percent of the dentists. Men comprise 25 percent of all teachers, but most of them are concentrated in certain teaching fields. In the professional fields, as elsewhere, the overwhelming preponderance of one sex or the other in particular occupations reflects widely held views about what kinds of work are appropriate for men and women.

Men have long been employed as nurses in mental hospitals, and the armed services have used men for nursing functions, especially in war, under the title of corpsmen or medical aidmen. The armed services have recently begun to offer commissions to male nurses, but so few men enter nursing schools that this departure from traditional sex distinctions is likely to have only slight practical significance. As nursing administration grows in importance, more men may be expected to enter the field, but it would be surprising if many were attracted to an occupation still regarded as peculiarly appropriate for women.

Although the great majority of teachers are women, the profession is not thought of as wholly a "women's" occupation. It has often been urged that more men should be induced to enter elementary and secondary teaching, not only in order to increase the supply and reduce turnover, but also because they might be more effective teachers for boys. Teaching already claims 60 percent of all women who graduate from college and go to work immediately, and many of the remaining women graduates enter teaching at a later time. Therefore, it would be necessary to train and employ more men in order to effectuate a striking increase in the proportion of college graduates who become teachers. With high levels of employment, however, major adjustments in pay structure and promotion opportunities would be required to attract and retain more men in the profession.

In the field of higher education, men teachers predominate, and shortages expected to occur as student enrollments increase by an estimated 40 or 50 percent by the mid-1960's may lead to the employment of more women. In 1955, the ratio of women to men among regular, full-time teachers was highest in teachers' colleges, where women constituted more than one third of the total. By contrast, women made up less than 14 percent of the regular, full-time teaching staff in nonpublic universities. In all types of higher educational institutions combined, men accounted for almost four out of five full-time teachers. In most college teaching fields, of course, men predominate, and in engineering and agriculture, men were over 99 and over 95 percent of all teachers, respectively, in 1955. While women are a minority of college teachers, they are strongly represented in education, some health fields, English, foreign languages, fine arts, and several other subject areas. In home economics and library science they accounted in 1955 for over 96 and 71 percent of the teachers, respectively.

The strength of the tradition that engineering is a masculine field makes it unlikely that women will be important in the relief of shortage situations there in the near future. The increase in the number of women engineers from under 1,000 to over 6,600 between 1940 and 1950 is striking, but this is of small moment in a profession with some 600,000 workers. While many employers hesitate to employ women engineers, many others are willing to do so, and the few women who graduate from engineering schools each year do not seem to have great difficulty now in securing acceptable jobs. Recent developments also suggest the possibility of sizable increases in the future in the employment of women as draftsmen and other kinds of auxiliary engineering personnel. A shift in emphasis in occupational guidance and counseling might encourage more women to enter these fields. The period of education and training for engineers and engineering technicians is about the same as for teaching or for certain nursing or medical technician occupations. Yet, few young women prepare for engineering and related occupations, largely because these have been traditionally regarded as masculine.

The extent to which the sex labeling of jobs and conventional views about the distinctive attributes of women are deterrents to the effective utilization of professional personnel has not yet been adequately studied. Past experience does indicate, however, that where rigid sex distinctions in professional occupations contribute to shortage situations, they are likely to be relaxed or even abandoned.

x. WOMEN IN THE ARMED SERVICES

THE PRESENT UTILIZATION of women by the armed services is another and special aspect of the general tendency toward opening up new areas of work for women outside the home. The recruitment, selection, training, and use of women for military functions pose certain internal problems for the armed services, but they also have significant implications for the use of women in many fields of civilian employment. Since activities related to defense and war have been for centuries an almost exclusively male domain, the introduction of women into military organizations constitutes one aspect of the radical change which has occurred in women's employment.

Although women have directly assisted the military in every crisis since the days of the Revolutionary War, it was not until 1948 that the Congress accorded to all women military personnel, as it had previously to Army and Navy nurses and medical specialists, permanent status in the regular and reserve components of their respective services—Army, Navy, Marines, and Air Force. With the passage of the Women's Armed Forces Integration Act in June, 1948, the fourth stage in an evolutionary development was reached. The first stage saw women, mainly family members of military personnel, as unpaid volunteers. The second involved women as civilian employees of the armed services, and the third, as volunteers serving in temporary or quasi-military units. Now they are regular members of the permanent military establishment. Service in the armed forces of the United States has never been compulsory for women.

As early as 1775, semiofficial groups of civilian women served with the military as cooks, canteen workers, nurses, and seamstresses. Recognition of the value of nursing care rendered by volunteers in the Civil War and by trained nurses employed under contract in the Spanish-American War led to the establishment of the Army Nurse Corps in 1901 and the Navy Nurse Corps in 1908 as definite components of the military. Members of these corps, however, were not accorded full officers' rank, pay, or other benefits.

During World War I, shortages of clerical workers led the Army to authorize the employment of civilian women at military installations and the assignment of women overseas as civilian employees. The Navy Department, in addition to employing women in civilian capacities, authorized the enlistment of women as full members of the Naval and Marine Reserves. Approximately 11,000 "Yeomanettes" and "Marinettes" served in the United States before their organizations were disbanded in 1919, and some 24,000 women served in the Army and Navy Nurse Corps.

PARTICIPATION OF WOMEN IN THE MILITARY DURING WORLD WAR II

Within six months after the United States entered World War II, the Congress authorized the establishment of the Women's Army Auxiliary Corps (WAAC) in May, 1942, to serve with the Army at home and overseas, without military status, in noncombat posts. Other legislation followed rapidly, authorizing the acceptance of women in the reserve forces of the other services: the WAVES (Navy) in July; the SPARS (Coast Guard) in November; and Women Marines in February, 1943. In July, 1943, a bill was passed which converted the WAAC to the Women's Army Corps (WAC) with temporary military status. A year later, the Army and Navy Nurse Corps were granted real, instead of relative, rank and other benefits. All of these six women's services were or became components of the military establishment for the wartime period. As such, they were subject to all military rules, regulations, and discipline, and their members were entitled to the same pay as men of the same grades and ranks. Women physicians, dietitians, and physical therapists also served on active duty, and, during the course of the war, those who were so engaged as civilian employees of the War Department were granted military status and offered commissions in ranks commensurate with their training and experience. Following the creation of the Air Force as a separate service, the Women's Air Force (WAF) was established in 1948.

The interest of the armed forces in establishing these women's services and the willingness of the Congress to authorize them were the result of several considerations. Various women's groups were exerting pressure to have women participate directly in the military effort. The difficulties that the armed forces encountered during World War I in securing adequate numbers of clerical workers were vividly recalled. Finally, there was some apprehension that the armed forces might be handicapped by manpower shortages if the war continued for several years.

During the course of World War II, a total of approximately 350,000 women saw active military duty, with 65,000 serving overseas. Women thus accounted for about 3 percent of some 12 million who were in active service during the war. Table 23 shows how the total number of women who served were distributed among the several services and corps.

Originally, the services assumed that women could be used effectively in only a small number of assignments—typing and clerical work, telephone switchboard operation, driving, and cooking. Their use in supervisory positions was not contemplated except on a very limited basis. The few jobs deemed suitable for women were identified separately, and assignments were re-

*Table 23. Number of Women in the Services and Nursing Corps
during World War II*

Army Nurse Corps (including dietitians and physical therapists)	60,000
Navy Nurse Corps	14,000
WAC	140,000
WAVES (including dietitians and physical therapists)	100,000
SPARS	13,000
Women Marines	23,000
Total	350,000

Source: Department of Defense

stricted accordingly. It was anticipated that the majority of women possessing the necessary skills for these assignments would need only a short period of training in military procedures.

The development of shortages in many skilled occupations very early in the war soon led the services to use women not only to fill requirements for a few specialized jobs, but also to supplement the available manpower in other occupations for which women either were or could be trained. As additional shortages of qualified men developed, the list of positions authorized for women was expanded, and the specialist training programs designed to qualify personnel for these positions were also open to women. The fact that women in service performed many jobs as well as servicemen and in some instances better— where, for example, patience and attention to detail were required—led to a complete reversal in policy.

The result was that all assignments were opened up to women, with the exception of a small number specifically designated unsuitable for physical or social reasons or prohibited by law. Women officers were used in staff planning and operational assignments and functioned as supervisors over both male and female personnel in many different situations. As the result of nursing shortages, greater use was made of nurses as teachers and supervisors, and the simpler nursing tasks were delegated to semi-professional or nonprofessional personnel.

During World War II, the Adjutant General estimated that women could fill about 1.5 million of the 7.7 million positions in the Army and Air Corps. In point of fact, the maximum strength of the women's services was never much in excess of 275,000 at any one time. There was no prospect whatever of recruiting much larger numbers by voluntary means, and as the war progressed there was little incentive to build the strength of the women's services to anything approaching the 1.5 million level. Yet, at no time was the recruiting of WAC personnel interrupted. The War Department recognized that recruiting costs were high, but it also believed that it was better to incur such costs in order to acquire trained women for clerical, medical technician, and other assignments than it was to train limited-service soldiers for such work. For many noncombatant positions women came to be recognized as more valuable to the war effort than men.

In their postwar evaluation, the armed forces reached the conclusion that the use of the women's services had been successful. They recognized, however, that recruitment had been hampered by the negative attitudes of the public towards military service for women and that the antagonism of many officers and enlisted men toward the use of women on military assignments impeded their effective utilization. Finally, the armed forces' appraisals showed that women had presented special problems in housing, personal safety, and procurement of clothing.

World War II helped to bring home to the senior military staff the importance of making maximum use of the potentialities of all citizens in any future emergency. Consequently, in their post-war planning for the women's services the armed forces tried to achieve a dual objective: to provide a mobilization base of trained personnel to facilitate the rapid recruitment, assignment, and utilization of volunteer women in case of war or national emergency; and to make available the skills of women for the accomplishment of the peacetime mission of the military.

CURRENT POLICIES AND PRACTICES

In 1956, approximately 34,000 women were serving on active duty, as shown in Table 24.

Table 24. Number of Women in the Services and Nursing Corps, April 30, 1956

	Officers (Including Warrant Officers)	Enlisted	Total
Army Nurse Corps	3,600		3,600
Navy Nurse Corps	2,101		2,101
Air Force Nurse Corps	2,482		2,482
Air Force Medical Specialist Corps	124		124
Army Medical Specialist Corps	500		500
WAC	904	7,893	8,797
WAVES	793	5,327	6,120
Marines	117	1,727	1,844
WAF	643	7,869	8,512
Total	11,264	22,816	34,080

Source: Department of Defense

In addition to the above, women also are commissioned in the Medical Corps (doctors), Dental Corps, and Medical Service Corps (biologists, chemists, pharmacists, biochemists, administrators, medical statisticians, etc.). At the present time, a very small number of women are serving on active duty in the armed services as physicians or dentists.

There are differences in administrative procedures among the women's services with respect to enlistment standards, officer procurement, training, assignments, and promotions. These, to a large extent, grow out of the varying traditions, purposes, and needs of each of the women's services and of their respective parent services. All of the women's services are composed of volunteers.

The various medical components which have been mentioned were established to perform specific professional functions, and all their members are officers. The women's general purpose services are composed of both officers and enlisted women. Members of these services—WAC, WAVES, Women Marines, and WAF—may perform most noncombat duties. Thus, they do not serve on aircraft engaged in combat missions or on naval vessels other than hospital ships or military transports.

Since 1948, the women's services have never approached the maximum strengths authorized by law—namely, 2 percent of the strengths of their respective parent services in the case of the WAC, WAVES, WAF, and Women Marines—although a major recruiting effort was made during the Korean hostilities. A major reason for the failure to reach authorized strength has been the desire of all the services to keep enlistment standards relatively high. In general, the women's services have accepted less than one third of those who apply.

MEDICAL SERVICES

Men and women are appointed in the different medical services in ranks commensurate with their age, professional qualifications, and civilian experience. In these services, the traditional distinctions between "men's" and "women's" occupations have, for practical purposes, been abandoned. Graduate nurses are commissioned in the Army, Navy, and Air Force Nurse Corps. Women with graduate training in dietetics, physical therapy, or occupational therapy, are commissioned in the Army and Air Force Medical Specialist Corps, as are men. In the Navy, women in these and allied scientific professions are commissioned in the Medical Service Corps. The Marine Corps does not have a medical service since medical care for their personnel is provided by the Navy. The Army accepts women for the Nurse and Medical Specialist Corps between the ages of 21 and 45, and the Air Force between 21 and 40. The Navy accepts nurses between the ages of 21 and 39½, and medical specialists between 20 and 33.

Newly commissioned officers are given a brief orientation course in military organizations, customs, and practices prior to their first job assignments. Officers in the medical services are responsible not only for patient care, but, to a greater extent than in many civilian medical institutions, also for instructing non-professional personnel, assisting in the preparation of training programs, providing counseling and guidance services, and conducting on-the-job training for related personnel. The greater use of professional personnel as administrators, supervisors, and teachers became necessary during World War II, and the practice has been continued and expanded since then. For example, dietitians often are responsible for departmental policies relating to the requisitioning of food and equipment, control of food costs, and management of food-service personnel. Nurses and therapists are charged with the direction, supervision, and on-the-job training of medical technicians and other personnel.

The military services provide advanced training courses to qualify nurses in special fields, among them anesthesia, psychiatric nursing, operating-room supervision, and hospital administration. All types of medical service officers are eligible for postgraduate study at civilian institutions, as well as for courses in administration conducted at such military schools as the Army's Medical Service School. Some Army Medical Specialist women attend the WAC Officer Advanced Course in preparation for higher-level staff duties.

Most of the members of the women's medical services are in the three lowest commissioned ranks, and the authorized personnel structures provide for relatively few openings for women at higher ranks. Prior to and during World War II, relatively few nurses rose above the rank of first lieutenant. In recent years, however, there has been a significant increase in the proportion of captains. It has been contended, nevertheless, that the authorized grade structures have not kept pace with the increased skills and responsibilities required of these women; that they do not provide reasonable opportunities for promotion; and, therefore, that it is difficult to secure and retain qualified personnel.

GENERAL PURPOSE SERVICES

To a striking degree the policies and practices in the WAC, WAVES, Women Marines, and WAF follow those established for men in their respective services. In fact, the basic policies are the same for men and women. Women are employed on jobs interchangeably with male personnel of like qualifications and abilities and, as is the case with men, are encouraged, and even in many ways required, to advance steadily to more skilled and higher positions.

There are, however, several significant differences. Enlistment requirements are more stringent for women and the minimum age for enlistment is higher. A woman must be unmarried to be initially accepted for service; if married while in service, she may remain unless she becomes pregnant. Women may not serve in ranks higher than colonel in the Army, Marines, and Air Force, or captain in the Navy. The important sources for securing male officers are the service academies and Reserve Officers Training Corps programs in colleges. There are no equivalents to these for the women's services. Until recently, women were excluded from formal enrollment as cadets in ROTC programs. Some women have been permitted to attend ROTC classes on college campuses and have received college credit for their work, but not commissions. In June, 1956, however, the Air Force decided to offer commissions to qualified college women who complete prescribed ROTC courses. The advisability of extending the ROTC program to include women has been discussed, and the point has been made that, since the services attempt to secure their women officers from among college graduates, the extension of the ROTC program to women would be justified as a way of providing a continuing source of junior officers.

Basic or boot training to orient enlisted women in the customs, traditions, and practices of their service is given at separate facilities, but most specialist and advanced training is offered in schools established for men. Specialist training is provided in such areas as finance, personnel administration and management, communications, transportation, supply, food service, and special services. Advanced training is given in technical subjects and staff and administrative management techniques to prepare personnel for higher-level jobs. For the most part, courses conducted for men are open to women, if the training prepares them for duty assignments authorized for women and if housing is available. On-the-job training supplements formal schooling for both men and women. School training and job assignments are rotated in a pattern designed to develop the capabilities of the individual.

Women are employed in most staff, operational, and technical positions at all echelons of the military establishment. Assignments of women to specific jobs are handled in the same manner and under the same procedures as for men. Although there is a natural tendency to place them where the need is greatest, the policy is to assign women in as many different jobs as possible. The reason for this policy is that it provides additional experience in the utilization of women, which would facilitate their widest possible use in the event of full mobilization. As a matter of basic policy, the armed forces in peacetime try to avoid placing personnel in dead-end jobs. In line with this objective, all enlisted jobs are structured into career fields which provide orderly routes for advancement. Enlisted women, consequently, are assigned only to career fields in which all steps of the promotion ladder are likely to be open to them.

RECRUITMENT, TRAINING, AND UTILIZATION

Applicants for enlistment in the women's services must be United States citizens, physically qualified, of high moral character, and without dependents under 18 years of age. They are also required to have a high school diploma, or evidence of equivalent education, and to attain a passing score on a qualification test. Enlistees must be at least 18 years old, and those under 21 must have their parents' written consent. Maximum ages for initial enlistment vary. The Navy acepts women up to age 26, the Marines to age 30, and the Army and Air Force to age 34. Minimum enlistment periods are generally the same for men and women—two years in the Army, three years in the Marines, and four years in the Navy. The exception is the Air Force, which has a minimum enlistment of three years for women and four years for men. Enlistment for longer periods is optional, and over two thirds of the women enlisting in the Army do so for at least three years. As with men, options to enlist for a specific school are offered by the Army and Navy.

The test administered to applicants is known as the Armed Forces Women's Selection Test. The passing score is higher than that set for men, and, indeed, is approximately the equivalent of the average score attained by men on the Armed Forces Qualification Test. Originally, women were given the same battery of tests as men, but studies indicated that women do better in training and on the job than could be predicted from scores based on tests designed for men. A new test was, therefore, devised for women in order to improve selection procedures.

All newly enlisted women in the WAC attend an initial eight-week training course which is similar to that given male recruits, except that combat subjects are excluded and greater emphasis is given to administrative subjects. At the end of this basic course, assignments are made either directly to jobs or to specialists' schools. The type of training and the job assignments are determined by the needs of the service and by the personal desires, capabilities, and aptitudes of the individual. Because many of the enlistees enter service shortly after the completion of civilian schooling, and more than half of them are under 20 years of age, counseling designed to help them make sound career choices is especially significant. More than three quarters of the basic trainees are sent to schools for specialist training. Intensive courses, lasting from six to eighteen weeks, are given in finance procedures, machine accounting, personnel administration and management, stenography, supply, cryptography, radio, food service, etc. Courses are offered to prepare women for medical and dental laboratory work, as medical, dental, and occupational and physical therapy technicians, and for pharmacy and X-ray work. Although on-the-job training is heavily relied upon for further development of skills, advanced school courses are also conducted and attendance is possible at any stage of military service. Leadership courses are provided for women who possess the necessary qualities to become noncommissioned officers.

Currently, jobs in eight of the Army's ten occupational fields, in thirty-two of the Air Force's forty-three, in twenty-five of the Navy's sixty-one, and in twenty-six of the Marine Corps' thirty-seven are authorized for enlisted women. In each of these fields, women are on an equal footing with men in regard to pay received, work performance expected, and opportunities for promotion.

Recruitment among college graduates for officer training candidates is the primary source for new officers in the women's services. All services also offer officer training to qualified enlisted women under 27 year of age who are outstanding in character and intelligence, and possess qualities of leadership. The Army also tenders direct commissions to qualified college graduates up to age 32, and the Air Force through age 39. Retention of these commissions is contingent upon successful completion of a basic officers' training course. Selections are made by boards of officers on the basis of personal interviews, scores attained on qualification tests, and examination of school records, references, and job experience.

Women officers are utilized interchangeably with men in staff and operational assignments in such fields as personnel and administration, intelligence, training and instruction, information and education, special services, logistics, budget and finance, civil affairs and military government, public information, and law. Women officers may be trained for and assigned to almost all duties except those which are recognized as tactical in nature. Each year some officers are sent to civilian colleges and universities for post-graduate study.

The wide range of positions now open to women in the armed forces underlines the changes which have taken place since the beginning of World War II. Originally, as has been seen, only a few assignments were open to them. Today, women are excluded only from positions which they cannot handle because of limitations of physical strength, from active combat posts, and from assignments where minimum privacy cannot be insured, as aboard a naval vessel. The fact that most types of assignments are theoretically open to women is partly balanced by other considerations which enter into their utilization within the armed forces. In many instances, particularly within the Navy, assignments otherwise suitable for women are limited because they would interfere with policies for male personnel. Thus, in order to insure the satisfactory operation of the policy of rotating men from shipboard to shore duty, certain shore assignments are reserved for men.

One of the pronounced advantages to the armed forces of having women in uniform is that it facilitates the manning of posts where it is difficult to attract and hold civilian personnel. The availability of housing, however, is an important determinant of actual assignment, and, chiefly for reasons of economy, it is not deemed advisable to assign less than about fifty enlisted women to an isolated installation.

A woman may apply for separation when she marries, if she has served a specified minimum period after the completion of military schooling. Consequently, the number of separations because of marriage is another factor influencing the utilization of women in the armed forces. Losses due to marriage occur mostly in the lower enlisted and officer grades. Most married women request release from military service when continued active duty would involve separation from their husbands. When both husband and wife are in service, efforts are made to assign them to the same stations, thereby encouraging the woman to remain on active duty. In spite of the loss because of marriage, a higher proportion of women than of men enlist for a second period of service. In the Army and Air Force, approximately half of the women who are eligible for reenlistment sign up for additional service. Advanced training is given, for the most part, to women who, it is believed, will continue in service for a period long enough to justify the investment. A small number of the women who leave active duty join the reserve forces and would be available for duty in an emergency.

CURRENT PROBLEM AREAS

Current military planning with respect to the utilization of women in the services has not yet taken full cognizance of four crucial questions: Can volunteering be relied upon to provide the armed forces with as many women as could be efficiently absorbed in times of mobilization? To what extent should the armed forces rely upon women in uniform rather than upon civilian personnel or men in uniform to fill a wide range of non-combat positions? To what extent should the armed services limit their utilization of women to a small group with relatively high qualifications? To what extent should the armed forces and civilian employers be permitted to compete, as they did during World War II, for the same groups of women?

The Congress regularized the women's services in 1948 in order to strengthen the nation's mobilization potential, but until these four questions are answered, a firm judgment on whether this purpose has been achieved cannot be reached. The answers cannot be provided by the military services alone, for they require the further development of general mobilization planning which takes into account the competing manpower claims of the armed forces, civilian industry, and civil defense needs. Reliance upon current enlistment criteria during full mobilization is likely to product direct competition between the armed services and civilian employers for the same women with relatively scarce skills.

In such planning, special attention will have to be paid to those segments of the total labor force made up of men and women with unusually high, and therefore relatively scarce, abilities or skills. Currently, armed services planning rests on the assumption that the use of women will be limited by the numbers who can be secured through voluntary enlistment. Should the large-scale use of women be required in a future mobilization, the experimentation of the armed services to date would not provide adequate guidance for their most effective utilization. The role of women in the armed forces has been restricted, in ways already indicated, by law and convention. It may, therefore, be argued that a thorough attempt has not yet been made to explore the military and social limits to which the utilization of women in the armed forces could be pressed.

Women have already been shown capable of performing a wide range of noncombat military functions. It might be advisable, therefore, to modify the policy of using a relatively small number of carefully selected women in a wide range of jobs, in order to learn more about how women of varying capacities and skills may be effectively utilized. Otherwise, if full mobilization compels the recruitment of women with significantly lower qualifications, the services will be faced with the problem of utilizing groups with which they have had little experience.

IMPLICATIONS FOR CIVILIAN LIFE

The developments of recent years in the utilization of women in the armed forces have significance for civilian life. Although the changes that have taken place within the armed forces during this period in the recruitment, training, assignment, and promotion of women still remain to be thoroughly studied, it is clear that they represent an important experiment in new ways of utilizing womanpower.

The experience of the armed forces with recruitment of women underlines the significance of cultural attitudes in influencing their availability for certain types of work. Many young women volunteered for active military duty during World War II in the face of opposition on the part of their parents, who viewed military service as an unsuitable activity for their daughters. The widely held conviction that military service is a function to be performed by men has some analogy with the conventional view that certain jobs belong to men and others to women. In spite of the growth of attitudes more favorable to the participation of women in the armed forces, there is still a significant body of opinion to the contrary. Its strength, it may be noted, reflects in part the relatively low esteem in which most Americans hold military service as a career for men, let alone women. The armed forces have drawn upon the assistance of leading women to interpret military service favorably to the young women of America in order to encourage enlistments.

What has happened in the armed services indicates that women are capable of performing a much wider range of functions than is still generally believed to be feasible. Today, the armed forces start with the presumption that women can fill almost all assignments. This means that the services have abandoned the rigid patterning of "men's" and "women's" jobs, and are making assignments increasingly in terms of the availability of skill without reference to sex. For example, women have been assigned to such characteristic "men's" jobs as mechanic and truck driver.

The contrast between the employment of women in the armed forces and in civilian life is nowhere sharper than with respect to the opportunities of women for training and promotions. Since the end of World War II, the armed forces have sought to improve career opportunities in the hope of attracting and holding able individuals. The women's services have benefited from the emphasis they have placed upon opportunities for training and promotion. As has been seen, however, women may not advance beyond the rank of captain in the Navy or colonel in the other services. Some have justified this limitation by pointing out that women do not participate in combat and that officers above these ranks should have had combat experience.

Within the military, basic personnel policies are designed to insure that women can add to their skills and be promoted if they are qualified. In civilian employment, it may be noted, women are sometimes preferred precisely because it is not thought necessary to provide them with training opportunities or promotions. In the armed services, one of the few remaining problem areas with respect to promotion is the limited number of higher grades available within the Army, Navy, and Air Force Nurse Corps and the Medical Specialist Corps. This situation, however, has been under consideration by the Congress, and remedial action is contemplated which would create a greater number of positions in the higher ranks. Turnover rates for women in the armed forces are relatively high, as they are for young women in industry. Yet, as has been observed, a considerable proportion of those who complete a single term do reenlist. This is attributed to the good career opportunities which many have found within the military establishment.

In many respects, the armed forces have been more venturesome than civilian industry in developing new approaches to the effective utilization of women. It is significant that the challenge to move in this direction has contributed to deepening their understanding of the many measures required to improve the utilization of men as well as women. Finally, the variety of experience obtained from the regularization of the women's services suggests what can be accomplished in utilizing women in occupational fields normally viewed as closed to them.

xi. WORK IN THE LIVES OF WOMEN

Two THEMES recur in the earlier chapters. One is the striking increase in opportunities which women have had during the past half century to participate in paid employment; the other is the extent to which their response to these opportunities has been conditioned by their concern with their functions as wives and mothers. In the past, some married women were compelled by economic necessity to work outside the home. But, for most married women, the option of working did not, for practical purposes, exist. Today, most married women are able to choose whether and how much they will work. Both men and women have options with respect to the effort they devote to work and to the degree to which they permit their jobs to rule their lives. By and large, however, only a small minority of men can exercise a choice between working and not working before they reach an acceptable age for retirement. This contrast underlies the fundamental difference between the work patterns of men and women.

The alterations which have taken place in the labor market, in family life, and in social attitudes, together with rapid urbanization, have influenced the behavior of women old enough to work, and also the ways in which the oncoming generation is brought up and prepared for life. Changes in the models of adult life which affect the attitudes and expectations of girls, as they are growing up, concerning future employment outside the home constitute a major theme of this chapter.

A schematic delineation of the place of work in the lives of women can be ventured only at the cost of ignoring diversities. The adult women in the labor force today, as has been seen, do not constitute a homogeneous group. Among them are women who grew up before World War I. At the opposite extreme are the young women born just before World War II, who first went to school when it ended. Within this span of years alone a host of significant changes occurred in the position of women in American society, their educational opportunities, the labor market, urban living, and the like. Much is known about the life experiences of the generation born early in this century. One can only guess about the future experiences of those who will live to welcome the new century.

Even if only women born during a single decade were considered—as, for instance, those now between the ages of twenty and thirty—one would still be faced by a bewildering variety of factors which affect the ways in which they respond to work. These will differ if a girl is brought up in a Negro sharecropping family in Georgia, or in the home of a Boston banker; if a girl drops out of school at the end of the first year in high school, or continues with her education until she acquires a Master of Arts degree; if the man she marries is an unskilled worker earning $45 weekly, or a successful doctor with an annual income of $25,000; if she lives in Pittsburgh, Fall River, or Santa Fe.

This analysis focuses on the younger generation of women living in urban communities who have had a high school or college education; who grew up neither in poverty-stricken homes nor in the homes of millionaires; who are married and have children; and whose husbands are at neither the lower nor upper extremes of the income scale. This emphasis is justified by the fact that by far the most striking change in women's employment has occurred among married women with children. This, of course, should not be taken to minimize the importance of work for the women who remain single, the married women who do not have children, and the women who lose their husbands through death or divorce. Among all these groups of women very substantial proportions are likely to be in the labor force. The circumstances of their adult lives, particularly those related to work, set them apart, however, in some degree, from women who have both husband and children.

The dominant social influences encountered during their formative years are the same for women who marry and for those who do not. Most of the girls who will not marry grow up with the belief that they will; most of those who will not have children anticipate that they will; and most of those who will lose their husbands do not expect to. It seems reasonable to assume that only a small proportion of the women who have neither husband nor children and spend all their adult years in paid employment were motivated from early childhood to realize their dreams and ambitions in and through work. No value judgment is made on the attainments of the small number of women who are so motivated, or on their contributions to society, in recognizing that they differ markedly from the overwhelming majority of women in the labor force.

THE OLDER PATTERN

The ideal model which the young girl early in the century—the grandmother of today's young girl—had before her was that of the woman who had the good fortune to find a successful husband and who was the mother of several healthy children. Marriage and motherhood were the touchstones of a successful adult life. Some young women in mill towns and Negro girls might have anticipated working most of their adult lives. The girl who grew up in a modest home might have expected to take a job when she left school and contribute most of her earnings to the running of the household. She would anticipate giving up her job when, in her early or middle twenties, she would marry and start her own family. Only if she subsequently lost her husband or was in dire straits would she be likely to seek a job. The girl whose family was well-to-do would grow up expecting not to work outside of her home at any time either before or after marriage, although she would probably look forward to participating in community and church affairs on a voluntary basis.

Around the turn of the century, a large number of girls finished high school, and some even went on to attend or complete college. Their secondary education was not vocationally directed —it did not prepare them specifically for work outside the home. Domestic work and most factory jobs did not require any special educational background. The high school or college graduate, however, was ready to assume a teaching post. Some exceptional young women, who usually came from middle- or upper-class families, and who had the opportunity to acquire a good education, could prepare themselves seriously for paid employment. Many feminists were "career women," who were, almost without exception, determined to enter into competition with men and to carve out for themselves a niche in the world of man's work. Many of these women, seeking the emancipation of their sex by demonstrating their competence in occupations monopolized by men, were even willing to pay the price of foregoing marriage and children in order to insure a career and win their independence.

The contrast between the past and present place of work in the lives of women is depicted by Figure 6. This shows labor force participation rates for women against significant points in their lives; namely, completion of school, marriage, birth of last child, entrance of last child into school, marriage of last child, and death of husband.

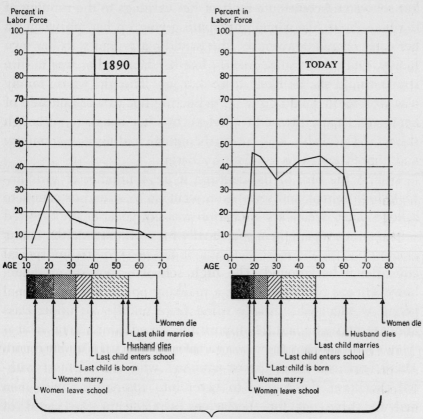

Figure 6. Work in Relation to Significant Stages in the Lives of Women, 1890 and Today

For sources of upper portion of the figure, see Figure 2. Lower portion based on data from Paul C. Glick, "The Life Cycle of the Family," *Marriage and Family Living*, Feb., 1955.

The figure shows how much later in their lives women leave school than they did in the past and how much earlier they marry. It indicates that they are younger when their children enter school and marry; that they live much longer; and that they are less likely to be widowed at an early age.

What are the models which influence the young girl growing up today? Even if her own mother does not hold a paying job, but devotes all of her time to running a household and caring for the children, she is likely to be acquainted with many married women who do hold jobs in addition to discharging their responsibilities at home. More likely than not, the young girl has had teachers who are married and have children of their own. She has heard and read about women successful in business, the arts, and in other fields who are married and have children. She may have had her attention called to those few women whose achievements equal those of their exceptionally successful husbands.

The young girl today learns early in her growing up that work outside the home can mean many different things in the life of a woman. At the same time, however, she takes it for granted that work will occupy a quite different place in her life than in her brother's. She has no reason to doubt from what she observes about her father and the fathers of her friends and neighbors that work is, so to speak, a "natural" activity of men, and that they are preoccupied by what happens to them in the world of work. Like her mother and grandmother before her, she will expect to marry and bear children. If she can hold down a job in addition —and even better, if she can manage to make a success of her work—well and good. But she is likely to feel that the primary challenge she faces is to succeed as wife and mother.

From one point of view, the differences which earlier set boys apart from girls in the games they played, the clothes they wore, and the freedom that each was allowed, are no longer so sharp. Today girls play baseball, tennis, and other games, as boys do. Today girls, like boys, are frequently dressed in dungarees. They spend their school years in close association with boys. If they are not permitted quite the same freedom as boys, they are at least no longer under the strict supervision which previously marked the childhood and adolescence of girls.

The increasing similarities in the bringing up of boys and girls have not obliterated, of course, significant differences which shape the ways in which both perceive their future lives. It is still usual for girls to play with dolls and boys with guns; for girls to wear dresses and boys, suits; for girls to help their mothers and for boys to help their fathers. The fact that boys and girls attend the same schools does not mean, as has been seen, that their educational experiences are identical. One who asks a group of seven or eight year olds what they want to be when they grow up will be impressed by the fact that the girls almost always specify wife and mother—in addition to teacher and nurse. Almost no boy ever comments on marriage and having children when he expresses his preference as among policeman, truck driver, fireman, ballplayer, engineer, or doctor. The differences in the activities of men and women, both in and outside the home, remain sufficiently striking so that few girls question that their sex will define the essential character of their lives, including, of course, the extent and kinds of work they will do.

Adolescent boys and girls do not have identical attitudes toward their schooling viewed in terms of preparation for later life. Boys are more likely than girls to recognize that their position in the world in later years will depend on their success in their jobs, which often will depend on how well they prepare themselves educationally. Although most girls expect to work before they marry, only a minority see their education as a means of preparing for a lifetime of work outside the home. The vast majority appear to be concerned with entry jobs, rather than with long-run occupational commitments. This does not mean, as has been seen, that girls do less well in high school than boys.

While they are still in school, a large part of the emotional energy of girls is devoted to social relations with young men, in anticipation of making a successful marriage. This, they are convinced, will be the crucial decision in their lives. Young men are, of course, preoccupied with their interest in women, but they are not likely to assume that the pattern of their adult lives will depend upon the marriage they make. What happens to the young man will obviously be significantly affected by the girl he marries and the life they fashion together. But he expects that her life will be overwhelmingly shaped by his success in work. The young woman is likely to take it for granted that her adult life will be largely determined by the man she marries.

WORK BEFORE MARRIAGE: THEN AND NOW

It has previously been pointed out that early in the century it was customary for young women from modest or low income families to go to work after they left school, although some parents still felt that their daughters' virtue might in consequence be endangered. It was not uncommon, even in families which could have made good use of additional earnings, for young women to be prevented from working outside the home for this reason. Early in the century, it was also true that the social standing of the business or professional man could be jeopardized if his adolescent daughters decided to go to work. Young ladies from upper income families might join a ladies' auxiliary and undertake voluntary work on behalf of a church, hospital, or some other appropriate community organization, but if they took a job either in an office or in a shop they risked precipitating a major family crisis. Even in a large urban community, the number of positions available to a well-educated young woman which were regarded as "respectable" was distinctly limited. This helps explain the resistance of many parents to their daughters' employment.

Today, almost every young woman takes it for granted that she will look for a job shortly after completing her schooling, even though she contemplates early marriage. The parents whose young daughter neither works nor studies are likely to view her behavior as odd and feel under some compulsion to alter it.

There are now few fields of employment which are not considered "respectable" for women. Also changed is the extent to which young people make decisions for themselves. The autocratic father who dictates to his adolescent daughter whether she should stay in school or go to work is far less common a figure than in the past. Nor is the father likely to determine what his daughter does with her earnings. Many young people who hold a job but continue to live at home pay the equivalent of board and rent, but others do not, and spend or save their income as they please.

In the period after departure from school, the quest for a mate remains primary with girls. There is a widespread impression that the choices young women make about occupations, and their behavior on the job, frequently testify to their predominant concern with marriage. Employment and personnel officers report that in the exceptionally strong labor market of recent years many young women, before deciding to take a particular job, want to know about the presence of eligible men in the work force. During the past decade, some young women have been unwilling to enter the nursing profession because of the unusual restrictions on their social life which its study and practice impose. For some young women the fact that so many young physicians are now married when they start their internships further reduces the attractiveness of nursing as a career, for previously a personable nurse had a good chance to marry a doctor.

The secondary position assigned to work by many young women is also suggested by the report that young women seeking white-collar jobs often are interested in working only near shopping areas. It also appears that young women often make a decision about a job in terms of hours and other working conditions which might interfere with a normal social life. Many employers are convinced that the job decisions of these young women are not significantly affected by such factors as high earnings and opportunities for advancement. The hours of work and the agreeableness of the working environment seem to weigh far more heavily with them.

WHY MARRIED WOMEN WORK

The variety of factors which bear upon the entrance or re-entrance of married women into paid employment after they have begun to rear a family have been discussed in earlier chapters. Here it is sufficient to call attention to those considerations which illuminate the place that work occupies at that stage of their lives. To begin with, there are many families in which the wife must take a job because the husband has become temporarily or permanently disabled, or because of emergency expenses. Even where there is no such compelling economic need, the wife's earnings are important. Relatively few families feel that they have all the money they genuinely need. Some women may work even for a small salary, though their expenditures are increased by the resultant outlays for clothes, transportation, and purchase of services which they might otherwise provide themselves. Nevertheless, there is a considerable net monetary advantage to most families when the wife works.

If a woman has worked during the early years of marriage before she has children, the pull back into the labor market is likely to be stronger than if she had never contributed to family income. In the American setting only the exceptional family voluntarily reduces its consumption level. This is a step usually taken only under severe compulsion. It is, moreover, difficult to maintain a family at its accustomed standard of living when one income earner is lost and additional members must be cared for, which is the case when children begin to arrive. If the additional income provided by the working wife does not make it possible to buy sought-after household and other durable goods outright, it will frequently facilitate their acquisition by installment buying. In a culture which encourages the aspiration for ever-rising consumption standards and material well-being, the drive is strong toward home ownership, the outfitting of the home with labor-saving devices and appliances, and the acquisition of other commodities which signify middle-class status. In fulfilling these consumption goals, as well as the desire for more education for the children and better medical care, the supplementary income may be decisive. Where the husband's income alone does not assure the desired standard of living, the wife may feel that she has a compelling reason to enter or re-enter the labor market.

Her earnings, however, may also mean something quite different to the married woman. They may give her a sense of security against future contingencies, or they may constitute the foundation for a sense of independence which she desires. If, for example, she first went to work when she was eighteen, married at twenty-one, and remained employed for two more years, she became accustomed to providing for her own personal needs. For these five years, she did not have to ask her father or her husband for money to buy a hat, a dress, or, for that matter, anything else that she wanted, though not necessarily needed. Having enjoyed this kind of personal independence, she may be eager to regain it by returning to work.

Considerations of a noneconomic nature, however, are also often influential in drawing married women back to work. Many women find the successful performance of household chores a burden. Some do not like to clean; some find cooking a continuing mystery. Others do not like to take care of children exclusively, and to be deprived of adult companionship. For them, the satisfactions found in working in an adult environment and in escaping from household duties, which they find boring, are the persuasive considerations. It may well be that among these women the option to go to work would frequently be accepted even if no monetary advantage accrued from holding a job.

A much larger group of married women, on the other hand, who find homemaking activities quite tolerable, may feel that the care of a small city apartment and one or two children, particularly after they have reached the age of six or ten, is less than a full-time challenge to their energies and interests. Should a woman want to, she can no doubt find enough work to occupy her completely in caring for even a small home and family; but there are many who are reluctant to spend all their time in home-making functions and who feel that unpaid work has little worth.

A woman's disposition to work outside the home becomes much greater in many cases as her children approach adolescence and require fewer hours of supervision. More important, she can anticipate the day when her family will shrink to two members, her husband and herself. If she already has some free time available, she will have that much more in the future. There are clear advantages in returning to work at an age when her chances of securing employment are relatively good. Not only will she have an easier time finding a job to her liking, but she may also be in a better position to accumulate pension and other benefits which may be helpful if she survives her husband, as she is likely to do.

Among the women who pursued their education to the completion of college or beyond, or who had specialized training preparing them for professional or semiprofessional occupations, giving up work because of marriage or childbearing may represent a serious break in what had been a planned career. If these women had an opportunity to work before or early in their marriages, and if they found their work satisfying, their desire to return to work is likely to be very strong. They might have been quick to give up their jobs, but they may find, after five or ten years of running a home and caring for children, that they feel restive because some of their expectations have not been realized. It is no deprecation of marriage and of the profound satisfactions of motherhood to observe that Americans are inclined to stress their positive and rewarding aspects and to play down their negative and costly ones. Many girls and boys, consequently, grow up with something less than realistic conceptions about married life. The more education a woman has —the more disciplined she has been about preparing herself for work—the more she may be impelled to seek satisfactions not found completely within the home.

Americans put a premium on leisure time, but not on wasting time. It should not be surprising, therefore, that some married women with one or two children feel uneasy when they find themselves with unused time on their hands. As in the past, a large number of married women extend the horizons of their lives by participating in voluntary activities. But many fields formerly the exclusive domain of volunteers have been increasingly taken over by professionally trained personnel. The major point, however, is that older women today can have vastly more free time than was possible thirty or fifty years ago, and, increasingly, those who do are motivated to put it to constructive use.

CONTINUED IMPORTANCE OF THE HOME

Each of these reasons—the desire to earn money, the preference for office or other work over unpaid household work, the search for meaningful activity when the family has shrunk or the children need less care, the interest in making use of one's earlier education and training, and, finally, the disinclination to waste time—exert a strong pull on married women to return to paid employment. However, most women are not in paid employment, and this warns against jumping to the conclusion that women no longer find significant satisfactions in their homemaking activities and in the rearing of children. What has happened is that a whole complex of developments has produced new options for married women which were not present previously. The fact that large numbers of married women at different points in their lives choose to return to paid employment does not mean that the home, children, and husband no longer have primacy for them. It has been seen that their behavior in the labor market proves the opposite.

Whether married women go back to full-time or to part-time work, whether they stay permanently or leave after a longer or shorter period—these and related aspects of their behavior in the labor market appear to be determined primarily by conditions at home and their reactions to them. If their homemaking duties require a high proportion of their total energies, they are much less likely to work a full week, every week. If they are in a position to take a full-time job and later are confronted with a problem at home—the illness of a child, for example—most women will respond by dropping out of the labor market.

It has been recognized that women are less willing than men to travel long distances to work because they fear they will have insufficient time in which to discharge their major responsibilities at home. Many women, including those from low-income families, are unwilling to consider positions which require overtime, no matter how liberally they may be paid for it. Maximizing their present or even their future income is not a primary concern.

Some women resent the lack of opportunities open to secure advanced training, which is the key to promotion, but many others avoid positions of increased responsibility. True, there are many men who shy away from more challenging jobs, preferring one of relative ease and lack of responsibility with less income to another of stress and strain and more income. Yet, it remains true that with men, by and large, the job is central; with women, the home. To a much greater extent than women, men want to get the job which pays the best; if necessary, they are more willing to travel long distances daily for some worthwhile differentials; more of them keep their eyes open for chances to improve themselves by securing additional training.

THE NEW PLACE OF WORK

The tremendous alteration which has occurred in the place of work in the lives of married women can be traced back to the 1930's, if not earlier, but some of its most significant aspects date from the period of World War II. Late in the 1940's it became clear that married women were in the labor market to stay. The developments of more recent years only reinforce the conviction that structural changes in the female labor force are occurring. Even though their full significance is not yet clear, it is safe to assume that more and more married women will spend more and more of their adult lives in paid employment—if they have the opportunities to do so. And it seems as if the opportunities will continue to exist.

It would be unreasonable to expect the major institutions of society which shape the lives of women—the home, the school the community—to reflect fully the new place of work in the lives of married women. Most young girls growing up today, however, probably perceive that the older model of a woman who finds all her satisfactions within marriage and the home is no longer appropriate. No one should expect them to understand fully the variety of ways in which their own lives may be affected by such changes as the lengthening of life and the improvement of the health of the entire population. These developments, in conjunction with the decline in the average age at which women marry and the tendency to concentrate childbearing in the early and middle twenties, help illustrate how strikingly the framework of women's adult lives has been transformed. But the young girl who grasps the general import of these developments will appreciate how large a span of her adult life may not be wholly or even partially devoted to the care and upbringing of her children and to homemaking functions, and that she may have a need to find other meaningful activities to occupy her.

Parents and teachers, products of earlier generations, also have need to understand the major changes which have already taken place and are currently under way in the place of work in the lives of women.

If young girls succeed in developing more realistic models for adult life, this alone will have important implications for their education. They may be less likely than in the past to think of their education primarily from the viewpoints of self-development, initial jobs, or insurance should something go wrong with their marriages. If young women explicitly recognize that much of their adult lives may be spent in paid employment, this will influence their educational planning, and possibly other aspects of their lives. To the extent that they appreciate that industry is abandoning old prejudices and is opening up more and more fields of work to women, they may pursue different educational programs from those they now follow, so as to secure a firmer base on which to build a more satisfactory occupational life.

PROBLEMS FACING WOMEN WHO RETURN TO WORK

How can the married woman in her middle or late thirties who begins to gain a little free time prepare herself for a return to work? If she had a college education, or if she worked for a few years after leaving school, much of her knowledge may have slipped from her in the intervening years. Such specific skills as she once possessed may have suffered from disuse. Having been out of the labor market for many years, she may have lost the assurance she once had about her ability to meet the demands of a job. Having been her own boss for many years, she may have doubts about keeping a schedule set by others.

Her problems multiply as she considers returning to work. At twenty-one, she was pleased with a proofreading job in a publishing house. At thirty-eight, after having carried major responsibilities for home and children, she is by no means certain that such work will satisfy her. She may feel that she has interests or talents of which she was previously unaware, but she may not yet have any clear perception of what they are, or how they can be satisfied or realized in the world of work with which she has had little contact in the intervening years. If she is primarily moved by a desire to get out of the home and earn an income of her own, she may be less perplexed by these considerations. But even then she may question whether she will be able to hold down a selling job which she knows she can get, because it means that she will have to be on her feet for eight hours a day. Or, although she knows that with some retraining she can bring her secretarial skills back to an acceptable level, she may still question whether she will be able to tolerate the routine aspects of the job.

Many women have need for counseling—for a chance to discuss their deeply felt but perhaps not clearly articulated hopes and doubts. Many need information about the jobs open to them in their home communities and the training opportunities of which they must take advantage if they are to prepare themselves for better jobs. But how many know that such help, however inadequate, is available, or know where to find it?

If an increase in options, a broadening of choice, is viewed as a boon, the greater opportunities which women now have for holding a job under conditions which make it possible for them also to discharge their homemaking responsibilities may be considered an important gain. Today, women may choose whether they want to do as their mothers and grandmothers before them did, and spend all of their time on homemaking and childrearing; or whether they prefer to devote themselves to a job; or whether they will venture to combine marriage and work.

But several other propositions must be inspected before the conclusion of clear gain can be accepted. No individual ever makes decisions free of social values and pressures. Improving one's standard of living is a characteristic American goal, and the question must be faced whether the large number of women who now choose to hold a job in addition to running their homes do so because they prefer a life of heightened activity, or whether they are responding in large measure to social presssures which they are unable to withstand. If a family's status is largely determined by the plane of living it enjoys, many married women may go to work because they do not want their family to lose out in the competitive drive for goods and services. What initially looked like a broadening of options may be more spurious than real. The costs of not responding in the affirmative may be too high for many married women to tolerate. They go to work because they feel they cannot afford to remain at home.

They may also feel themselves under pressure to find an outlet for the free time which they begin to have as their children grow up. They might prefer to idle it away or spend it in other than gainful activity, but they are made uneasy when they see their neighbors going to work. In some instances, they may even fear criticism from their husbands or others because they are not holding a job, or be encouraged by them to return to work. Yet, a decision in favor of running the home in combination with a job does not mean that uncertainties and anxieties are banished. True, most women will be unlikely to reach such a resolution without the tacit, if not active, support of their husbands. But there are times when they may be concerned about whether they are, in fact, contributing as much as they could to the satisfaction and contentment of their husbands' and children's lives. They are likely to be especially uneasy about the impact of their working on the development of their children. It is widely believed that it is important for mothers to remain at home through the period of their children's adolescence, and some authorities warn that the employment of mothers outside of the home may contribute to juvenile delinquency. Even if mothers do satisfy themselves, on reflection, that they are not neglecting their children by working, they still may not be able fully to escape insecurities engendered by such warnings.

Even in the absence of compelling economic necessity, young women of the present generation must meet and resolve many problems in reaching a decision about combining marriage and work. They will start with the realization that married women can and do work for much, if not most, of their lives. Many may plan to realize important values through work, and to do so they may seek to make the most of their educational opportunities.

Before their educations are completed, however, this question will be posed for many of the new generation: can they prepare themselves properly for careers in view of the current strong pull toward early marriage? The adolescent girl who wants to marry early and have children may not look ahead to the possibility of working later in life. Even if she does, it is psychologically difficult for her to plan so far in advance for work which will not begin until she reaches her middle or late thirties. Those who do prepare for and plan to enter a career upon graduation encounter another problem when they marry: can they in fact fully discharge their family responsibilities and yet have the time and energy to work outside the home? If they decide to interrupt their work while their children are young, they must then seek ways to maintain their skills for as many as ten to fifteen years of homemaking.

Many women have, obviously, already found their answers to these difficult questions. Many more are and will be seeking effective ways of fulfilling their major functions as wives and mothers, while also realizing their potentialities as workers in the arts, science, industry, commerce, and government. The possibilities which women now have for encompassing within their lives both homemaking and work outside the home constitute a new development in American society.

XII. PUBLIC POLICY ISSUES

THE MOMENTOUS changes in women's employment since the close of the nineteenth century— whether in the size and relative importance of the female labor force, in the occupational, age, and marital characteristics of women workers, or in the significance of paid employment in the lives of American women— have been evolutionary in character. They were not shaped according to preconceived purposes shared by the society as a whole. Except for the years of World Wars I and II, no conscious effort was made as a matter of public policy to expand the employment of women. Only in very recent years, as has been seen, has much deliberate thought been given to womanpower as a critical aspect of the nation's total manpower resources.

This does not mean, however, that there has been no significant relationship, except during periods of wartime emergency, between public policies and women's employment. Quite the contrary. Government policies at the local, state, and Federal levels have had a direct bearing upon the development and utilization of the country's womanpower resources, just as the growth and changing composition of the female labor force have had reciprocal effects upon public policies.

The employment of women outside the home precipitates issues of public policy which have no parallel in the case of men workers. In the United States, as in other countries, work outside the home always tends to be evaluated, in greater or lesser measure, in terms of its impact on women's childbearing and childrearing functions. The employment of women has led to the emergence of public policy issues for still another reason—namely, that work outside the home has been one of several means through which women have sought to overcome widely held assumptions about their inferiority and to achieve a status in the society equal to that of men.

RANGE OF POLICIES AFFECTING WOMANPOWER

A great variety of public policies have exercised and continue to exert some influence upon the development and utilization of the country's resources of womanpower. In creating and maintaining a school system which undertakes, as one of its major purposes, to prepare girls as well as boys for the world of work, the society has enormously encouraged the growth of the female labor force. The connection between the establishment of a secondary public school system and the expansion of women's employment in office and clerical work and in other fields has been noted in Chapter IV. The degree to which girls currently make use of their high school experience for occupational purposes and the important contribution which publicly supported colleges and universities make to training young women for professional and semiprofessional occupations have also been detailed.

Less fundamental and pervasive in their effects on the growth and composition of the female labor force were the efforts made during World Wars I and II to increase the total labor supply by making greater use of women workers. World War II, however, did set developments in motion which carried over after the close of hostilities, and which accelerated long-run forces operating to expand the female labor force. In particular, the war experience helped alter attitudes among employers toward women workers and among women toward employment outside the home. World

War II also laid the basis for the regularization of the women's services in the military establishment, thereby opening new opportunities to them and introducing new utilization practices.

Governmental action has also stimulated the growth of the female labor force through policies which have helped to maintain high levels of employment. Among them, the continuing and large-scale expenditures for national defense during the many years of the cold war are particularly significant. These expenditures have stimulated demands for almost all types of workers, and have expanded employment opportunities for women, as in the aircraft and electronics industries and in clerical and office work. Governmental expenditures for research and development, which create heavy demands for engineering and scientific manpower, have also provided new employment opportunities for women in professional and technicians' occupations.

Federal, state, or local governmental agencies and services, which provide vocational guidance or assist in placing workers who seek employment, help in converting a potential labor supply into an actual one, and thus contribute to increasing the size of the female labor force. The evidence, however, does not clearly indicate whether these guidance and placement services have altered the occupational distribution of women workers or the level of work which they perform. The current program of the U. S. Department of Labor to induce employers to abandon their negative attitudes towards older workers and to facilitate their employment is worthy of special note. It has a specific bearing on widening the range of job opportunities open to older women.

Shortages of teachers have led states and localities to institute programs designed to expand the supply. At the Federal level, the Women's Bureau and the U. S. Office of Education took the lead in forming the Committee on New Teachers for the Nation's Classrooms, which has sponsored a state and local program for the recruitment and preparation of well qualified mature college graduates. This program, which involved over 100 colleges and universities in 1956, operates on the assumption "that a woman with broad liberal arts training, often with children of her own, ought to be able to acquire the additional knowledge and techniques" to meet her state's requirements for teaching in a minimum period of time.

Continued high demands for nursing personnel have also led to governmental action, and in 1952 public training programs were in operation for practical nurses in communities in 38 states, most with the assistance of Federal funds for vocational education. In 1956, a special Federal program was established to encourage the expansion of practical nurse training, of college training of graduate nurses, and of graduate training of public health personnel.

The Women's Bureau offers perhaps the clearest example of a continuing governmental interest in fostering the employment of women. The emergency mobilization of women workers during World War I led to the creation of a Woman-in-Industry Service in the Department of Labor, the functions of which anticipated many of the services undertaken by the Women's Bureau in advancing the welfare and status of women both as workers and citizens. The act of June, 1920, which established the Women's Bureau within the Department of Labor, charged it with responsibility for formulating "standards and policies which shall promote the welfare of wage-earning women, improve their working conditions, increase their efficiency, and advance their opportunities for profitable employment."

These examples only suggest the many ways in which the community, acting through Federal, state, and local governments, influences the scale and characteristics of women's employment. It has been maintained, for example, that laws which restrict immigration, prescribe higher age limits for compulsory school attendance, and set ceilings on hours of work, have all helped to expand the female labor force because they have had the effect of reducing the availability of men for employment. But so many other factors have also played a part in the expansion of the female labor force that it is difficult to demonstrate this plausible contention. Even tax policy may have an indirect influence on the employment of women. An innovation in Federal income tax provisions was made in 1954 to help women who must work and who are also responsible for the care of children, by permitting limited deductions for child care expenditures. The part which the school lunch program—an outgrowth of agricultural policy—has played in facilitating the employment of mothers of school age children also remains a matter of conjecture. All levels of government, particularly since 1940, have contributed directly to expanding the range of opportunities open to women in government employment. But it remains unknown to what extent the absence of differential treatment of men and women workers, which marks personnel policies covering those in public employment, has influenced the policies of private employers toward women workers.

States and localities establish license or certification requirements for individuals entering not only professional and semi-professional employment but also a few skilled trades. The basis for this governmental policy, and for periodic—usually upward—revision of the standards of preparation and competence for the occupations covered, is protection of the public interest. Both men and women are affected by licensing provisions, but they have a special significance for women workers because of their discontinuity in paid employment, and because of the large number of women in licensed occupations. In teaching and nursing, as has been seen in Chapter IX, changes in licensing qualifications create difficulties in adding to the supply of personnel from among those who initially qualified under the earlier standards and wish to return to employment after a lapse of years. Yet, the higher standards for employment in teaching, nursing, and other licensed occupations have not prevented the growth of these occupations.

SOCIAL ATTITUDES AND PUBLIC POLICY

Developments during the past seventy-five years make it clear that Americans have not generally disapproved of women participating in paid employment. From the viewpoint of public policy, whether or not women should work outside the home is not an open issue, and, in a strict sense, never has been. It would, however, be misleading to convey the impression that all public policies directly or indirectly affecting the employment of women have invariably contributed to the expansion of job opportunities for them, and, therefore, to the growth of the female labor force. Americans have had, and continue to have, severe reservations about married women with small children working outside the home. They have also been disposed to view with disfavor the competition which women may offer men, especially heads of families, when jobs are scarce. They have been sufficiently concerned with the maternal function of women, with their wellbeing and that of children, as well as with what constitutes suitable work for women, to adopt legislation which regulates and controls the fields and conditions of work for women.

Public opinion poll data indicate that Americans overwhelmingly disapprove of having the mother of young children go to work when her husband is able to support her. Even during World War II, a substantial minority of the population did not approve of having married women take jobs in war industry. Public opinion surveys in 1943 showed that more than half of the married men who were questioned were unwilling to have their wives take defense jobs. More than half of the mothers questioned stated that they would not take war jobs, even if free care was provided for their children in day nurseries. At the same time, majority sentiment approved having married women without children take jobs in war plants. After the war, there was overwhelming disapproval of full-time work for mothers of young children, but an almost even division of opinion on having mothers of older children work outside the home.

Both men and women generally take it for granted that the male is the family breadwinner and that he has a superior claim to available work, particularly over the woman who does not have to support herself. The strength of this conviction manifests itself most clearly in times of unemployment. Thus, during the depression of the 1930's, the idea that married men should be given preference over married women for jobs had very widespread approval. Employers rarely hesitated to dismiss women employees as soon as they married. The results of a 1936 poll show that four fifths of the women and a somewhat larger proportion of the men questioned believed that a married woman should not take a full-time job unless she had to support herself. A majority of both the men and women questioned in a national public opinion poll in 1939 indicated their sympathy with proposals which would prohibit married women from being employed by private industry or state and local governments, if their husbands' annual earnings were above a certain minimum. The rule against hiring both husband and wife, which was once widespread in public and academic employment, the older practice of paying men schoolteachers more than women, and the policy still followed in some communities of higher salary schedules for teachers with dependents, reflect in varying degrees the conviction that the male is the breadwinner of the family.

During World War II, this belief was manifested in public opinion poll results showing overwhelming sentiment in favor of drafting single women for military service in preference to fathers. Acceptance of the man's primary claim to employment also appeared in the results of a 1946 opinion survey showing that about three fourths of all those questioned, and even seven tenths of the employed women interviewed, believed that an employer should discharge an efficient woman worker whose husband could support her, in preference to an inefficient man who had a family to maintain. Today, under conditions of high employment, there is little opportunity to test the strength of such attitudes. Several leaders of predominantly male trade unions, however, have ventured the judgment that, if another major depression were to occur in the near future, their members would be strongly opposed to the continued employment of married women where they seemed to be competing with men for scarce jobs. Some business leaders also believe that heavy unemployment would be accompanied by the reappearance of unfavorable attitudes toward the employment of married women.

PROTECTIVE LEGISLATION

The point was made earlier that the society has long differentiated between women workers and workers in general in its public policies. Modern labor legislation in the United States began with the regulation of child labor, and the next group of workers to be the object of special protective legislation were women. State legislation affecting women workers dates back to the 1870's, and it has grown enormously in scope and complexity since the 1890's. Special protection for women in paid employment constitutes an expression of public policy which recognizes that women are, on the average, physically not as strong as men, that not all occupations are considered suitable for them, that their responsibility for bearing and rearing children justifies efforts to prevent them from working in hazardous occupations or under injurious conditions, and that they are less able to protect themselves.

Today, laws which establish standards for the employment of women are found on the statute books of every state and of the

District of Columbia, Alaska, Hawaii, and Puerto Rico. There is great diversity in the scope of the legislation and in its enforcement. In some states, women's employment is subject to extensive regulation, but in others only a few aspects are subject to legislation. The most frequent type of legislation is that which governs hours of work, including maximum daily and weekly hours, day of rest, meal and rest periods, and night work. Such laws are on the statute books of 45 states. Forty-three states set limits to the hours which women may be employed in one or more industries. Fifteen states establish a six-day week for women in some or all industries, and an additional 7 do this for men and women workers. The meal periods of women workers are specially regulated in 23 states, and 8 states provide special rest periods for women in certain industries. Night work for adult women is limited in one fashion or another in 20 states, with 13 of them prohibiting adult women from working in certain industries or occupations, and the others regulating the number of hours women may work, or the conditions of night work.

Ten states currently regulate the weight which may be lifted or carried by women workers, and 24 states prohibit their employment in one or more occupations. Employment in mines is prohibited in 17 states; 9 have prohibitions against the employment of women in barrooms; and 8 do not permit women to work at certain other jobs which are regarded as especially hazardous or injurious. The laws of Ohio, for example, do not allow women to work in mines, dispense alcoholic beverages, handle baggage or freight, engage in trucking work, be employed as bellhops or at blast furnaces, drive taxis, or engage in still other kinds of work. Three states regulate the industrial homework of women and minors, and another 17 have laws which cover industrial homework for all persons. Laws prohibiting the employment of women immediately before or after childbirth are in effect in half a dozen states.

Minimum wage statutes affecting women have been adopted by 29 states, and in 5 of them the legislation also extends to men or minors or both. Sixteen states, the female labor force of which accounts for approximately half of all women workers in the nation, have laws establishing the principle that wage rates in various industries and employment fields are to be based on the job and not on sex. The significance of these equal pay laws, most of which have been placed on the statute books in recent decades, will be considered later.

PROTECTIVE LEGISLATION AND WOMEN'S EMPLOYMENT

The laws designed to protect women workers have sought to accomplish their purpose without adversely affecting the opportunity of women to work. The proponents of such legislation maintain that resulting improvements in wages, hours, and working conditions have helped to foster the employment of women. There is, therefore, good reason to inquire whether these laws influence either employment opportunities or the ways in which women workers are utilized. There is no need to evaluate in this context the adequacy of existing laws which regulate women's employment, or the many proposals for their revision, improvement, and wider application. Nor is it necessary to consider the problems of administration and enforcement which arise in connection with them, the degree to which they have contributed to raising the standards of employment for men, or the large body of labor legislation which affects men and women workers alike.

The period during which legislation affecting women workers has developed has also witnessed the continuous growth of the female labor force. It could be argued, therefore, that the laws designed to protect women workers have not restricted their employment opportunities. Yet, it can be shown that specific statutes were intended to prevent the employment of women in certain industries, jobs, and locations, and not always for the stated purpose of serving the best interests of the women themselves. Employers, in opposing special protective laws for women, have frequently insisted that one consequence of their enactment would be a replacement of women workers by men. To the extent that the competitive position of women workers in the labor market is altered by regulations applying to them alone, such legislation obviously does have a direct impact upon their employment opportunities.

Thus, laws prohibiting night work did reduce employment opportunities for particular groups of women workers before World War II, and were strongly objected to by the women affected. There is evidence that maximum hour laws have, in certain instances, led employers to substitute men for women workers and to assign men to women's jobs for overtime work. Legislation banning split-shift arrangements also appears to have restricted employment opportunities for small numbers of women. In a few instances, protective legislation was frankly intended to drive women out of an employment field. Thus, the molder's union, after trying to dislodge women from the industry by preventing its members from helping to train them, secured legislation in several states in the second decade of the century which, in effect, prohibited the employment of women as coremakers. A representative of the union, testifying in 1945 in favor of equal rights for women before a Senate committee, declared "that this restrictive legislation did produce marked effects, which means that it helped the organization in its effort to exclude women. . . ." Another witness asserted that New York's legislation of 1919 regulating employment in local transportation "was put through by sentimental women, aiding and abetting the mens' labor unions. We called it 'uplift legislation.' It uplifted the women out of paying jobs." Those who have wanted to assure complete equality between the sexes by constitutional amendment have generally attacked legislation which affects women workers exclusively as discriminatory, because it serves as a device for preserving jobs for men.

At different times protective laws have had the effect of reducing employment opportunities for women not only in coremaking and local transportation, but also in bookbinding, printing, restaurant work, and still other fields. The total number of women affected, either directly or indirectly, however, appears to be quite small. On the basis of such studies as have been made, minimum wage laws affecting women workers exclusively cannot be said to have resulted in any significant replacement of women workers by men. The impact of such laws upon hiring policies, the composition of the work force, technological innovations, and the structuring of jobs still remains to be thoroughly investigated. While some laws have deterred some employers from hiring women, many laws patently have had no practical effect in closing out employment opportunities, for the employers who were affected had no real incentive to hire women.

The few searching inquiries which have been conducted point to the conclusion that the restrictive consequences of special protective legislation for women are, on balance, relatively slight. This was the judgment reached in Dr. Elizabeth Faulkner Baker's volume on *Protective Labor Legislation*, which appeared in 1925, and in the Women's Bureau's study, *The Effects of Labor Legislation on the Employment Opportunities of Women*, published in 1928. Even though Dr. Baker held that laws protecting women exclusively prejudiced the effort to gain equal status with men, she concluded that the only significant groups of women denied opportunities by such laws were the small numbers employed in predominantly male occupations. The Women's Bureau, firmly committed to the protection of women workers, took the position that their exclusion from some jobs was wholly justified because the work would be harmful; that, in other instances, the jobs which were not available to women as a result of legislation were so undesirable that they were not worth holding; and that, in still other cases, employers made adjustments to the laws so that no restriction in employment resulted.

Although the question has since been repeatedly debated, no large-scale studies have been undertaken since the 1920's to ascertain the precise consequences for women's employment of this body of special legislation. The difficulties attending any effort to assess the specific influence exercised by such legislation upon employment opportunities and utilization practices should not be minimized. Compared with changes in the economy, in technology, in levels of employment, in such demographic factors as age of marriage, fertility rates, childbearing patterns, and life expectancy, or in levels of education, social attitudes, and in aspirations for higher living standards, protective legislation seems to have had only minor consequences on the total range of employment opportunities open to women or on their utilization.

The view that protective labor laws are not significant determinants of women's job opportunities is confirmed by the fact that as conditions in the labor market have changed, their application and enforcement have been modified. Thus, as a general rule, enforcement has been less strict when there has been a high demand for women workers and it has been in the public interest to attract more women into employment. During the 1930's, there was an increase in laws having restrictive consequences, and more of an effort was made to enforce them. In the very tight labor market of the war years, on the other hand, there were relaxations in the laws which previously had barred women from certain occupations, or prevented them from working at night or for more than a maximum number of hours. These relaxations were effected by authorizing exceptions through administrative or legislative action. Thus, more than 200 plants in New York state were granted permits during World War II allowing them to employ women at grinding operations, and a small number of women were also permitted to work in core-making. The granting of such special permits was contingent on the maintenance or introduction of good working conditions. In California, exceptions were made to the night work laws to permit the employment of women in the aircraft industry and elsewhere. Similar modifications occurred in 22 other states where protective laws restricted the utilization of women workers.

This flexibility in application was temporary, and in the less tight labor market of the later 1940's, the protective laws were more strictly enforced, but not nearly as rigidly as before the war. Another change in enforcement came with the high demand for workers during the Korean mobilization. Since the early 1950's, there have been protests from some employers and women workers against the enforcement of laws prohibiting night work and split shifts or curtailing overtime work.

In the course of the employer conferences summarized in Chapter III, a special effort was made to assess the extent to which labor legislation applying exclusively to women influences their employment opportunities. The consensus was that it is usually of small moment. Some employers said, however, that the lack of uniformity in state legislation posed special problems and occasionally restricted employment opportunities for women. Employers also noted that in some localities restrictive legislation prevented women with high seniority from electing night work, even though they preferred to work at night, because wage rates were higher and hours shorter, and because it interfered less with their homemaking responsibilities. Cases were reported which suggested that a certain number of women were cut off from jobs because banks and insurance and other companies could not hire them for clerical work at night.

Differences in the length of required periods for meals create occasional problems for employers in industries where a mixed work force is present. Prohibitions against the employment of women in jobs requiring the lifting and carrying of heavy weights were said to be largely outmoded because of technological advances. However, instances were reported which indicated that such legislation strengthened the employer's preference for men, if they were available. Generally speaking, employers seemed to feel that existing regulatory laws required them to make only minor adjustments if they wished to continue to employ women.

The most that can be said, therefore, on the basis of limited testimony from employers, is that protective legislation does have some adverse effect upon the employment opportunities of an unspecified but small number of women in certain localities and in certain fields of employment. There is no question, however, that it is far less significant an influence on the employment of women than are the conventional views found in employer circles about the distinctive attributes or qualities of women workers and the sex-labeling of jobs.

Some union leaders believe that the existence of differential legislation provides employers with a justification for hiring men for work which women have in fact done or could undertake. Unions are now convinced that legislation which improves working standards for women also has a beneficial effect on men workers.

POLICIES AFFECTING WORKING WIVES AND MOTHERS

In view of the growing importance of work outside the home for married women and mothers, public policies which specifically relate to their participation in paid employment deserve separate consideration. Married women now suffer few legal restrictions on their economic activities. Several states still require a wife to secure the consent of her husband or of a judge before engaging in an independent business. But this reminder of the married woman's subordinate position in the past, however important it is symbolically, is of relatively slight practical importance.

Somewhat more significant is the body of law governing the relations between husband and wife which recognizes the husband's rights to his wife's domestic services and her duty to provide them, and his right to choose and change their domicile. In law, husband and wife also have a joint obligation to live together and mutual rights to each other's society and companionship. In theory, the wife's employment is subordinate to her husband's claim to her services or to his decision to change their domicile. In practice, however, the law also holds that the husband has an obligation to exercise his rights reasonably, and that such matters as the choice of a domicile or whether his wife works are to be settled by joint decisions. For practical purposes, therefore, the body of law governing the relations between husband and wife provides no obstacles to the married woman who wants to go to work.

The married woman's behavior in the labor market, as has been seen, is conditioned by her childbearing, childrearing, and homemaking functions. This creates special problems in the administration of the state unemployment laws, because eligibility for compensation rests, among other things, on the claimant's availability for work. Most states apply essentially the same principles to men and women in determining eligibility for unemployment benefits. The characteristic behavior of women in the labor market, however, has led most states to make a variety of special provisions in their laws for women seeking compensation. A number of states provide that married women who, in order to meet their home responsibilities or marital obligations, temporarily quit work or leave one job to seek another, are not eligible for unemployment compensation. In a few states, married women who leave a job to move to another locality with their husbands, and are unable to locate a job there, are also ineligible for compensation. As a general rule, women who state that they are available only for part-time jobs are held ineligible for compensation when they are unemployed. Also ineligible are women who, because they have to nurse infants or prepare meals for older children, specify that they are available for work only with a particular employer or in the neighborhood in which they live. However, the denial of benefits is unusual when unemployed women refuse to take jobs during hours which would severely conflict with their household duties.

Working wives and mothers are also affected by rules which make them ineligible for compensation when they are unemployed because of pregnancy. In most states, women who are laid off or discharged by their employers because of pregnancy are still considered available for work and, therefore, eligible for unemployment compensation. In some states, however, either because of legislation prohibiting their employment just before or after childbirth, or because of unemployment compensation rulings, a pregnant woman who leaves a job or is dismissed by her employer is denied benefits during specified periods of time. Where this situation obtains, the pregnant woman may have a strong incentive for concealing her condition or, if she is engaged in work which is harmful to her, for not giving it up in order to seek a more suitable job. She risks either temporary loss of wages or early discharge if her pregnancy is discovered, and is not eligible for benefits when she leaves one job to find an easier one.

While some working wives and mothers may be adversely affected with respect to unemployment benefits because their personal circumstances limit their availability for work, there is no evidence that this situation deters them from entering paid employment. In the decade following 1946, it may be noted, women accounted for more than a third to over one half of all unemployment compensation claimants. For women workers in general, unemployment benefits are a higher proportion of earnings than is the case for men, since most compensation provisions of the unemployment laws favor workers who receive low wages.

In addition to those already mentioned, several other public policies affect the relationship of wives and mothers to employment. These include measures or practices which provide income for married women who have to stop working because of pregnancy; which give women job security when they stop working because of pregnancy; which establish facilities for the care of children of working mothers; and which provide financial assistance to mothers in families where the husband is not present. Six states, as has been seen, have laws prohibiting the employment of women just before or just after childbirth. Rhode Island, which is not among these states, does provide, through its Temporary Disability Insurance Act, for the payment of cash benefits to women who leave work for a period of six weeks before and six weeks after childbirth. Other states which have also established disability insurance systems expressly exclude pregnancy as a ground for compensation. One Federal Law, the Railroad Retirement Act of 1946, also provides for the payment of maternity benefits for the women workers covered by it.

Maternity leave arrangements which provide job security are a relatively new development in the United States and reflect the growing importance of married women in the labor force. Collective bargaining agreements and programs established by employers on their own initiative give many married women in private employment this form of job protection. Policies regulating sickness and annual leave provide both job protection and income to women employed in the Federal civil service and by most state governments when they are absent from work because of pregnancy. Additional leave without pay for maternity purposes is also customary in public employment. A survey by the National Education Association in 1951 indicated that about half the school systems in the country had established regular maternity leave programs.

The use of public funds to maintain facilities which provide care for the children of working mothers is also a fairly recent development. Broadly speaking, these facilities are designed to protect the child, rather than to make it easier for the mother to hold a job. The prevailing attitude is that the society's interests are best served by having mothers remain at home to care for their children, but there is some sentiment in favor of using public funds for child care where the mother is compelled to work. Only in recent years has it been argued that there is reason for expanding child care facilities in order to enable mothers who do not have to work to do so.

World War II, as has been seen, created a need for facilities to provide care for the preschool and school-age children of working mothers. Early in the war, emergency funds were made available to help states develop community programs for the care of children of employed mothers. Beginning in 1942, Federal grants were made under the Lanham Community Facilities Act to local agencies in critical war industry areas to help them operate child care facilities such as nursery schools, day care centers, and supervised play and recreation groups. Almost all of the grants went to local school systems, but some were made to public welfare and housing agencies. State and local funds were also used to operate these different child care facilities, and fees were charged for their use. State funds were appropriated for child care purposes in New York, Connecticut, Pennsylvania, and Washington. At their peak, the programs assisted by Federal grants provided care for about 29,000 children in school-age centers, another 26,000 in combined nursery and school-age centers, and 81,000 in nursery schools.

A number of the public programs continued for a short time after the war, but no Federal funds have been allocated for child care purposes since 1946. Appropriations made under the community facilities act adopted during the Korean conflict could not be used for child care purposes. In 1956, only three states were operating any kind of child care programs. New York maintained several centers, but only for the children of migratory agricultural workers. In Massachusetts, several local school systems were aided by state funds to provide care for children of employed mothers. California, which has a more ambitious program, makes state funds available to provide care for the children of migratory agricultural workers and to local school systems to maintain day care centers. These centers can be used by mothers who are compelled to work, as well as by those employed in certain fields where there are shortages of personnel. Whether and how much of a fee is paid for the care provided depends upon the number of parents working, family income, and the number of children in the family. Two cities also operate centers for children whose parent or parents, though employed, cannot provide for their care. Detroit's centers enroll a small number of children, and New York City's serve about 5,000.

The programs which provide public funds to mothers of minor children in the absence or death of the father warrant brief attention, because they have a bearing upon the degree to which some women are under compulsion to seek employment. Under the Federal-state program of Aid to Dependent Children, needy mothers whose husbands may or may not be living, as well as other adults, receive monthly payments to help them care for dependent children. In August, 1956, this program aided some 608,000 families to care for over 1,693,000 dependent children at a total cost of $54.7 million. The average monthly family payment came to $90.

In only a few states is this form of assistance to women responsible for dependent children substantial enough to constitute a genuine alternative to employment. But even where the payments seem barely sufficient to prevent destitution, as in most Southern states and some others, they may still relieve some of the economic pressure upon widows, divorcees, women separated from their husbands, and unwed mothers. For many women in need, however, the assistance provided is so inadequate, in contrast to even minimum earnings from work, that it probably deters few recipients who can work from seeking employment.

More substantial payments not contingent upon need are available to widows under the provisions of the Old Age and Survivors' Insurance program and the Railroad Retirement Act of 1946. A widow with two dependent children whose husband was covered by these insurance measures can receive as much as $200 a month. Moreover, additional family earnings from employment up to $1,200 a year do not jeopardize the payment of the full benefits to which the survivor is entitled. It appears likely that these insurance systems tend to encourage many widows to seek part-time employment. Benefit payments are also available to the survivors of members of the armed forces whose deaths were service-connected and in some cases where they were not. In combination with other sources of income, either earned or unearned, such benefits could obviously reduce the economic pressure on some widows to seek employment.

According to the Social Security Administration, in 1953 there were a total of about 800,000 widows less than 65 years old with children under 18. Of this number, some 300,000 were the recipients of benefits under Old Age and Survivors' Insurance; about 100,000 were paid benefits by the Veterans Administration; less than 50,000 received benefits under the Railroad Retirement Act, and about 100,000 received Aid to Dependent Children assistance. A small proportion of these widows received income from more than one of these sources, and about 400,000 derived income from employment. How many widows were foregoing insurance benefits because they were working is not known.

EQUAL RIGHTS

Most groups seeking to improve the standards of women's employment or to expand the job opportunities open to women are not calling for striking innovations in public policy in order to achieve these objectives. Nevertheless, protests against attitudes and practices which are prejudicial to the interests of women workers, or to their effective utilization by employers, are repeatedly and frequently voiced. Instances of overt discrimination are also cited by those affected. For example, the American Society of Women Accountants has joined other professional women's groups in demanding a change in the selection process of the Federal civil service, because the right of "the appointing officer to specify sex for any position has led to discrimination against women accountants." However, the charge that women workers generally are the objects of discriminatory practices is now not made with either the same regularity or intensity as in the past.

A proposed amendment designed to secure full equality of legal rights for women was first introduced in the U.S. Senate in 1923. In its most recent form, the heart of the amendment simply declares that "Equality of rights under the law shall not be denied or abridged by the United States or by any State on account of sex." Its advocates contend that an equal rights amendment is essential for eliminating rules of law and legislation which apply to women alone, or which differentiate between men and women with respect to economic, social, and political rights. In their eyes, discrimination against women exists whenever women are treated differently from men.

Action on an equal rights amendment has been pressed in every Congress since 1923, and in 1946 it received approval by a majority, but not the required two thirds, in the Senate. An equal rights amendment was carried in the Senate in 1950 and again in 1953 by more than the required two-thirds vote. On both occasions, however, it was adopted with the added proviso that it "shall not be construed to impair any rights, benefits, or exemptions now or hereafter conferred by law upon persons of the female sex." In the opinion of the proponents of an equal rights amendment, this qualification had the effect of destroying its purpose.

Most of the organizations which advocate the principle of full equality with respect to women's opportunities for training, employment, and promotion believe that this objective will not be achieved through legislation alone, or even by an amendment to the Constitution. Over forty women's organizations, as well as the Women's Bureau, are on record as opposing the equal rights amendment on various grounds: that it is not a suitable means for securing the ends sought; that it would pose insuperable difficulties, particularly for the states, in interpretation and implementation; that the full range of its consequences cannot be anticipated; that it might upset the existing body of law governing family relationships and property; that it would destroy laws specially designed to protect women; that there are fundamental differences between the sexes which require differential treatment of men and women by the law. The proponents of the measure insist that women are still so extensively deprived of personal, property, family, and other rights by law that their status is distinctly inferior to that of men, and that this situation will be effectively remedied only by an equal rights amendment. On the question of protective legislation in particular, they argue that new and improved laws which protect both men and women equally would represent a gain over those which now affect women exclusively. Some equal rights amendment advocates maintain that special legislation for particular groups of citizens, such as mothers, would be constitutional under the amendment. The National Federation of Business and Professional Women's Clubs and the General Federation of Women's Clubs, both of which have large memberships, and the National Association of Women Lawyers, the American Society of Women Accountants, and the National Women's Party are among the women's organizations championing an equal rights amendment. An amendment has also been endorsed by the platforms of the Republican and Democratic parties—since 1940 by the former, and since 1944 by the latter—and has been supported by the National Education Association.

EQUAL PAY LEGISLATION

In the past, as has been seen in Chapter VIII, it was common for men to be paid significantly more than women for similar work. This was the situation in such different fields as factory employment and teaching, and though it was protested by many women workers, it was generally accepted. Today, the principle of equal pay for equal work is widely, if not universally, endorsed. Differences between men's and women's rates for similar work have narrowed considerably in recent years and in many instances have disappeared entirely. It is difficult to ascertain how large and widespread existing wage differentials are, because, as has been noted, men and women are usually found in different kinds of jobs. Equal pay for equal work is now an objective of trade unions, employers' organizations, and governmental units and agencies, as well as of many women's organizations. As a principle, it is supported by three main lines of argument. It is held that, as a matter of equity, women should receive the same wages or salaries as men when they perform the same work. Second, it is viewed as an effective means for maintaining men's wage rates against the competition of "cheap" women's labor. Finally, equal pay is justified on the ground that it helps to increase total purchasing power.

While the sentiment in favor of equal pay is overwhelming, its proponents differ over the methods for securing it. Employer groups hold that it should be achieved by voluntary action. Thus, the National Association of Manufacturers, which has declared that "the principle of equal pay for equal work performance within the structure of the local business establishment is sound and should be observed," has joined with the U.S. Chamber of Commerce and individual employers in opposing equal pay legislation.

Unions which have long been committed to the principle of equal pay have stressed its implementation through collective bargaining. They are now, however, also on record as favoring equal pay legislation. The Congress of Industrial Organizations strongly supported Federal legislation at hearings in 1945 and subsequently. Although individual unions affiliated with the American Federation of Labor had earlier endorsed state equal pay laws, the Federation itself did not support Federal legislation. A resolution adopted at the founding convention of the joint AFL-CIO in December, 1955, led the Executive Council of the organization to endorse, six months later, Federal legislation aimed at providing equal pay for comparable work for women workers.

Women's organizations have helped create a favorable climate of opinion for the equal pay principle through their educational efforts, and differences among them over the equal rights amendment have not prevented them from joining forces to lobby for equal pay legislation. Together with trade unions and civic groups, key women's organizations helped found the National Equal Pay Committee in 1953, which seeks, through legislation, collective bargaining agreements, and voluntary action, to eliminate inequalities in the wage rates of men and women for the same kind of work.

The rapid growth of the female labor force in recent years has been reflected in the increasing emphasis placed upon governmental action to assure equal pay. The equal pay principle, which has applied in the Federal civil service since 1923, is also followed in setting wage rates for other civilian employees of the Federal government. In about half the states, wage rates for public employees are set without regard to sex. Local communities have also acted to remove inequalities in pay based on sex for teachers and other public employees. Of more than 400 cities with a population of 30,000 or above covered in a National Education Association survey, only 4 percent had higher salary schedules for men than for women in 1952-53.

Michigan and Montana were the first states to adopt equal pay laws, both in 1919. Arkansas, California, Colorado, Connecticut, Illinois, Maine, Massachusetts, New Hampshire, New Jersey, New York, Oregon, Pennsylvania, Rhode Island, and Washington, as well as the Territory of Alaska, have all adopted equal pay statutes since 1943. Just how much the existing laws have achieved in equalizing wage rates for men and women working on the same or equivalent jobs is open to dispute. They have, of course, helped in the educational campaign for equal pay. They have also encouraged the growth of job evaluation and classification systems which determine wages on the basis of training, skill, work performance, etc., and which sometimes disclose the existence of differentials based on sex. State equal pay legislation does not appear to have prompted employers to shift from women to men workers. On the other hand, there is some evidence that a number of employers have responded to the laws by reclassifying jobs so as to maintain traditional inequalities.

Many of the state laws have been criticized because of their provisions exempting specified groups of employers or employees from the statutes and permitting factors other than sex to affect wage differentials. The statutes also vary in the effectiveness of their enforcement machinery and the penalities they establish. The growing sentiment for a Federal equal pay law since the close of World War II can be traced in part to dissatisfaction with state legislation and in part to the slow pace with which wage differentials have been reduced through collective bargaining agreements. Many unions have long issued declarations in favor of equal pay, and where women have traditionally constituted a large proportion of the total membership—as in the needle trades for example—equal pay has not been a problem for many years. In other instances, where the membership is predominantly male, local unions have not always adhered to the equal pay policies adopted by the national organizations. Some collective bargaining contracts provide for wage differentials based on sex, and four states with equal pay laws specifically permit this practice. In recent years, major gains have been made through collective bargaining, as in the meat packing industry, to reduce and even wipe out wage inequities based on sex. Available studies suggest that about one fourth of the workers covered by collective bargaining agreements are employed under contracts which contain equal pay clauses. Such provisions are far more common in manufacturing than in other industries.

The character of union organization among women workers helps explain the emphasis now given to legislation as a means of eliminating wage inequalities. The estimated 3,000,000 women union members comprise a little more than one sixth of total union membership and account for less than one seventh of the women in the labor force. Substantial numbers of women union members are found in industries in which women constitute significant proportions of the work force, as, for example, in the needle trades, textiles, electrical goods manufacturing, and communications. At the same time, other employment fields in which women are strongly represented are poorly organized, as in office, clerical, and sales work. Union membership among women workers is heavily concentrated in a relatively small number of organizations. About half of all women union members are found in about one tenth of all the national and international unions, and at least half of the membership in each of these unions is female.

Long before the first equal pay bill was introduced into the Congress, the Federal government had contributed to the elimination of wage inequalities in private, as well as in public, employment. During World War I, the War Labor Board adopted the principle of equal pay for equal work for women employed in jobs normally filled by men. During World War II, beginning in November, 1942, the official policy of the National War Labor Board was that men and women should receive equal pay "for comparable quality and quantity of work on the same or similar operations. . . ." The Wage Stabilization Board, established as a result of the Korean conflict, adopted the same policy in November, 1951. Bills requiring employers engaged in interstate commerce to establish equal pay rates for equivalent or comparable work for men and women have been introduced in every Congress since 1945. Growing sympathy for such a Federal measure appears not only in the testimony presented during the Congressional hearings on equal pay bills in 1945, 1948, and 1950, but also in the fact that such legislation was endorsed by the two major parties in 1952. In his 1956 State of the Union message, the President, declaring that "the principle of equal pay for equal work without discrimination because of sex is a matter of simple justice," urged its implementation by an act of Congress. Those who oppose this step contend that the magnitude of the difficulties which would be faced in administering and enforcing a Federal equal pay law has not been appreciated, and that the problem of wage inequalities based on sex can be solved in other and better ways.

FUTURE PROBLEM AREAS

Groups seeking to advance the interests of women in paid employment are currently much concerned with equal pay legislation and an equal rights amendment. Interestingly enough, comparatively little public attention is now being given to other forms of governmental action which might be aimed at this objective. The increasing participation of mothers in paid employment has not been accompanied by a general demand for an expansion of public child care facilities, and there is little sentiment in favor of moving in this direction merely in order to make it easier for mothers to go to work. Nor does there appear to be any significant body of opinion which looks to legislation as a means of establishing maternity leave programs which provide both income and job security. The return to work among older women has brought a growing recognition that they face special problems with respect to training and guidance. Thus far, however, there has been little detailed consideration of the extent to which the community should be charged with responsibility for helping them solve these problems, or of the ways in which such a responsibility can best be discharged.

If there are new developments in public policy in the future, they are likely to turn on the presence of large numbers of wives and mothers in the labor force. Judging by the past, it may be taken for granted that some of the striking changes which have marked women's employment in recent years will influence future public policy issues. As of the moment, however, the form these future developments may take is still obscure.

BIBLIOGRAPHY

Abbott, Edith. Women in Industry. New York, 1909.

Abelson, Robert P. Sex Differences in Predictability of College Grades. Educational Testing Service. Princeton, 1951.

Adams, Leonard P. Wartime Manpower Mobilization. Cornell Studies in Industrial and Labor Relations. Vol. 1. Ithaca, 1951.

Altman, Ralph. Availability for Work: A Study in Unemployment Compensation. Cambridge, Mass., 1950.

American Management Association. Supervision of Women on Production Jobs. Special Research Report No. 2. New York, 1943.

American Nurses Association. Facts about Nursing, 1955-56 edition. New York, 1956.

——Nurses Invest in Patient Care. Preliminary Report on a Five-Year Program of Studies of Nursing Functions. May, 1956.

Applebaum, Stella B. Working Wives and Mothers. Public Affairs Pamphlet No. 188. New York, 1952.

Arnstein, Margaret. "Getting the Record Straight," Nursing Outlook, June, 1954.

Arthur, Julietta K. Jobs for Women over Thirty-five. New York, 1947.

Association for Higher Education. Current Issues in Higher Education, 1955. Proceedings of the Tenth Annual National Conference on Higher Education. Washington, D.C., 1955.

Baetjer, Anna M. Women in Industry: Their Health and Efficiency. Philadelphia, 1946.

Baker, Elizabeth Faulkner. Protective Labor Legislation: With Special Reference to Women in the State of New York. New York, 1925.

Baker, Helen. Women in War Industries. Princeton University, Industrial Relations Section. Research report series No. 66. Princeton, 1942.

Baker, Laura Nelson. Wanted: Women in War Industry. New York, 1943.

Beard, Mary R. Woman as Force in History: A Study in Traditions and Realities. New York, 1946.

Beauvoir, Simone de. The Second Sex. New York, 1953.

Bixler, Norma. "Married Women Workers in the War," *The Antioch Review*, September, 1945.

Blank, David M., and George J. Stigler. Demand for and Supply of Scientific and Technical Personnel. National Bureau of Economic Research. To be published 1957.

Bliven, Bruce, Jr. The Wonderful Writing Machine. New York, 1954.

Bowlby, John. Maternal Care and Mental Health. World Health Organization. Geneva, 1951.

Bray, Douglas W. Issues in the Study of Talent. New York, 1954.

Brown, Kenneth E. "National Enrollments in High School Science," *The Science Teacher*, March, 1956.

"Bryn Mawr Studies Its Ph.D.'s," *Journal of the American Association of University Women*, October, 1954.

Bureau of Labor Standards, Department of Labor. Annual Digest of State and Federal Labor Legislation, various numbers. Washington, D.C.

——Labor Laws and Their Administration: Proceedings of the Thirty-sixth Convention of the International Association of Governmental Labor Officials, Providence, R. I., May 25-27, 1953. Bulletin 169. 1954.

——Resumé of the Proceedings of the Eighteenth National Conference on Labor Legislation. Bulletin 154. 1952.

Bureau of Labor Statistics, Department of Labor. Labor Laws and Their Administration: 1937. Proceedings of the Twenty-third Convention of the International Association of Governmental Labor Officials. Bulletin 653. Washington, D.C., 1937.

——Women in the Social Sciences. Cora E. Taylor. 1954.

——Women Production Workers in the Machinery Industries: Employment Distribution, Earnings. Report No. 98. January, 1956.

Bureau of the Census, Department of Commerce. Census of Population: 1950. Vol. II, Characteristics of the Population. Vol. IV, Special Reports. Washington, D.C.

——Current Population Reports:

　Series P-20. Population Characteristics, various numbers.

　　　　P-50. Labor Force, various numbers.

　　　　P-57. Monthly Report on the Labor Force, various numbers.

　　　　P-60. Consumer Income, various numbers.

——Report on Population of the United States at the Eleventh Census, 1890, Part II. 1897.

——Sixteenth Census of the United States: 1940. Comparative Occupation Statistics for the United States, 1870 to 1940. Alba M. Edwards. 1943.

Butler, Elizabeth B. Women and the Trades: Pittsburgh, 1907-1908. New York, 1909.

Butts, Freeman R., and Lawrence A. Cremin. A History of Education in American Culture. New York, 1953.

Campbell, Helen. Women Wage Earners. Boston, 1893.

Cantril, Hadley, ed. Public Opinion: 1935-1946. Princeton, 1951.

Caplow, Theodore. The Sociology of Work. Minneapolis, 1954.

Carroll, Aileen L. "A Refresher Course is a Community Service," *American Journal of Nursing*, May, 1953.

Central Michigan College. A Cooperative Study for the Better Utilization of Teacher Competencies. A Report of the First Two Years of the Study. Mount Pleasant, Mich., 1955.

Church, Ruth E. "Womanpower Today and Tomorrow," *American Journal of Nursing*, April, 1953.

Civilian Production Administration, Bureau of Demobilization. Industrial Mobilization for War. History of the War Production Board and Predecessor Agencies, 1940-1945. Vol. I: Program and Administration. Washington, D.C., 1947.

——Minutes of the Advisory Commission to the Council of National Defense, June 12, 1940 to October 22, 1941. Historical Reports on War Administration. Documentary Publication No. 1. 1946.

——Minutes of the War Production Board, January 20, 1942 to October 9, 1945. Historical Reports on War Administration. Documentary Publication No. 4. 1946.

——Policies of the National Defense Advisory Commission and the Office of Production Management, May 1940 to April 1942. Historical Reports on War Administration. War Production Board Special Study No. 23. 1946.

Cole, Charles C. Encouraging Scientific Talent. National Science Foundation. New York, 1956.

Commission on Financing Higher Education. Nature and Needs of Higher Education. New York, 1952.

Committee on the Function of Nursing, Eli Ginzberg, Chairman. A Program for the Nursing Profession. New York, 1950.

Commons, John R., and Associates. History of Labor in the United States, 1896-1932. Vol. 3, by Don R. Lescohier and Elizabeth Brandeis. New York, 1935.

Conference on the Role of Women's Colleges in the Physical Sciences. Held at Bryn Mawr College. 1954.

Council for Financial Aid to Education, Inc. Proceedings of Conference on Special Problems Faced by Women's Colleges in Gaining Support from Business Corporations. Held at Barnard College, New York, May 25, 1955.

——The Women's Colleges in the Nation's Service. New York, 1955.

Cunningham Drug Company Foundation. For Better Nursing in Michigan. Based on a report prepared by Division of Nursing Resources, Public Health Service, U. S. Department of Health, Education, and Welfare. Detroit, 1954.

Dahm, Margaret M. "Temporary Disability Insurance — Experience Under Existing Laws," *Monthly Labor Review*, June, 1956.

Department of Defense. Careers for Women in the Armed Forces. Washington, D.C., 1955.

Department of Health, Education, and Welfare. Annual Report, 1955. Washington, D.C., 1956.

——Health Manpower Source Book. Publication No. 263, Sections 1, 2, 5. 1952, 1953, 1954.

——Public Health Service. Chart Book on Health Service Manpower. 1956.

Department of the Navy, Bureau of Naval Personnel. Selection and Classification Tests for Women. Barbara Wand and William G. Mollenkopf. Technical Bulletin 54-11. Washington, D.C., June, 1954.

Deutsch, Helene. The Psychology of Women: A Psychiatric Inquiry. New York, 1945.

Deutscher, Irwin. A Survey of the Social and Occupational Characteristics of a Metropolitan Nurse Complement. Publication 105, Community Studies, Inc., Kansas City, Mo., November, 1956.

Ditzion, Sidney. Marriage, Morals and Sex in America: a History of Ideas. New York, 1953.

Dolan, Eleanor F. "Educational Goals for College Women," *Association of American Colleges Bulletin*, October, 1953.

Dornbusch, Sanford M. The Family in the Labor Force. Ph.D. Thesis, microfilm, University of Chicago, 1953.

Durand, John D. The Labor Force in the United States, 1890-1960. New York, 1948.

——"Married Women in the Labor Force," *American Journal of Sociology*, November, 1946.

Dyer, Henry S. College Board Scores, Their Use and Interpretation. College Entrance Examination Board. New York, 1953.

Educational Policies Commission. Education for All American Youth: A Further Look. Washington, D.C., 1952.

——Policies for Education in American Democracy. Washington, D.C., 1946.

Educational Testing Service. Final Report, 1954, National College Freshman Testing Program. Princeton, 1954.

——Final Report, 1955, National College Sophomore Testing Program. 1955.

——Institutional Testing Program. Summary Statistics, 1953-54, Graduate Record Examinations. 1954.

Endicott, Frank S. Trends in the Employment of College and University Graduates in Business and Industry, 1955. Ninth Annual Report, Northwestern University, Evanston, Ill., 1954.

Fauri, Fedele F. "The Shortage of Social Workers: A Challenge to Social Work Education," *Social Work Journal*, April, 1955.

Foster, Robert G., and Pauline Park Wilson. Women After College: A Study of the Effectiveness of Their Education. New York, 1942.

Fuller, Frances M., and Mary B. Batchelder. "Opportunities for Women at the Administrative Level," *Harvard Business Review*, January-February, 1953.

Fund for the Advancement of Education, The. Teachers for Tomorrow. Bulletin No. 2. New York, November, 1955.

Gafafer, W. M. "Industrial Sickness Absenteeism Among Males and Females during 1950." *U. S. Public Health Reports*, November, 1951.

General Electric Company. The Homemaking Habits of the Working Wife. New York, 1952.

Ginzberg, Eli, Sol W. Ginsburg, Sidney Axelrad, and John L. Herma. Occupational Choice: An Approach to a General Theory. New York, 1951.

Glick, Paul C. "The Life Cycle of the Family," *Marriage and Family Living*, February, 1955.

Graduate Education for Women: The Radcliffe Ph.D. A Report by a Faculty-Trustee Committee. Cambridge, 1956.

Groves, Ernest R. The American Woman: The Feminine Side of a Masculine Civilization. New York, 1944.

Gruenberg, Sidonie M., and Hilda Sidney Krech. The Many Lives of Modern Woman. New York, 1952.

Hansl, Eva vom Baur. Trends in Part-Time Employment of College Trained Women. New York, 1949.

Harris, E. M. Married Women in Industry. Institute of Personnel Management, Occasional Papers No. 4. London, 1954.

Hauser, Philip M. "Mobility in Labor Force Participation," in E. Wight Bakke and others, Labor Mobility and Economic Opportunity. New York, 1954.

Havemann, Ernest, and Patricia Salter West. They Went to College. New York, 1952.

Hawes, Elizabeth. "The Woman Problem," *The Antioch Review,* March, 1945.

Hilton, Mary N. "Earnings and Employment of Women Factory Workers, April 1954," *Monthly Labor Review,* October, 1955.

Hollinshead, Byron S. Who Should Go to College? New York, 1952.

Hottel, Althea K. How Fare American Women? A Report of the Commission on the Education of Women of the American Council on Education. Washington, D.C., 1955.

International Labour Office. The War and Women's Employment: The Experience of the United Kingdom and the United States. Montreal, 1946.

Jaffe, A. J., and Charles D. Stewart. Manpower Resources and Utilization: Principles of Working Force Analysis. New York, 1951.

Kass, Babette, and Rose C. Feld. The Economic Strength of Business and Professional Women. New York, 1954.

Kitagawa, Evelyn M. Relative Importance — and Independence — of Selected Factors in Job Mobility, Six Cities, 1940-1949. University of Chicago, 1953.

Klarman, Herbert E. "Requirements for Physicians," *American Economic Review,* May, 1951.

Klein, Viola. The Feminine Character. London, 1946.

Komarovsky, Mirra. Women in the Modern World: Their Education and Their Dilemmas. Boston, 1953.

Leopold, Alice K. "Federal Equal Pay Legislation," *Labor Law Journal,* January, 1955.

Lester, Richard A. Hiring Practices and Labor Competition. Princeton University, Industrial Relations Center, 1954.

Long, Clarence D. "Impact of Effective Demand on the Labor Supply," *American Economic Review,* May, 1953.

——Labor Force in War and Transition: Four Countries. National Bureau of Economic Research. Occasional Paper No. 36. New York, 1952.

——The Labor Force in Wartime America. National Bureau of Economic Research. Occasional Paper No. 14. New York, 1944.

——Labor Force, Income, and Employment. National Bureau of Economic Research. Mimeographed. 1950.

Luetkens, Charlotte. Women and a New Society. London, 1946.

Lundberg, Ferdinand, and Marynia Farnham. Modern Woman: The Lost Sex. New York, 1947.

McBride, Katherine E., "What is Women's Education?" *The Annals of the American Academy of Political and Social Science,* May, 1947.

Maul, Ray C., "Is the Science Teacher Shortage a Curriculum Factor?" *The Science Teacher,* May, 1956.

——Teacher Supply and Demand in the United States. National Education Association. Washington, D.C., 1948, 1949, 1950, 1951, 1952.

Mead, Margaret. Male and Female. New York, 1949.

——"Some Theoretical Considerations on the Problem of Mother-Child Separation," *American Journal of Ortho-psychiatry,* July, 1954.

Merriam, Ida C. "Social Welfare in the United States, 1934-1954," *Social Security Bulletin,* October, 1955.

Metropolitan Life Insurance Company. "Children in Broken Families," *Statistical Bulletin,* February, 1955.

Meyer, Annie Nathan, ed. Women's Work in America. New York, 1891.

Miller, Frieda S. "Household Employment in the United States," *International Labour Review,* October, 1952.

"Mobilization of Manpower and Pressing the Fight for Freedom: Part I: Womanpower in War." Academy of Political Science, *Proceedings,* Vol. XX, 1942-44, No. 3.

Montagu, M. F. Ashley. The Natural Superiority of Women. New York, 1953.

Mueller, Kate Hevner. Educating Women for a Changing World. Minneapolis, 1954.

Muntz, Earl E. "Unemployment Compensation and Women Workers," *American Economic Security,* July-August, 1956.

Myrdal, Alva, and Viola Klein. Women's Two Roles: Home and Work. London, 1956.

National Education Association. "First-Year Teachers in 1954-55," *Research Bulletin,* February, 1956.

——"Teacher Supply and Demand in Degree-Granting Institutions, 1954-55," *Research Bulletin,* December, 1955.

——"Teacher Supply and Demand Report," *Journal of Teacher Education,* March, 1953, 1954, 1955, 1956.

National Manpower Council. A Policy for Scientific and Professional Manpower. New York, 1953.

——A Policy for Skilled Manpower. New York, 1954.

——Proceedings of a Conference on the Utilization of Scientific and Professional Manpower. New York, 1954.

National Metal Trades Association. Women in Industry. Chicago, 1943.

National Science Foundation. Education and Employment Specialization in 1952 of June 1951 College Graduates. Washington, D.C., 1955.

——Fifth Annual Report. 1955.

New York State Education Department. Demand and Supply of Teachers in the Upstate New York Public Schools. Louis H. Conger. Albany, June, 1955.

——Division of Research. A Survey of Nursing Personnel Resources in Hospitals in New York State. Albany, 1956.

Norris, Louis William. "How to Educate a Woman," *The Saturday Review,* November 27, 1954.

Office of Community War Service. Teamwork in Community Services, 1941-1946. Washington, D.C., 1946.

Office of Defense Mobilization. Mobilization and Health Manpower: II. A Report of the Subcommittee on Paramedical Personnel in Rehabilitation and Care of the Chronically Ill. Report to the Director of Office of Defense Mobilization by the Health Resources Advisory Committee. January, 1956.

Office of Education, Department of Health, Education, and Welfare. Biennial Survey of Education in the United States, 1950-52. Chapters 1-5. Washington, D.C., 1954-55.

——Earned Degrees Conferred by Higher Educational Institutions, 1953-1954. Circular 418. 1955.

——Factors Affecting the Improvement of Secondary Education. Circular 404. 1954.

——Final Reports of War Training Programs. Bulletins 9-14. 1946.

——A Look Ahead in Secondary Education. Report of the Second Commission on Life Adjustment Education for Youth. Bulletin 4. 1954.

——Offerings and Enrollments in Science and Mathematics in Public High Schools. Pamphlet 118. 1956.

——Why Do Boys and Girls Drop Out of School, and What Can We Do About It? Circular 269. 1953.

Ostheimer, Richard H. A Statistical Analysis of the Organization of Higher Education in the United States, 1948-1949. New York, 1951.

——Student Charges and Financing Higher Education. New York, 1953.

Palmer, Gladys L. Labor Mobility in Six Cities. Social Science Research Council. New York, 1954.

Palmer, Gladys L., and Ann R. Miller. Work-Attachment Patterns in Six Cities. Industrial Research Department, Wharton School of Finance and Commerce, University of Pennsylvania. 1953.

Parker, Cornelia Stratton. Working with the Working Woman. New York, 1922.

Parnes, Herbert S. Research on Labor Mobility: An Appraisal of Research Findings in the United States. Social Science Research Council. Bulletin 65. 1954.

President's Commission on the Health Needs of the Nation. Building America's Health. A Report to the President. 5 vols. Vol. 2, America's Health Status, Needs and Resources; and Vol. 3, A Statistical Appendix. Washington, D.C., 1952.

"Rich Middle-Income Class, The," *Fortune*, May, 1944.

Ruml, Beardsley, and Sidney G. Tickton. Teaching Salaries Then and Now: A 50-Year Comparison with other Occupations and Industries. The Fund for the Advancement of Education. Bulletin No. 1, 1955.

Russell, John Dale. "New Factors Affecting Equality of Opportunity in Higher Education," in Approaching Equality of Opportunity in Higher Education. American Council on Education. Washington, D.C., 1955.

Saenger, Gerhart. "Male and Female Relations in the American Comic Strip," *Public Opinion Quarterly*, Summer, 1955.

Saunders, Lyle. "The Changing Role of Nurses," *American Journal of Nursing*, September, 1954.

Schaffter, Dorothy. What Comes of Training Women for War? Commission on the Implications of Armed Services Education Programs. American Council on Education. Washington, D.C., 1948.

Scheinfeld, Amram. Women and Men. New York, 1948.

Schnelle, Kenneth E. Manpower Resources in a Tight Labor Market. Minnesota Division of Employment Security. St. Paul, 1952.

Schottland, Charles I. "Toward Greater Security in Childhood," *Social Security Bulletin*, April, 1955.

Seymour, W. H. "Pros and Cons of Women in Business," *Commercial and Financial Chronicle*, August 11, 1955.

Slocum, Walter L. Occupational Planning by Undergraduates at the State College of Washington. Rural Sociology Series on Youth, No. 10. Bulletin 547. February, 1954. Washington Agricultural Experiment Stations, Institute of Agricultural Sciences, State College of Washington. Pullman, Wash.

Snoke, Albert W., and Richard B. Ogrean. "Nursing Service and Education," *Hospitals, Journal of the American Hospital Association*, January 1 and 16, 1956.

Social Security Board, Bureau of Employment Security. Occupations Suitable for Women. Washington, D.C., 1942.

Society of Women Engineers. Women in Engineering. Patricia L. Brown, ed. New York, 1955.

Solomon, Benjamin. "The Growth of the White-Collar Work Force," *Journal of Business*, October, 1954.

Spahn, Roberta R. "Some Facts about the Nursing Shortage," *American Journal of Nursing,* July, 1954.

Stearns, Harold E., ed. Civilization in the United States: An Inquiry by Thirty Americans. New York, 1922.

Stice, Glen, William G. Mollenkopf, and Warren S. Torgerson. Background Factors and College-Going Plans Among High-Aptitude High School Seniors. Educational Testing Service. Princeton, August, 1956.

——A Study of the Factors Affecting the College-Going Plans of High Aptitude High School Seniors. Educational Testing Service. Princeton, 1955.

Stigler, George J. Trends in Employment in the Service Industries. National Bureau of Economic Research. General Series, No. 59. Princeton, 1956.

Strong, Edward K. Vocational Interests of Men and Women. Stanford, Calif., 1943.

Terman, Lewis M., and Catherine C. Miles. Sex and Personality. New York, 1936.

Tompkins, Ellsworth. "Where are the Boys?" *School and Society,* July 2, 1949.

Tompkins, Ellsworth, and Walter H. Gaumitz, "Reducing Drop-Outs," *The Bulletin,* National Association of Secondary-School Principals, December, 1950.

Treadwell, Mattie E. The Women's Army Corps. Washington, D.C., 1954.

UNESCO. World Survey of Education. Paris, 1954.

U. S. Bureau of Labor. Eleventh Annual Report: Work and Wages of Men, Women, and Children. Washington, D.C., 1895-96.

——Fourth Annual Report: Working Women in Large Cities. 1888.

——Report on Conditions of Women and Child Wage Earners in the United States. 19 vols. 1910-13.

——Sixth and Seventh Annual Reports: Cost of Production. 1890-91.

U. S. Congress, Joint Committee on Atomic Energy. Engineering and Scientific Manpower in the United States, Western Europe and Soviet Russia. Joint Committee Print, 84th Congress, 2nd Session. Washington, D.C., 1956.

——Subcommittee on Research and Development of the Joint Committee on Atomic Energy. Hearings on the Shortage of Scientific and Engineering Manpower. 84th Congress, 2nd Session. April 17, 18, 19, 25, 26 and May 1, 1956. Statement of Dr. Robert H. Carleton, Executive Secretary of the National Science Teachers Association.

U. S. House of Representatives, Committee on Interstate and Foreign Commerce. Hearings before a Subcommittee on the Health Amendments Act of 1956. 84th Congress, 2nd Session. Washington, D.C., June 13, 14 and 15, 1956.

——Committee on the Judiciary. Hearings, Equal Rights Amendment to the Constitution and the Commission on the Legal Status of Women. 80th Congress, 2nd Session. March 10 and 12, 1948.

U. S. Senate, Committee on the Judiciary. Hearings, Equal Rights Amendment. 79th Congress, 1st Session. Washington, D.C., September 28, 1945.

——Hearings, Amend the Constitution Relative to Equal Rights for Men and Women. 79th Congress, 1st Session. February 21-March 31, 1945.

"Vocational Guidance and Training for Women," *International Labour Review*, July, 1952.

War Manpower Commission. History of the Mobilization of Labor for War Production during World War II. Constance A. Kichel. 1946. Incomplete manuscript filed in Library, Bureau of the Budget, Executive Office of the President.

War Production Board. War Production in 1944. Report of the Chairman. Washington, D.C., June, 1945.

Wells, Jean A. "Labor Turnover of Women Factory Workers, 1950-1955," *Monthly Labor Review*, August, 1955.

West, Margaret D. "Estimating the Future Supply of Professional Nurses," *American Journal of Nursing*, October, 1950.

Whelpton, Pascal K. Cohort Fertility, Native White Women in the United States. Princeton, 1954.

White, Lynn, Jr. Educating Our Daughters—A Challenge to the Colleges. New York, 1950.

Wilcock, Richard C. "New Firms and the Labor Supply in Small Communities," *Current Economic Comment*, November, 1954.

Wilcock, Richard C., and Irwin Sobel. "Labor Market Behavior in Four Midwestern Shoetowns," *Industrial and Labor Relations Review*, October, 1955.

——"Secondary Labor Force Mobility in Four Midwestern Shoetowns," *Industrial and Labor Relations Review*, July, 1955.

Willett, Mabel H. The Employment of Women in the Clothing Trade. New York, 1902.

Wolfle, Dael. America's Resources of Specialized Talent. The Report of the Commission on Human Resources and Advanced Training. New York, 1954.

Women's Bureau, Department of Labor. Bibliography on Employment Problems of Older Women. Multilith D-70. Washington, D.C., 1954.

Bibliography on Night Work for Women. August, 1946.

Changes in Women's Employment during the War. Special Bulletin 20. June, 1944.

Changes in Women's Occupations 1940-1950. Bulletin 253. 1954.

Digest of State Equal-Pay Laws. June 1, 1955.

The Effective Use of Womanpower. Report of the Conference—March 10 and 11, 1955. Bulletin 257. 1955.

The Effects of Labor Legislation on Employment Opportunities of Women. Bulletin 65. 1928.

Employed Mothers and Child Care. Bulletin 246. 1953.

Employing Women in Shipyards. Bulletin 192-6. 1944.

Employment after College: Report on Women Graduates, Class of 1955. 1956.

Employment Opportunities for Women. Medical Service Series. Bulletin 203. Parts 1-5 and 8. 1952-54.

Employment Opportunites for Women. Science Series. Bulletin 223. Parts 1-4 and 6-8. 1948 and 1949.

Employment Opportunities for Women. Social Work Series. Bulletin 235. Parts 1-8. 1951 and 1952.

Employment Opportunities in Characteristic Industrial Occupations of Women. Bulletin 201. 1944.

Equal Pay Indicators. 1952.

Equal-Pay Primer. Leaflet 20. 1955.

Handbook of Facts on Women Workers. Bulletin 237. 1950.

An Idea in Action: New Teachers for the Nation's Children. Pamphlet 2. 1956.

Maternity Protection of Employed Women. Bulletin 240. 1952

1954 Handbook on Women Workers. Bulletin 255. 1954.

"Older" Women as Office Workers. Bulletin 248. 1953.

Older Women Workers. 1945.

Part-Time Jobs for Women: A Study in Ten Cities. Bulletin 238. 1951.

Planning Services for Children of Employed Mothers: A Report Prepared by a Subcommittee of the Interdepartmental Committee on Children and Youth. May, 1953.

Professional Engineering: Employment Opportunities for Women. Bulletin 254. 1954.

Progress of Women in the United States, 1949-1951. Report Prepared for the 7th Assembly of the Inter-American Commission of Women at Santiago, Chile, May 30-June 14, 1951. 1951.

Women's Bureau, Department of Labor *(continued)*
Progress toward Equal Pay in the Meat-Packing Industry. Bulletin 251. 1953.
Report of the National Conference on Equal Pay, March 31-April 1, 1952. Bulletin 243. 1952.
State Minimum-Wage Laws and Orders. Bulletin 247 and supplements 1-3. 1953-56.
The Status of Women in the United States, 1953. Bulletin 249. 1953.
Suitability for Women of Nontraditional and Industrial Occupations, with Special Reference to Lathe Operators' Jobs in Machine-Shop Production. Lillian V. Inke. March, 1954.
Training Mature Women for Employment. Bulletin 256. 1955.
The Woman Wage-Earner. Elizabeth D. Benham. Bulletin 172. 1939.
Womanpower Committees during World War II, United States and British Experience. Bulletin 244. 1953.
Women as Workers: A Statistical Guide. 1953.
Women in Higher-Level Positions. Bulletin 236. 1950.
Women in the Federal Service. Part I: Trends in Employment, 1949; Part II: Occupational Information, 1950. Bulletin 230. 1949 and 1950.
Women Workers and Their Dependents. Bulletin 239. 1951.
Women Workers in Ten War Production Areas and Their Postwar Employment Plans. Bulletin 209. 1946.
Women's Employment in Aircraft Assembly Plants in 1942. Bulletin 192-1. 1942.
Women's Jobs: Advance and Growth. Bulletin 232. 1949.
Women's Occupations through Seven Decades. Janet M. Hooks. Bulletin 218. 1947.
Women's Wartime Hours of Work. Bulletin 208. 1947.
"Women's Opportunities and Responsibilities." *The Annals of the American Academy of Political and Social Science,* May, 1947.
Woody, Thomas. A History of Women's Education in the United States. 2 vols. New York, 1929.
Woytinsky, W. S. Employment and Wages in the United States. The Twentieth Century Fund. New York, 1953.
Woytinsky, W. S., and E. S. Woytinsky. World Population and Production, Trends and Outlook. The Twentieth Century Fund. New York, 1953.
Yale University and the Fairfield Connecticut Public Schools. Yale-Fairfield Study of Elementary Teaching. Report for 1954-55. New Haven, 1956.

INDEX

Abilities and traits of women, 54, 88, 93-94, 104-05, 121-22, 167-68, 170, 191, 193, 214-15, 220, 226-30, 323, 336; health, 134, 145, 229-30, 317; intelligence and aptitudes, 93, 99, 184-85, 206-08, 227-29; personality and motivation, 92-95, 103-04, 184-88, 214, 229-30, 237, 241, 251, 315-16; physical characteristics, 91, 95-96, 145, 226-29, 329

Absenteeism, 94, 97, 154, 156, 163, 229-30, 253

Age of women, childbearing and, 68, 69, 84, 132-34, 264, 307, 317; college graduation and, 198, 217; job opportunities and, 103-04; labor force participation and, 66-84 *passim*, 125-133, 139, 141, 221, 246-47, 307; marriage and, 66-67, 69, 74, 79-80, 83-84, 131-35, 264, 307, 317; occupational distribution and, 67, 69, 80, 120, 247-49; population, in the, 129, 133, 137; *see also* Older women

Agriculture, *see* Farm workers; Rural women

Aid to Dependent Children program, 341-42

American Banking Association, 210

American Federation of Labor, 346

American Nurses Association, 261, 278

American Red Cross, 48

American Society of Women Accountants, 343, 345

Armed forces, women in, 51, 230, 285 *ff*; during World War II, 286-90, 323-24

Asheville, N C., 86

Attitudes toward women's employment, 49, 53, 71, 85 *ff*, 121, 150-54, 218, 226, 232-37, 282, 289, 300, 327-29; changes in, 51, 89-90, 124, 132-41 *passim*, 305-12, 323; employers', 86 *ff*, 150-65 *passim*, 226-39 *passim*, 249, 323, 328, 336 (*see also* Employers, policies and practices of); married women, 75, 77, 85, 93, 136-37, 161-62, 166, 305-06, 312-15, 327-29; men

workers', 88-91, 104-07, 152, 161, 226, 233-34, 237, 327-28; women's, 69, 88-95 *passim*, 104-07, 153, 160-62, 166, 230, 237-38, 250-253, 303-316, 323, 327-29; *see also* Abilities and traits of women, personality and motivation; Discrimination against women; Expectations of girls and women; "Men's" and "women's" jobs; Reasons for working and not working; Tradition, influence of

Automation, 141-42

Baetjer, Anna M., 227, 230

Baker, Elizabeth Faulkner, 333

Bay City, Mich., 280-81

Birth rate, changes in 129, 132-34, 263, 266; *see also*, Childbearing

Boston, 82-86 *passim*

Buffalo, 81

Business, women in, 62, 86 *ff; see also* Employers' policies and practices; Managers, officials, and proprietors, women as; Manufacturing industries; Sales occupations; Supervisors, women as

Carleton, Robert H., 273

Census, U. S. Bureau of the, 48, 57-81 *passim*, 110-13, 121-130 *passim*, 157, 183, 197, 248, 278

Chamber of Commerce, U. S., 346

Characteristics of women, *see* Abilities and traits of women

Chicago, 86

Child care centers, 147, 149, 327, 339-41, 350

Childbearing, 77, 134, 323, 330, 337-38; age of mother and, 68, 69, 84, 132-134, 264, 307, 317; duration of marriage and, 68-69, 74-75; education of mother and, 74-76, 193-94, 264; length of period of, 69, 133-34, 307; *see also* Birth rate, changes in; Children; Maternity leave and benefits

Childlessness, 68, 77